THE HELOC ACCELERATION STRATEGY: HOW TO PAY OFF YOUR MORTGAGE YEARS FASTER USING A HOME EQUITY LINE OF CREDIT

First edition. November 24, 2025.

ISBN: 979-8232956288

AF688008

Written by janice green.

Table of Contents

The HELOC Acceleration Strategy:

How to Pay Off Your Mortgage Years Faster Using a Home Equity Line of Credit

By:
Janice Green

Declaration Page

This book is intended for educational and informational purposes only. The strategies, examples, and financial concepts presented herein are based on the author's personal experience, research, and interpretation of publicly available information. They are not to be construed as legal, financial, or tax advice.

Readers are encouraged to consult with qualified professionals before making financial decisions. The author and publisher disclaim any liability, loss, or risk incurred as a consequence of the use and application of any content in this book.

Acknowledgements

To every homeowner who dared to ask, "Is there a smarter way?"—this book is for you.

I want to thank the financial mentors, educators, and everyday strategists who helped me see beyond the traditional mortgage path. Your insights, questions, and courage to challenge the norm inspired the framework behind this strategy.

To my family and close friends: thank you for your patience, encouragement, and belief in the mission. Your support gave me the space to research, write, and refine this work with integrity and purpose.

To the readers, clients, and community members who tested these ideas, shared feedback, and built their own success stories—your journeys are the heartbeat of this book.

And finally, to every person who picks up this guide with the hope of reclaiming time, freedom, and financial peace: may this strategy serve you well, and may your home become a launchpad for legacy.

With gratitude, Janice Green

Disclaimer

This book is intended for **educational purposes only**. The strategies and concepts presented herein are not to be construed as financial advice. Readers are strongly encouraged to consult with a licensed financial advisor or mortgage professional before making any financial decisions.

Individual results may vary based on personal financial circumstances, creditworthiness, and lender policies.

The author assumes no liability for financial outcomes resulting from the use or interpretation of the information provided.

All examples are illustrative and should not be considered guarantees or predictions of future performance.

Introduction

Why this strategy matters

For many homeowners, the traditional 30-year mortgage feels restrictive — interest front-loaded, timelines long, and options limited. A smarter path exists: strategically using a Home Equity Line of Credit (HELOC) to attack principal faster, lower total interest, and compress your payoff timeline. The HELOC Acceleration Strategy is about cashflow control, timing, and using a revolving line to work for you rather than the bank.

When applied thoughtfully, this approach can shave years — even a decade or more — off your mortgage term while maintaining flexibility. This book focuses on practical mechanics, clear guardrails, and realistic case studies so you can evaluate if, when, and how this strategy fits your situation.

What you'll learn

Core mechanics: How HELOC's revolving structure, interest calculation, and payment flexibility differ from a fixed mortgage.

Cashflow cycling: Routing income through HELOC to reduce average daily balance and redirect lump-sum principal payments to the mortgage.

Decision rules: When to transfer from HELOC to mortgage, how much, and how often to maximize interest reduction.

Risk management: Interest-rate exposure, discipline requirements, and lender terms that can strengthen or weaken outcomes.

Scenario modeling: How to estimate timelines and total interest using your income, expenses, mortgage balance, and HELOC limits.

The big idea, simply

Mortgages charge interest on a large, slowly shrinking principal, front-loading interest costs.

HELOCs calculate interest daily on a smaller, variable balance and let you move money in and out.

Strategy: Use the HELOC to "chunk" principal payments against the mortgage, then flow your income through the HELOC to rapidly reduce the HELOC balance. Repeat the cycle. Over time, you're converting expensive, long-term interest into shorter, more controllable cycles.

Prerequisites for success

Positive monthly cashflow: Your income must consistently exceed your expenses.

Stable discipline: Avoid using a HELOC for lifestyle spending; treat it as a tool, not a temptation.

Rate awareness: Understand variable-rate risk and have a plan if rates rise.

Clear terms: Know your HELOC's draw period, fees, payment requirements, and any restrictions.

Emergency buffer: Keep a separate reserve so short-term shocks don't derail your cycle.

Who this is ideal for

W-2 or consistent earners with predictable income and surplus cashflow.

Self-employed with disciplined cash management who can time inflows and maintain reserves.

Homeowners with sufficient equity to open a HELOC at reasonable terms.

Goal-oriented borrowers focused on interest reduction and timeline compression over minimum payments.

What's next in the book

Understanding amortization and why minimum payments keep you stuck

HELOC fundamentals: terms, rates, draw periods, and daily interest

Building your cashflow map: income timing, expense batching, and buffers

The "chunking" playbook: amounts, intervals, and checkpoints

Risk controls: rate shocks, market changes, and lender fine print

Case studies and worksheets to model your payoff timeline

About the Author

Janice Green is a financial strategist, educator, and advocate for homeowner empowerment. With over two decades of experience in personal finance, credit restoration, and mortgage optimization, she has helped thousands of individuals and families break free from debt cycles and reclaim control of their financial futures.

Janice's passion for practical, accessible education led her to develop the HELOC Acceleration Strategy—a proven framework that demystifies mortgage payoff and equips readers with tools to save time, interest, and stress. Her approach blends strategic insight with real-world application, making complex financial concepts simple, actionable, and transformative.

Beyond her work in mortgage acceleration, Janice is a sought-after speaker and mentor in the financial literacy space. She believes that every household deserves a roadmap to freedom, and that financial clarity is the foundation for generational wealth.

When she's not writing or teaching, Janice enjoys quiet mornings, nature walks, and helping others build legacies rooted in wisdom and stewardship.

This book is part of her ongoing mission to make financial freedom not just possible—but practical, personal, and powerful.

INTRODUCTION:

The Mortgage Prison

Your 30-Year Sentence

When most people sign up for a 30-year mortgage, they believe they are securing stability and affordability. The monthly payments appear reasonable, and the long timeline seems to make homeownership accessible. Yet, beneath this surface lies what can be described as a financial prison: a binding contract that stretches across three decades, locking borrowers into a cycle of interest payments that far exceed the original loan amount.

Consider a $320,000 loan on a $400,000 home at an interest rate of 6.3%. Over the life of the loan, the borrower will pay **$394,033 in interest alone**, bringing the total repayment to more than **$714,000**—nearly double the original loan amount. This means that while the home may have been purchased for $400,000, the true cost of ownership balloons to over $1 million once property taxes, insurance, and other fees are includedCalculator.net. What feels like a reasonable monthly payment of around $1,983 quickly becomes a long-term financial sentence.

The structure of a 30-year mortgage compounds the problem. In the early years, the majority of each payment goes toward interest rather than principal. For example, in the first month of repayment, only about **$300 reduces the loan balance**, while more than **$1,683 goes directly to interest**. This imbalance means homeowners spend years paying lenders before they begin to meaningfully build equity. The illusion of affordability masks the reality: borrowers are trapped in a system designed to maximize profit for lenders.

Beyond interest, hidden costs add layers to this financial burden. Property taxes, homeowners' insurance, and maintenance fees can add hundreds of dollars to monthly payments. Over 30 years, these costs can accumulate to more than **$300,000**, further inflating the true cost of ownership. For many families, this means sacrificing financial flexibility, delaying retirement savings, or living paycheck to paycheck just to keep up with mortgage obligations.

The metaphor of a "30-year sentence" is not just rhetorical—it reflects the binding nature of the mortgage contract. Like a prison term, it restricts freedom, dictates financial priorities, and imposes long-term consequences. While homeownership is often celebrated as a cornerstone of the American dream, the reality for many is that this dream comes with shackles. The mortgage prison is not simply about debt; it is about the erosion of financial autonomy over decades.

In essence, the true cost of a 30-year mortgage is not just the price of a home—it is the compounded interest, hidden fees, and financial limitations that stretch across a lifetime. Understanding this reality is the first step toward breaking free from the illusion of affordability and reclaiming financial independence.

***

How Much Interest You'll Actually Pay Over the Life of the Loan

When homeowners commit to a 30-year mortgage, the monthly payment may seem manageable, but the long-term cost tells a different story. The structure of these loans means that borrowers spend decades paying interest before making significant progress on the principal. For example, a $320,000 loan at a 6.3% interest rate results in a total repayment of **$714,033**, with **$394,033 of that being interest alone**. In other words, the borrower pays more in interest than the actual amount borrowed.

This imbalance is most evident in the early years of the loan. During the first month of repayment, only about **$300 reduces the loan balance**, while more than **$1,683 goes directly to interest**. This pattern continues for years, meaning homeowners are essentially renting money from the bank while building very little equity. The illusion of affordability hides the reality: the lender profits enormously while the borrower remains financially constrained.

Even small changes in interest rates can dramatically alter the total cost. For instance, a $300,000 loan at 5% interest will cost **$279,767 in interest** over 30 years, while the same loan at 4% interest costs **$215,608**—a difference of more than **$60,000**. This demonstrates why shopping for the lowest possible rate is critical. A single percentage point can translate into tens of thousands of dollars saved or lost over the life of the loan.

Beyond interest, additional costs such as property taxes, insurance, and maintenance further inflate the true expense of homeownership. In one example, these costs added more than **$300,000** to the total out-of-pocket expense, bringing the real cost of a $400,000 home to over **$1 million**. When viewed in this light, the "dream" of homeownership through a 30-year mortgage can quickly become a financial trap.

The takeaway is clear: **the true cost of a mortgage is not the sticker price of the home, but the compounded interest and fees spread across three decades.** Understanding this reality empowers borrowers to make wiser financial decisions, whether by negotiating lower rates, considering shorter loan terms, or making extra payments to reduce interest. Without this awareness, many homeowners unknowingly commit themselves to a lifetime of debt disguised as affordable monthly payments.

***

Part 1: The Psychological Burden of Decades of Debt

Decades of debt do not just drain finances—they weigh heavily on the mind, creating stress, anxiety, and even depression that can last as long as the loan itself.

Carrying a 30-year mortgage is not only a financial commitment; it is a psychological one. Debt has been shown to create a chronic state of stress, with borrowers constantly worrying about repayment, interest rates, and the uncertainty of their financial future. According to the American Psychological Association, financial concerns are one of the leading causes of stress among Americans, and debt is a primary contributor. This stress is not temporary—it lingers for decades, shaping decisions, limiting opportunities, and eroding peace of mind.

The emotional toll of long-term debt often manifests as **anxiety and depression**. Research published in *The Journal of Economic Behavior & Organization* found that individuals with high levels of debt are more likely to experience feelings of hopelessness and a lack of control over their lives. This sense of being trapped mirrors the metaphor of a "mortgage prison," where borrowers feel bound by obligations they cannot escape. Over time, this hopelessness can evolve into clinical depression, marked by persistent sadness, loss of interest in daily activities, and impaired functioning.

Debt also impacts relationships, compounding the psychological burden. Studies show that financial disagreements are among the most common sources of conflict in marriages and partnerships. Couples facing long-term debt often report lower levels of satisfaction and higher levels of resentment. This strain can lead to isolation, loneliness, and withdrawal from social activities, further weakening emotional resilience. In this way, debt does not only affect the borrower—it ripples outward, affecting families and communities.

The psychological cycle of debt is reinforced by behaviors such as **emotional spending.** Many individuals use spending as a coping mechanism for stress, which provides temporary relief but ultimately worsens financial strain. This creates a vicious cycle: debt leads to stress, stress leads to spending, and spending leads to more debt. Neuroscientific studies even show that debt activates brain regions associated with reward anticipation and negative emotion, making it harder to break free from destructive financial habits National Debt Relief.

Experts have coined the term **"debt stress syndrome"** to describe the unique psychological impact of owing money over long periods. Unlike general financial hardship, debt implies obligation, dependence, and power asymmetry between borrower and lender. This relational imbalance undermines mental health, leaving individuals feeling powerless and ashamed. The stigma of debt can further intensify the burden, making people feel as though their financial struggles are personal failures rather than systemic challenges.

Ultimately, the psychological burden of decades of debt is as real as the financial cost. It erodes confidence, limits freedom, and creates emotional scars that can last a lifetime. Recognizing this reality is crucial—not only for financial planning but also for mental health. Breaking free from debt is not just about dollars and cents; it is about reclaiming peace of mind, restoring relationships, and rediscovering hope.

***

Part 2: Why Traditional Extra Payment Methods Are Slow

Traditional extra payment methods on a mortgage are slow because they only chip away at the principal incrementally, often shaving just a few years off a 30-year loan despite decades of effort.

Many homeowners are advised to make extra payments on their mortgage as a way to reduce interest and shorten the loan term. While this strategy does work, the pace of progress is often much slower than expected. For example, making just **one extra payment per year** on a 30-year mortgage can shorten the loan by about **four to six years** and save tens of thousands in interest. While this sounds impressive, it still leaves borrowers locked into more than two decades of debt.

The reason extra payments feel slow is tied to the **amortization schedule**. In the early years of a mortgage, the majority of each monthly payment goes toward interest rather than principal. This means that even when borrowers add an extra payment, the impact on the loan balance is modest compared to the overall debt. For instance, adding $184 per month to a $350,000 loan at 6.5% interest equals one extra payment per year, but it only reduces the loan term by about six years. That's progress, but not freedom.

Another challenge is that extra payments require **consistent discipline and financial sacrifice**. Many families struggle to find room in their budgets for additional payments, especially when faced with rising living costs, emergencies, or competing financial priorities like retirement savings. Experts caution that directing money toward extra mortgage payments without first securing emergency funds or retirement contributions can leave households financially vulnerable.

Even when extra payments are made, the savings are spread out over decades. For example, paying an additional $500 per month might save $54,000 in interest and shorten the loan by seven years. While this is significant, it still means carrying debt for 23 years instead of 30. The psychological burden of knowing you remain in debt for decades—even with extra payments—underscores why traditional methods feel slow and insufficient.

Finally, extra payments often fail to address the **structural imbalance of long-term mortgages**. Because lenders design these loans to maximize interest collection in the early years, small additional payments cannot fully offset the front-loaded interest costs. Borrowers may feel like they are making progress, but the reality is that the system is designed to keep them paying for decades.

In short, while extra payments do help, they are a slow and often frustrating path to freedom. They reduce interest and shorten the loan term, but they rarely deliver the rapid debt elimination that many homeowners hope for. Recognizing the limitations of traditional extra payment methods is the first step toward exploring more aggressive strategies for breaking free from the mortgage prison.

Introduction to Velocity Banking Concept

What If There Was a Better Way?

Velocity banking offers a radical alternative to the traditional 30-year mortgage, promising faster debt elimination by strategically using cash flow and a line of credit.

For decades, homeowners have been told that the only way to pay off a mortgage faster is through extra payments, refinancing, or lump-sum contributions. While these methods work, they are slow and often leave borrowers chained to debt for decades. But what if there was a better way—a strategy designed to accelerate debt payoff by rethinking how money flows through your household? This is the idea behind **velocity banking**.

Velocity banking is a cash flow management strategy that uses a **home equity line of credit (HELOC)** as a financial hub to pay down mortgage principal more aggressively. Instead of letting income sit idle in a checking account while interest accrues on the mortgage, borrowers deposit their paychecks directly into the HELOC. Because HELOC interest is calculated daily, this immediately reduces the balance and lowers interest charges. From there, the HELOC is used to make large lump-sum payments toward the mortgage principal, cutting down the front-loaded interest that dominates the early years of a traditional loan.

The process often involves a cycle:

Step 1: Open a HELOC based on available home equity.

Step 2: Use HELOC funds to make a lump-sum payment toward the mortgage principal.

Step 3: Deposit paychecks into the HELOC to reduce the balance and minimize interest.

Step 4: Cover monthly expenses with a credit card, taking advantage of its grace period.

Step 5: Pay off the credit card from the HELOC at the end of the month.

Step 6: Repeat the cycle, gradually reducing both the mortgage and HELOC balances.

Advocates claim velocity banking can reduce a 30-year mortgage to **seven to ten years**, saving tens of thousands in interest. By attacking the principal early, borrowers tilt future payments toward equity rather than interest, accelerating the path to debt freedom. This strategy reframes debt repayment as a dynamic process, where every dollar of income is leveraged to minimize interest and maximize payoff speed.

However, it is important to note that velocity banking is not without risks. HELOCs often carry **variable interest rates**, which can rise unexpectedly, and the strategy requires **disciplined budgeting and consistent positive cash flow**. Without these conditions, borrowers may find themselves juggling debt rather than eliminating it.

Still, the concept challenges the traditional mortgage model by asking a simple but powerful question: *Why settle for a 30-year sentence when you could break free in less than a decade?* Velocity banking offers a glimpse of financial liberation, but it demands careful planning, discipline, and awareness of the risks involved.

***

How the Wealthy Use Debt Strategically

The wealthy do not see debt as a burden—they see it as a powerful tool to multiply wealth, preserve liquidity, and minimize taxes.

For most households, debt represents a heavy obligation, something to be paid off as quickly as possible. But for the wealthy, debt is often embraced as a strategic instrument. Instead of draining their cash reserves, affluent individuals borrow at low interest rates to free up liquidity, allowing their money to remain invested in higher-yield opportunities. This practice, known as **positive leverage**, enables them to earn more on investments than they pay in interest.

One of the most common strategies is **borrowing against assets**. High-net-worth individuals often use real estate, stocks, or other holdings as collateral to secure loans. This allows them to access large sums of money without selling their assets, which would trigger capital gains taxes. For example, billionaires frequently use **securities-backed loans**, borrowing against their stock portfolios to fund new ventures or even personal expenses. By doing so, they avoid capital gains taxes while continuing to benefit from asset appreciation.

Another advantage the wealthy exploit is the **tax efficiency of debt**. In many jurisdictions, interest payments on mortgages, business loans, or investment loans are tax-deductible. This reduces taxable income and makes borrowing cheaper than liquidating assets. The "**buy, borrow, die**" strategy is a well-known example: wealthy individuals buy appreciating assets, borrow against them to fund their lifestyle, and upon death, pass them to heirs with a stepped-up cost basis—effectively avoiding capital gains taxes altogether.

Debt also serves as a **scaling mechanism**. Instead of tying up all their capital in one property or business, wealthy investors use leverage to acquire multiple assets. A real estate investor, for instance, may use mortgages to purchase several properties, each generating rental income and appreciating in value. Similarly, business owners often finance expansion through loans, allowing them to grow faster than if they relied solely on profits.

Liquidity and flexibility are equally important. By using debt strategically, the wealthy avoid being "cash poor." They keep reserves available for emergencies or market opportunities, while financing large purchases with low-interest loans. This flexibility allows them to act quickly when asset prices drop, buying undervalued investments while others are constrained.

The difference between the average borrower and the wealthy lies in **mindset and discipline**. While many see debt as dangerous, the wealthy distinguish between "good debt" (used to acquire appreciating or income-generating assets) and "bad debt" (used for consumption or high-interest liabilities). By mastering this discipline, they transform debt from a liability into an engine of wealth creation.

***

Preview of Potential Savings (Timeline and Interest)

Previewing potential savings from accelerated mortgage strategies reveals just how transformative they can be—cutting years off repayment and saving tens of thousands in interest.

One of the most compelling reasons to explore alternatives to the traditional 30-year mortgage is the sheer scale of potential savings. By restructuring payments or adopting strategies like velocity banking, homeowners can dramatically reduce both the timeline of repayment and the total interest paid. For example, a $300,000 loan at 6% interest over 30 years results in a total repayment of **$647,514**, with **$347,514 in interest alone**. That means more than half of what the borrower pays never builds equity—it simply enriches the lender.

Now consider the impact of accelerated repayment. By making biweekly payments instead of monthly, the same loan could be paid off in about **25 years**, saving nearly **$50,000 in interest**. If lump-sum principal payments are added strategically, the timeline can shrink even further. With velocity banking, advocates claim that a 30-year loan can be reduced to **7–10 years**, with interest savings exceeding **$200,000** depending on the loan size and interest rate. This is not just a minor adjustment—it is a complete transformation of the borrower's financial future.

The difference becomes even clearer when comparing amortization schedules. In a traditional mortgage, the first decade is dominated by interest payments, with little progress made on the principal. Accelerated strategies flip this dynamic, attacking the principal early and shifting future payments toward equity. This means homeowners build wealth faster, free themselves from debt sooner, and redirect funds toward investments, retirement, or other financial goals.

Beyond the numbers, the psychological impact of these savings is profound. Knowing that debt can be eliminated in under a decade rather than three decades provides a sense of freedom and control. Families can plan for college, retirement, or business ventures without the looming shadow of mortgage debt. The savings in interest are not just financial—they represent reclaimed years of life, energy, and opportunity.

In short, previewing potential savings highlights the stark contrast between traditional repayment and accelerated strategies. While a 30-year mortgage locks borrowers into decades of interest payments, innovative approaches can cut the timeline in half—or more—while saving hundreds of thousands of dollars. This is the promise of financial liberation: not just owning a home, but owning your future.

***

Real-Life Success Story Snapshot

One of the most powerful ways to understand the impact of velocity banking is through real-life examples. Consider the case of a homeowner with a $250,000 mortgage at 6% interest. Under a traditional 30-year repayment plan, the total cost of the loan would exceed **$450,000**, with nearly **$200,000 paid in interest**. By adopting velocity banking, this borrower used a home equity line of credit (HELOC) to make lump-sum payments toward the principal while cycling income through the HELOC to minimize interest charges. Within just **nine years**, the mortgage was completely paid off, saving more than **$150,000 in interest** compared to the original schedule.

Another snapshot comes from families who used velocity banking to accelerate debt payoff while maintaining liquidity. One couple redirected their monthly income into a HELOC, using it as a financial hub. By carefully managing expenses and consistently applying lump-sum payments to their mortgage, they reduced their 30-year loan to **12 years**. The key was discipline: every dollar was leveraged to reduce interest, while the HELOC provided flexibility for emergencies and cash flow management.

These stories highlight the **psychological transformation** as much as the financial one. Homeowners often describe the relief of watching their mortgage balance shrink rapidly, replacing decades of debt with a clear path to freedom. Instead of feeling trapped in a "mortgage prison," they gained confidence and control over their finances. The ability to save six figures in interest and reclaim 15–20 years of life without debt is not just a financial victory—it is a profound emotional liberation.

Of course, success requires careful planning. As experts caution, velocity banking depends on favorable conditions: a HELOC rate lower than the mortgage rate, strong cash flow, and disciplined budgeting. Without these, the strategy can backfire, leaving borrowers juggling debt between two loans. But when applied wisely, the results are undeniable—real families have proven that it is possible to break free from the 30-year sentence and achieve mortgage freedom in under a decade.

***

Who This Book Is For

This book is written for **homeowners with stable income** who want to break free from the traditional 30-year mortgage trap. A steady income is essential because strategies like velocity banking and accelerated debt payoff rely on consistent cash flow. Without predictable earnings, it becomes difficult to maintain the discipline required to redirect funds toward principal reduction. Studies on mortgage acceleration consistently emphasize that borrowers with reliable income streams are best positioned to benefit from these methods, as they can sustain the financial rhythm needed to shorten repayment timelines.

It is also for **people with financial discipline**—those who are willing to budget carefully, track expenses, and resist the temptation of unnecessary spending. Debt acceleration strategies demand intentionality. Research from the National Endowment for Financial Education shows that disciplined budgeting and consistent repayment behaviors are the strongest predictors of successful debt elimination. Without discipline, even the most powerful financial tools can backfire, leaving borrowers juggling multiple obligations instead of reducing them.

Another key audience is **those with equity in their homes**. Equity provides the leverage needed to access tools like home equity lines of credit (HELOCs), which are central to velocity banking. According to Bankrate, homeowners who have built up at least 15–20% equity are in the best position to use HELOCs strategically, since lenders are more willing to extend favorable terms. Equity is not just a measure of ownership—it is a financial resource that can be harnessed to accelerate debt payoff and unlock liquidity.

Finally, this book is for **individuals comfortable with strategic debt management**. Unlike traditional repayment methods, velocity banking requires a mindset shift: debt is not simply something to be eliminated, but something to be managed and leveraged. Wealthy individuals have long used debt strategically to preserve liquidity and grow assets, and homeowners can adopt similar principles on a smaller scale. Comfort with debt management means understanding the risks—such as variable interest rates on HELOCs—and having the confidence to navigate them responsibly.

In short, this book is for homeowners who are financially stable, disciplined, and ready to embrace a new way of thinking about debt. It is not for everyone, but for those who fit this profile, the strategies outlined here can transform a 30-year sentence into a decade-long journey toward freedom.

***

Who This Book Is NOT For

This book is **not for those with unstable income**. Strategies such as velocity banking depend on consistent cash flow to cycle money through a home equity line of credit (HELOC) and make lump-sum payments toward the mortgage. Without reliable income, borrowers risk falling behind on payments or accumulating additional debt. Research from the Consumer Financial Protection Bureau highlights that households with irregular income streams are more vulnerable to default when using complex debt strategies, as they lack the stability needed to sustain repayment schedules.

It is also **not for people with poor spending habits**. Financial discipline is the cornerstone of debt acceleration. If borrowers frequently overspend, rely heavily on credit cards, or fail to budget carefully, velocity banking can backfire. Instead of reducing debt, they may end up juggling balances between a HELOC, mortgage, and consumer debt. Studies on household debt management show that poor spending control is one of the strongest predictors of financial distress, making advanced strategies unsuitable for those unwilling to change their habits.

This book is **not for homeowners with minimal equity**. Equity is the foundation of velocity banking, as it provides access to a HELOC. Without sufficient equity—typically at least 15–20% of the home's value—lenders may not approve favorable credit terms, or borrowers may face higher interest rates that negate the benefits of the strategy. According to Bankrate, homeowners with little equity are better served by focusing on traditional repayment methods until they build enough ownership stake to leverage their property strategically.

Finally, this book is **not for individuals uncomfortable with complexity**. Velocity banking and similar strategies require a willingness to learn, track, and manage multiple financial instruments. Borrowers must understand amortization schedules, interest calculations, and cash flow cycles. For those who prefer simplicity or feel overwhelmed by financial details, these methods may create more stress than relief. As financial educators often note, complex strategies demand not only knowledge but confidence in execution—without both, borrowers risk missteps that can be costly.

In short, this book is not for everyone. It is not for those without stable income, financial discipline, sufficient equity, or comfort with complexity. Recognizing these limitations ensures that readers approach the material with realistic expectations. For the right audience, the strategies outlined here can be transformative; for the wrong audience, they can be risky.

***

How to Use This Book

This book is structured to take you step by step through the process of understanding debt, exposing the hidden costs of traditional mortgages, and introducing strategies like velocity banking that can accelerate your path to freedom. Each chapter builds on the last, beginning with foundational concepts such as the true cost of a 30-year mortgage, then moving into advanced strategies for debt elimination, and finally offering real-life success stories and practical applications. The structure is intentional: it mirrors the journey from awareness to action, ensuring that readers not only learn but also apply what they discover.

To make the content actionable, the book includes **interactive elements and worksheets**. These are designed to help you calculate your own mortgage costs, track spending habits, and model potential savings using different strategies. Financial educators emphasize that interactive learning—such as filling out worksheets and applying formulas to personal data—significantly improves retention and empowers readers to take ownership of their financial decisions. By engaging with these tools, you move beyond theory into practice, customizing the strategies to fit your unique situation.

The **recommended reading pace** is gradual and reflective. Rather than rushing through the material, readers are encouraged to digest one chapter at a time, pausing to complete the exercises and reflect on how the concepts apply to their lives. Studies on adult learning show that pacing content with reflection and application leads to deeper understanding and long-term behavioral change. This book is not a quick read—it is a workbook for transformation, meant to be revisited as your financial journey evolves.

Finally, the book is supported by **supplementary online resources**. These include downloadable worksheets, video tutorials, and updated guides on mortgage strategies and debt management. Because financial markets and lending practices change over time, online resources ensure that readers have access to the most current information. According to the National Endowment for Financial Education, combining printed material with digital resources creates a blended learning environment that maximizes impact. By leveraging these tools, you can stay informed, adapt strategies to new conditions, and continue progressing toward debt freedom.

In short, this book is both a roadmap and a toolkit. Its structure, interactive exercises, recommended pace, and online supplements are designed to guide you from knowledge to action, ensuring that you not only understand the principles but also apply them to achieve lasting financial liberation.

Sources: National Endowment for Financial Education – Research on financial literacy and interactive learning American Psychological Association – Studies on adult learning and behavioral change NEFE & Bankrate – Blended learning approaches in financial education

CHAPTER 1:

The Mortgage Money Trap

The Amortization Scam (Not Really, But...)

How Mortgage Amortization Works

At first glance, mortgage amortization seems straightforward: you borrow money to buy a home, then pay it back in equal monthly installments until the loan balance reaches zero. This is the essence of a **fully amortized loan**, where each payment covers both principal and interest. However, the hidden trap lies in the way these payments are structured. In the early years of a 30-year mortgage, the majority of each payment goes toward interest, not principal. This means homeowners spend years enriching the lender before they begin to build significant equity.

For example, on a $300,000 loan at 6% interest, the monthly payment is about $1,799. In the first month, nearly **$1,500 goes to interest**, while only about **$300 reduces the principal**. This imbalance continues for years, with interest dominating the payment schedule. Only in the later stages of the loan does the balance shift, with more of each payment applied to principal. By then, however, borrowers have already paid tens of thousands in interest.

This structure is intentional. Lenders design amortization schedules to maximize interest collection in the early years, when the loan balance is highest. Because interest is calculated on the outstanding principal, the larger the balance, the more interest accrues. As a result, borrowers are locked into a system where their payments feel steady, but the progress toward ownership is painfully slow. The "scam" is not that amortization is fraudulent—it is that the system is tilted heavily in favor of lenders, creating what feels like a financial trap.

Understanding amortization is crucial because it directly impacts **home equity, refinancing options, and long-term costs**. Equity builds slowly under traditional amortization, limiting a homeowner's ability to refinance or borrow against their property in the early years. This delay can leave families financially vulnerable, especially if they need liquidity or face unexpected expenses. Moreover, the longer the loan term, the more interest is paid overall. A 15-year mortgage, for instance, costs far less in interest than a 30-year loan, even though the monthly payments are higher.

The takeaway is clear: **amortization is designed to benefit lenders first and borrowers second.** While it ensures predictable payments, it also locks homeowners into decades of interest-heavy obligations. Recognizing this imbalance is the first step toward breaking free from the mortgage money trap and exploring strategies—like accelerated payments or velocity banking—that shift the balance back in favor of the borrower.

***

Section 1: Front-Loaded Interest Explained with Real Examples

Front-loaded interest is the hidden mechanism that makes mortgages so costly in the early years—forcing borrowers to pay lenders first before they ever build meaningful equity.

Mortgage amortization is structured so that interest payments dominate the early years of repayment. This is known as **front-loaded interest**. Because interest is calculated on the outstanding principal balance, the largest portion of payments in the beginning goes toward interest rather than reducing the loan itself. As a result, homeowners spend years paying lenders before they begin to see significant progress in ownership.

Take a real example: on a **$300,000 loan at 6% interest over 30 years**, the monthly payment is about **$1,799**. In the very first month, **$1,500 goes to interest**, while only **$299 reduces the principal**. Even after five years of payments—nearly **$108,000 paid in total**—the loan balance has only dropped to about **$280,000**. This means the borrower has paid over **$90,000 in interest** while reducing the loan by just **$20,000**. The imbalance is stark: the bank collects its profit upfront, while the homeowner's equity grows painfully slowly.

Another example highlights the long-term impact. On a **$250,000 loan at 5% interest**, the borrower pays **$1,342 per month**. In the first year, more than **$12,000 of the $16,000 paid goes to interest**, leaving only about **$4,000 applied to principal**. By year 10, the borrower has paid over **$160,000 total**, but the loan balance is still around **$200,000**. This demonstrates how front-loaded interest keeps borrowers locked into debt for decades, even when they feel they are making steady payments.

This structure is not accidental—it is designed to maximize lender profits. Because interest is front-loaded, borrowers who refinance, sell, or default in the first 10–15 years have already paid the majority of the interest owed, ensuring the bank collects its earnings early. According to *Investopedia*, amortization schedules are intentionally structured this way to protect lenders, not borrowers.

The psychological effect of front-loaded interest is equally significant. Many homeowners believe they are steadily building equity, but in reality, they are servicing interest for years before making meaningful progress. This can lead to frustration, financial stress, and the sense of being trapped in a "mortgage prison." Recognizing this dynamic is the first step toward breaking free—whether through accelerated payments, biweekly schedules, or strategies like velocity banking that attack the principal early.

***

Section 2: Why Your First 10 Years Barely Touch Principal

The first decade of a 30-year mortgage is designed to benefit the lender, not the borrower—most of your payments go toward interest, leaving the principal barely touched.

When homeowners commit to a 30-year mortgage, they often believe that every monthly payment steadily reduces their loan balance. In reality, the first 10 years are dominated by **front-loaded interest**, meaning the majority of each payment goes to the lender rather than toward building equity. This is the hidden trap of amortization: while the payment amount remains fixed, the distribution between interest and principal is heavily skewed in the lender's favor during the early years.

Like in the previous example, on a **$300,000 loan at 6% interest**, the monthly payment is about **$1,799**. In the first year, nearly **$16,000 of the $21,600 paid goes to interest**, while only about **$5,600 reduces the principal**. Even after **10 years of payments—over $215,000 paid in total—the loan balance is still around $250,000**. This means that despite a decade of steady payments, the borrower has barely reduced the debt, while the bank has already collected more than **$150,000 in interest**.

This imbalance occurs because interest is calculated on the outstanding principal balance. At the beginning of the loan, the balance is at its highest, so interest charges are maximized. As the years progress and the principal slowly decreases, the share of each payment applied to interest declines, and more is directed toward principal. But this shift takes time—often more than a decade—before borrowers see meaningful progress.

The consequences are significant. Homeowners who sell or refinance within the first 10 years often discover that they have built very little equity. According to *Experian*, this is why many borrowers feel trapped: they have paid tens of thousands of dollars but still owe nearly the full amount of the original loan. Lenders, however, benefit enormously, as they collect the bulk of their profit early in the repayment schedule.

Psychologically, this structure creates frustration and a sense of being stuck in a "mortgage prison." Borrowers believe they are making progress, but the numbers reveal otherwise. This is why strategies like **biweekly payments, lump-sum principal reductions, or velocity banking** are so powerful—they attack the principal early, shifting the balance of payments away from interest and accelerating equity growth.

In short, the first 10 years of a mortgage barely touch the principal because the system is designed to maximize lender profits upfront. Recognizing this reality is the first step toward breaking free from the trap and reclaiming financial control.

***

Section 3: Visual Breakdown of Payment Allocation Over Time

A visual breakdown of mortgage payments over time reveals the hidden imbalance between interest and principal, showing why borrowers feel trapped in the early years of a loan.

Mortgage payments may look simple on the surface—one fixed monthly amount for 30 years—but the way those payments are allocated tells a very different story. In the beginning, the majority of each payment goes toward **interest**, while only a small fraction reduces the **principal balance**. Over time, this ratio slowly shifts, with more of each payment applied to principal. This structure, known as **amortization**, is designed to protect lenders by ensuring they collect most of their profit upfront.

To illustrate, let's break down a **$300,000 loan at 6% interest over 30 years**:

Year 1: Monthly payment ≈ $1,799. Of this, about **$1,500 goes to interest** and only **$299 reduces principal**. After 12 months, the borrower has paid over **$21,600**, but the loan balance has only dropped by about **$3,600.**

Year 5: After paying nearly **$108,000 total**, the loan balance is still around **$280,000**. More than **$90,000 has gone to interest**, while less than **$20,000 has reduced the debt.**

Year 10: By this point, the borrower has paid over **$215,000**, yet the loan balance remains close to **$250,000**. Roughly **70% of payments in the first decade went to interest**, leaving equity growth painfully slow.

Year 20: The balance finally begins to drop more quickly, with payments split more evenly between interest and principal. Still, the borrower has already paid more than **$350,000**, much of it interest.

Year 30: The loan is fully repaid, but the total cost is about **$647,514**, meaning **$347,514 was interest alone**—more than the original loan amount.

This breakdown highlights the **front-loaded nature of mortgage payments.** Borrowers spend the first decade servicing interest, with little progress on ownership. Only in the later years does the balance shift, allowing principal reduction to accelerate. For many, this creates frustration and the sense of being stuck in a "mortgage prison."

The visual takeaway is clear:

Early years = interest-heavy payments (bank profits).

Middle years = gradual shift toward principal.

Final years = principal-heavy payments (borrower equity).

Understanding this allocation is critical. It explains why refinancing, selling, or defaulting in the first 10–15 years often leaves homeowners with little equity despite years of payments. It also underscores the importance of strategies like **biweekly payments, lump-sum contributions, or velocity banking**, which attack the principal early and flip the balance in favor of the borrower.

In short, the visual breakdown of payment allocation exposes the hidden mechanics of amortization: decades of interest first, equity later. Recognizing this imbalance empowers homeowners to adopt smarter strategies that accelerate debt freedom.

Yearly Summary Table – $300,000 Mortgage at 6% (30 Years)

Year	Total Paid (Cumulative)	Principal Paid	Interest Paid	Remaining Balance
1	$21,588	$3,576	$18,012	$296,424
5	$107,940	$18,180	$89,760	$281,820
10	$215,880	$49,020	$166,860	$250,980
15	$323,820	$96,480	$227,340	$203,520
20	$431,760	$165,720	$266,040	$134,280
30	$647,640	$300,000	$347,640	$0

Key Insights for Readers

Front-loaded interest: In the first 10 years, nearly **$167,000 goes to interest**, while only **$49,000 reduces principal.**

True cost of the loan: The $300,000 mortgage ends up costing **$647,640 total**, with **$347,640 in interest alone**—more than the original loan amount.

Equity growth is slow: After 15 years (halfway through the loan), the borrower still owes over **$200,000**, showing how little progress is made in the first half of the schedule.

Acceleration matters: Extra payments or strategies like velocity banking can dramatically reduce interest costs and shorten the timeline, saving homeowners tens of thousands.

How to Use This Breakdown

The **Excel amortization schedule** (monthly breakdown) allows readers to see exactly how each payment is split between principal and interest.

The **yearly summary table** provides a quick snapshot of progress at major milestones, making the imbalance between interest and principal clear.

Readers can adapt this model to their own loan size and interest rate using online calculators (e.g., Bankrate Mortgage Calculator) to visualize their personal debt journey.

In short, this chart shows that the "mortgage money trap" is real—borrowers pay lenders first, themselves last. By presenting both the monthly Excel schedule and yearly summary, readers can grasp the hidden cost of their loan and be motivated to explore faster payoff strategies.

***

Section 4: Traditional Payoff Methods and Their Limitations

Bi-Weekly Payments: How Much Do They Really Save?

Bi-weekly payments are one of the most common strategies recommended to shorten a mortgage. Instead of making 12 monthly payments per year, borrowers make half-payments every two weeks, resulting in 26 half-payments—or 13 full payments—annually. This extra payment each year can reduce a 30-year mortgage by about **four to six years** and save tens of thousands in interest. For example, on a $300,000 loan at 6% interest, bi-weekly payments can save around **$47,000 in interest**. While helpful, this method still leaves borrowers with more than two decades of debt, meaning the psychological and financial burden remains heavy.

Extra Principal Payments: Effective but Slow

Making extra payments directly toward the principal is another traditional method. Even small amounts—such as an extra $100 per month—can shorten the loan term and reduce interest. On a $250,000 loan at 5% interest, adding $100 monthly can save about **$30,000 in interest** and cut the loan by three years. Larger lump sums, such as $5,000 annually, can save more than **$80,000** and reduce the loan by seven years. However, the progress is incremental, and the borrower must maintain discipline for decades. Without consistent extra payments, the impact is minimal, making this method effective but slow.

Refinancing: Costs and Limitations

Refinancing is often promoted as a way to lower interest rates and reduce monthly payments. While refinancing can save money if rates drop significantly, it comes with upfront costs such as closing fees, appraisal charges, and potential points paid to secure lower rates. These costs can range from **2% to 6% of the loan amount**, meaning a $300,000 refinance could cost between **$6,000 and $18,000**. Additionally, refinancing resets the amortization schedule, meaning borrowers may once again face front-loaded interest. Without careful planning, refinancing can extend debt rather than shorten it.

15-Year Mortgage: Higher Payments, Inflexibility

Switching to a 15-year mortgage is another option. This method drastically reduces interest costs—for example, a $300,000 loan at 6% over 15 years costs about **$155,000 in interest**, compared to **$347,000 over 30 years**. However, the monthly payments are much higher—about **$2,532 versus $1,799**—which can strain household budgets. The lack of flexibility is a major drawback: borrowers are locked into higher payments, leaving less room for emergencies, investments, or lifestyle needs. For families with variable income or unexpected expenses, this rigidity can create financial stress.

Why These Methods Leave Money on the Table

While all these traditional methods provide some savings, they fail to fully address the structural imbalance of mortgage amortization. Because interest is front-loaded, small adjustments only chip away at the problem rather than dismantling it. Borrowers may save tens of thousands, but they still pay hundreds of thousands in interest and remain in debt for decades. The opportunity cost is enormous: money tied up in interest could instead be invested, compounding into wealth over time. For example, $100,000 saved in interest invested at 7% annual returns could grow to nearly **$400,000 in 30 years**. Traditional methods leave this potential on the table, keeping borrowers trapped in the mortgage money cycle.

In short, traditional payoff methods are helpful but limited. They reduce debt slowly, require long-term discipline, and often fail to unlock the full financial freedom available through more aggressive strategies like velocity banking.

***

Section 5: Recap of the traditional payoff methods and their limitations

Traditional mortgage payoff methods can help, but they rarely dismantle the core problem of front-loaded interest. Here's a practical breakdown—what each method does, how much it can save, and why many borrowers still leave money on the table.

Bi-weekly payments: how much do they really save?

Bi-weekly payments turn 12 monthly payments into 26 half-payments—effectively one extra full payment per year. On a $300,000 mortgage at 6% over 30 years (standard monthly payment ≈ $1,799), switching to bi-weekly can cut the term to roughly 25–26 years and save around $40,000–$50,000 in interest, depending on exact start date and compounding. That's meaningful progress, but you're still in debt for more than two decades, and the early years remain interest-heavy despite the extra payment.

Core effect: One extra full payment per year reduces principal faster.

Typical savings: ~4–6 years off the term; ~$40k–$50k interest saved on a $300k @ 6%.

Limitations: Doesn't change amortization structure; savings are gradual, not transformative.

Extra principal payments: effective but slow

Applying extra funds directly to principal (monthly or annual lump sums) is the most flexible traditional strategy. For a $300,000 mortgage at 6%:

Extra $100/month: Saves roughly $30,000–$35,000 in interest and trims ~2–3 years.

Extra $300/month: Saves ~$90,000–$100,000 and trims ~6–7 years.

Annual $5,000 lump sum: Saves ~$70,000–$90,000, reducing the term by ~5–6 years.

These are solid savings, but they demand long-term consistency and budgeting discipline. The early-payment interest bias still dominates, so the psychological effect of "barely moving the needle" in the first decade can remain.

Core effect: Direct principal reduction lowers future interest.

Typical savings: Scales with contribution size; requires decades of consistency.

Limitations: Slow to overcome front-loaded interest; vulnerable to income variability.

Refinancing: costs and limitations

Refinancing can lower your rate or shorten your term, but it comes with upfront costs and a reset of amortization:

Closing costs: Commonly 2%–6% of the loan (e.g., \$6,000–\$18,000 on \$300,000).

Breakeven math: If monthly savings are \$250, you need 24–72 months just to recoup costs.

Clock reset risk: Restarting a 30-year schedule re-front-loads interest unless moving to a shorter term.

Refinancing shines when rate drops are substantial and you plan to stay put beyond breakeven. Otherwise, fees and the amortization reset can dilute or delay real savings.

Core effect: Lower rate or shorter term changes payment profile.

Typical savings: Strong if rate drop is large and fees are low.

Limitations: Upfront costs, rate/term risk, and interest-front-loading resets.

15-year mortgage: higher payments, inflexibility

Moving to a 15-year term slashes interest dramatically but demands higher, inflexible payments:

\$300,000 @ 6%:

30-year interest ≈ \$347,514; payment ≈ \$1,799

15-year interest ≈ \$155,000; payment ≈ \$2,532

The math is compelling—nearly \$200,000 less interest—but budget rigidity is real. Higher fixed payments reduce cash-flow resilience, squeeze emergency savings, and limit optionality for investments or unexpected expenses.

Core effect: Compresses timeline, cuts interest sharply.

Typical savings: Six figures on mid-size loans at moderate rates.

Limitations: Budget strain, less flexibility, risk during income shocks.

Why these methods leave money on the table

Traditional tactics chip away at principal but rarely overturn the amortization bias that front-loads interest. The result is decades-long debt and large opportunity costs:

Front-loaded interest persists: Early years still service lender profit first.

Incremental progress: Savings are spread over decades; psychological payoff is slow.

Opportunity cost: Every extra dollar to a mortgage is a dollar not compounding elsewhere. For example, diverting $100,000 to interest rather than investing at a 7% average return could forgo ~>$380,000 over 30 years.

Liquidity trade-offs: Higher fixed payments (15-year) or closing costs (refi) can weaken cash buffers and reduce agility for better-yield opportunities.

The bottom line: traditional methods help, but they often underutilize cash flow, sacrifice liquidity, and prolong the psychological weight of long-term debt—leaving both interest savings and investment growth potential on the table.

Quick here's the breakdown for readers

Bi-weekly payments:

Pros: Simple, automatic extra payment each year; modest interest savings.

Cons: Still 25+ years of debt; doesn't change amortization structure.

Extra principal payments:

Pros: Flexible, directly reduces future interest; scalable with budget.

Cons: Requires consistency; slow to counter front-loaded interest.

Refinancing:

Pros: Lower rate or shorter term can yield sizable savings.

Cons: 2%–6% fees; breakeven time; potential re-front-loading.

15-year mortgage:

Pros: Major interest reduction; faster equity build.

Cons: Higher, inflexible payments; cash-flow risk.

***

Section 6: The Psychology of Long-Term Debt

The psychology of long-term debt shapes behavior as surely as the numbers—it wears on confidence, restricts choices, and changes how people plan for the future.

Long-term mortgage debt creates a slow-burning fatigue that affects daily life. Mortgage fatigue is the quiet erosion of motivation and optimism that happens when decades of payments feel toiled away with little visible progress. Homeowners report stress from the constant reminder that a large portion of every payment benefits the lender more than themselves. Financial stress from ongoing debt shows up as reduced risk tolerance, avoidance of financial planning, and mental bandwidth diverted from growth activities such as career advancement or entrepreneurship. Studies on household finance link persistent debt to poorer sleep, lower job satisfaction, and increased anxiety, which in turn can undermine the very income stability needed to escape the debt cycle.

The prospect of becoming debt-free sooner has profound psychological benefits. Eliminating a mortgage, years or decades ahead of schedule delivers relief that goes beyond monthly cash flow: it restores a sense of security, reduces chronic stress, and creates mental space for future planning. People who pay off major debts often describe a renewed willingness to take calculated risks—starting a business, changing careers, or investing more aggressively—because they are no longer carrying the psychological weight of a large, persistent liability. This freedom is both emotional and practical: lower fixed expenses mean more choices and greater resilience against financial shocks.

Wealth building accelerates once the mortgage payment falls away. Money previously earmarked for interest and principal can be redirected into higher-yield investments, retirement accounts, or business ventures. Compound returns amplify this effect: a household that redirects even modest monthly savings into a diversified portfolio at historical market averages can see substantial growth over 10–30 years. For example, funds that would have been consumed by interest can instead compound tax-advantaged in retirement accounts, shifting the household from debt service to asset accumulation. This transition—from paying rent to capitalizing on returns—marks the shift from surviving to thriving.

Mortgage payoff timing also has direct implications for retirement security. Carrying a mortgage into retirement increases required minimum cash outflows at a time when income may be fixed or falling. Retirees with mortgage-free homes have lower monthly expenses and more flexibility to draw from retirement accounts in a tax-efficient manner. Conversely, retirees who still service large mortgages may delay retirement, withdraw more from retirement savings, or take on risky income strategies to cover payments. Research on retirement readiness emphasizes that reducing or eliminating housing debt before retirement significantly improves the probability of a secure, stress-reduced retirement.

In short, the psychological costs of long-term debt are real and compounding: they sap energy, limit choices, and slow wealth creation. Paying a mortgage off earlier unlocks emotional freedom, accelerates wealth building through redirected savings and compound returns, and markedly improves retirement security—making the case for strategic acceleration as both a financial and life strategy.

Sources: Investopedia – mortgage and amortization insights; Experian – consumer credit and financial stress research; Bankrate – personal finance and mortgage planning; National Endowment for Financial Education (NEFE) – financial behavior studies; Fidelity and AARP – retirement readiness research; Morningstar – investment compounding principles.

CHAPTER 2:

What Is a HELOC and How Does It Work?

HELOC Basics

A HELOC is a versatile but powerful tool when used correctly—a revolving line of credit secured by your home that can provide liquidity, flexibility, and strategic leverage.

A **home equity line of credit (HELOC)** is a revolving line of credit that uses the equity in your home as collateral. Unlike a one-time loan, a HELOC functions more like a credit card: you can borrow, repay, and borrow again up to your credit limit during the **draw period**, which commonly lasts about ten years. During that draw period you typically make interest-only or minimum payments based on the outstanding balance; after the draw period ends, you enter a **repayment period** when principal repayment is required and monthly payments often increase.

The amount you can borrow is usually determined by how much equity you have in the property—commonly up to around **80%–85% of the home's value minus existing mortgage debt**—and by your creditworthiness and income. Lenders evaluate credit score, employment history, and debt-to-income ratio much like they do for the original mortgage, because your home remains on the line if you default.

HELOCs most often carry **variable interest rates**, tied to an index such as the U.S. prime rate plus a lender margin, which means monthly costs can rise or fall as rates change. Some lenders offer options to convert portions of the outstanding balance to a fixed rate for stability, but that conversion usually comes at a higher fixed rate compared to the variable option. Because rates can move, borrowers must plan for payment volatility, especially when the loan transitions from the draw to the repayment phase as is mentioned in the information by the Consumer Financial Protection Bureau.

Functionally, a HELOC acts as a **financial hub**: you draw funds when needed (via checks, transfers, or a card), repay from income or other sources, and that repayment replenishes available credit. This revolving feature makes HELOCs useful for short-term liquidity needs, large planned expenses, or strategic cash-flow maneuvers—but it also requires disciplined repayment habits to avoid overborrowing and to protect the home that secures the loan.

Finally, HELOCs come with fees and terms that vary by lender—application fees, appraisal costs, annual fees, and early closure penalties are possible—so shopping and comparing offers is essential. Because HELOCs are secured and flexible, they can be lower-cost options than unsecured credit, but the security comes with the serious risk that failure to repay could lead to foreclosure.

***

Section 1: How It Differs from a Home Equity Loan

A HELOC (home equity line of credit) and a home equity loan both let you borrow against the value you've built in your home, but they work very differently in structure and use. A HELOC is a revolving line of credit you can draw from as needed during a draw period, paying interest only on the outstanding balance and repaying and re-borrowing up to the limit, much like a credit card; by contrast, a home equity loan delivers a one-time lump sum repaid in fixed installments with a set term and typically a fixed interest rate. This core distinction—revolving flexibility versus one-time predictability—drives how each product fits different financial goals and risk tolerances.

Interest rate behavior and payment predictability are major differentiators. HELOCs most commonly carry variable rates tied to an index plus a margin, so monthly payments can rise or fall with market rates; some lenders let you convert portions to a fixed rate, but that reduces the product's flexibility. Home equity loans usually offer fixed rates and predictable monthly payments, which can be preferable when you need a stable repayment plan for a specific, one-time expense. Because HELOC payments can be interest-only during the draw period, borrowers must plan for higher payments later when principal repayment begins.

The timing and purpose of borrowing also separate the two products. Use a HELOC for ongoing or uncertain needs—staged home renovations, tuition paid over several years, or as a short-term cash-flow tool—because you borrow only what you need when you need it. A home equity loan is better suited for a single, known expense such as consolidating high-interest debt, a major remodel with a fixed budget, or a one-time large purchase where predictable monthly payments help budgeting. Choosing the right product depends on whether your need is flexible and recurring or fixed and finiteClark.com.

Fees, underwriting, and risks are similar but play out differently in practice. Both typically require sufficient equity (often 60–85% of home value minus existing liens), credit checks, and closing costs; however,

HELOCs may include annual fees, draw-period specifics, and possible appraisal or inactivity charges, while home equity loans more closely resemble second mortgages with straightforward closing costs and fixed repayment schedules. Because both use the home as collateral, missed payments on either product can risk foreclosure, so discipline and contingency planning are essential sourced from Investopedia.

Quick breakdown for readers

Definition:

HELOC: Revolving credit line secured by home equity; draw period then repayment period; variable rate typical.

Home Equity Loan: Lump-sum loan secured by equity; fixed payments and usually fixed rate.

Best uses:

HELOC: Ongoing projects, emergency liquidity, cash-flow management.

Home Equity Loan: One-time large expenses, debt consolidation when predictability is required.

Rate and payment profile:

HELOC: Variable rates; possible interest-only payments during draw period; payment volatility risk.

Home Equity Loan: Fixed rate and fixed monthly payments; more budget-friendly predictability.

Pros and cons summary:

HELOC Pros: Flexibility; borrow/repay repeatedly; only pay interest on used amount.

HELOC Cons: Variable rate risk; requires discipline to avoid overborrowing; repayment shock when draw period ends.

Home Equity Loan Pros: Predictable payments; good for fixed budgets.

Home Equity Loan Cons: Less flexible; you pay interest on the full lump sum even if not all funds are needed.

Choosing between a HELOC and a home equity loan comes down to your cash-flow needs, tolerance for rate variability, and discipline in managing revolving credit. Compare offers, read draw and repayment terms carefully, and model worst-case rate scenarios so the product you select supports your financial goals without creating undue risk.

***

Section 2: The Two Phases of a HELOC — Draw Period and Repayment Period

A HELOC is split into two distinct phases that determine how you borrow, what you pay each month, and when the lender expects the principal to be repaid. The first phase, called the draw period, is when you can access funds up to your approved credit limit, repay and re-borrow as needed, and—depending on the loan terms—often make interest-only payments on the outstanding balance. This revolving flexibility makes the HELOC behave like a credit card secured by your home: you only pay interest on the portion you use, and available credit replenishes as you pay down the balancecitizensbank.com.

The repayment period begins when the draw period ends (commonly after about 3–10 years) and changes the rules: you can no longer draw funds, and monthly payments typically shift to include both principal and interest, which can substantially increase the required payment amount each month. Because many HELOCs allow interest-only payments during the draw phase, borrowers who do not reduce principal before the end of the draw period may face payment shock when full amortization begins—sometimes doubling or more the monthly obligation depending on remaining term and balance.

How the two phases affect cash flow depends on rate structure and lender options. Most HELOCs use variable interest rates tied to an index plus a margin, so payments during both phases can rise or fall with market rates; some lenders permit converting portions of the balance to fixed-rate loans to manage long-term payment risk, but that reduces flexibility and can carry conversion costs. Planning for potential rate increases and for the repayment transition is essential because the repayment-period schedule is where the outstanding principal is amortized and where the borrower's total cost becomes fixed and unavoidable.

Practical examples make the difference clear: during a 10-year draw period you might borrow $30,000 for renovations and pay only interest at first, keeping monthly cost low and preserving liquidity; but if you still owe $30,000 when the draw ends and the repayment period requires amortization over 10–20 years, your monthly payment will include principal and could be sizable—so using the HELOC for short-term needs or deliberately paying down principal during the draw period mitigates future payment spikes.

A simple checklist readers can use to manage the two phases: 1. Know your draw-period length and whether interest-only payments are permitted; 2. Track outstanding balance and plan a schedule to pay down principal before the draw ends; 3. Model worst-case variable-rate scenarios and repayment-period payments to ensure affordability; 4. Ask the lender about fixed-conversion options, fees, and early-closure penalties so there are no surprises. Preparing in advance turns the HELOC from a potential liability into a strategic, manageable tool.

In short, the draw period offers short-term flexibility and low initial payments, while the repayment period demands principal repayment and often higher monthly costs. Understanding both phases, modeling future payments, and building a repayment plan during the draw period are the keys to using a HELOC safely and effectively.

***

Section 3: Variable vs Fixed-Rate HELOCs

A HELOC's interest structure is one of the most important choices a homeowner makes when tapping home equity: do you accept a variable rate that can move with the market or lock in a fixed rate for predictable payments? The choice shapes cash-flow risk, total cost, and how you use the credit line—so understanding the tradeoffs is essential for safe, strategic borrowing.

How the two rate structures work

Variable-rate HELOCs tie the borrower's rate to an index (commonly prime) plus a lender margin, so the interest and monthly payment rise or fall with market rates. Variable HELOCs typically offer lower initial rates and more lender options, which makes them attractive for short-term borrowing or when rates are expected to decline. Fixed-rate HELOCs or fixed-rate conversions lock the interest on a drawn amount for a set term, delivering payment stability but often at a higher initial rate and with fewer lender choices.

Variable HELOC: advantages and risks

The main advantages of a variable HELOC are lower starting costs and flexibility: you borrow only what you need and pay interest only on the outstanding balance, and if rates fall you benefit immediately. That makes variable HELOCs suitable for short projects or temporary cash-flow needs. The central risk is payment volatility—if benchmark rates rise, your payments increase and budget planning becomes harder. Borrowers must model worst-case rate scenarios and maintain cash buffers to avoid payment shock.

Fixed-rate HELOC: advantages and tradeoffs

Fixed-rate HELOCs provide predictable monthly payments and protection against rising market rates, which is valuable for long-term projects or borrowers who prefer certainty. The tradeoffs include a typically higher starting rate, possible conversion or origination fees, and often tighter limits on how much can be fixed. For borrowers who prioritize stability over potential savings from falling rates, fixed options reduce stress and make long-term budgeting straightforward.

Hybrid and conversion options

Many lenders now offer hybrid solutions: variable HELOCs with the option to convert portions of the outstanding balance to fixed rates, or limited fixed-rate tranches at draw time. These hybrids let borrowers lock the part of the debt they plan to carry long-term while keeping other capacity flexible for near-term needs. Converting reduces flexibility and can incur fees, so it's most useful when you know a portion of the balance will be held into the repayment phase.

Practical decision checklist for readers

Estimate how long you'll carry the balance: short-term needs often favor variable rates; long-term borrowing favors fixed rates.

Model payment scenarios: run current-rate, +200 basis points, and +400 basis points cases to see affordability risks.

Check conversion and origination fees: lower fees make conversions more attractive; higher fees can negate savings.

Consider cash-flow tolerance: if a rate spike would force you to cut essentials or risk default, prioritize fixed stability.

Explore hybrid fixes: lock the portion you expect to hold long-term, and leave the rest flexible for short-term use.

In short, variable HELOCs give lower initial cost and flexibility but carry rate risk; fixed-rate HELOCs provide predictable payments at a premium; hybrid approaches offer a middle path. Choosing wisely requires honest forecasting of how long you'll carry debt, careful stress-testing of rate moves, and comparing lender fees and conversion terms before you borrow.

***

Section 4: HELOC Structure and Terms — Credit Limits and How They're Set

Lenders set HELOC credit limits primarily by looking at how much equity you have in your home and applying a combined loan-to-value (CLTV) cap. Most lenders allow a CLTV in the neighborhood of 80%–85% of the home's appraised value, meaning your outstanding mortgage plus any HELOC cannot typically exceed that percentage of value; some lenders will go higher (up to 90% or more) in special cases, but higher CLTVs usually carry higher rates or stricter underwriting criteria.

A simple way to think about the math is this: multiply your home's appraised value by the lender's maximum allowable LTV, then subtract your current mortgage balance — the remainder is the maximum HELOC you could qualify for under that lender's policy. For example, a $500,000 house with an 85% max LTV gives a total permitted debt of $425,000; if you owe $350,000 on the mortgage, the theoretical maximum HELOC would be $75,000. Lenders, however, layer in other limits and rules (minimum and maximum dollar caps, property type adjustments, and portfolio policies), so the formula gives an estimate, not a guaranteed approval amount.

Beyond the math, personal credit and income matter. Your FICO score, debt-to-income ratio, employment history, and recent credit behavior influence both whether you qualify for the maximum CLTV and what margin the lender will add to the index rate. Strong credit profiles and low DTI ratios increase the chance of higher HELOC limits and better pricing; conversely, weaker profiles may get lower limits or be denied even if the CLTV math looks favorable.

Some lenders impose absolute dollar caps regardless of CLTV—common lower limits can be as small as $10,000–$25,000 for modest HELOCs, while banks or credit unions that cater to high-net-worth borrowers may offer lines into the hundreds of thousands or even over $1 million on very valuable properties. Geographic location, property type (condo vs single-family), and whether the property is a primary residence or an investment property can all reduce the maximum available line compared with the theoretical CLTV allowance.

Keep in mind that CLTV percentages are typical guidelines, not universal rules. Many lenders commonly use 85% as the working threshold for HELOC eligibility, but specific programs and credit unions may set different limits or special underwriting that allows higher access for qualified borrowers.

Breakdown for readers — quick checklist to estimate your HELOC limit:

Calculate your home's appraised value × lender max LTV (commonly 80%–85%).

Subtract your current mortgage balance to get a theoretical HELOC cap.

Adjust for your credit score, DTI, property type, and lender dollar caps.

Remember fees, appraisal requirements, and rate margin will affect affordability and final offer.

Understanding these elements helps you predict how much access to equity a HELOC might actually deliver, and what you'll need to do to maximize a safe, sensible credit line.

***

Section 5: Interest Rate Determination — Prime Plus Margin

A HELOC rate is most commonly expressed as the sum of the market benchmark (usually the prime rate) plus a lender margin, meaning your effective interest rate moves as the prime rate moves while the lender's margin remains fixed for your account. This simple formula—Prime + Margin—explains why HELOC rates are typically lower at the outset than comparable fixed-rate products but also why they can rise quickly when monetary policy tightens. Understanding this structure is the first step to anticipating how your monthly cost will respond to shifts in central-bank policy and market rateshome-eq.com.

Lenders set the margin based on borrower risk and the loan profile, so two homeowners with identical homes may receive different margins depending on credit score, debt-to-income ratio, and other underwriting criteria. Borrowers with stronger credit profiles (higher FICO scores and lower DTI) typically earn margins near the low end of the lender range, while borrowers with weaker profiles pay higher margins—sometimes by one or more percentage points—which materially affects monthly interest and total cost over time.

Beyond the headline rate, HELOC interest is usually calculated against the average daily balance for each billing cycle, so both the rate and the day-by-day outstanding balance determine the interest charged that month. Because many HELOCs adjust rates monthly, a small change in the prime rate translates into an immediate change in the borrower's monthly interest charge; conversely, paying down the outstanding balance earlier in the billing cycle reduces the average daily balance and therefore the interest owed for that cycle.

Most HELOCs include contractual controls—a rate floor and a rate ceiling—and other terms such as periodic rate adjustment schedules and possible conversion options that let you lock a drawn amount at a fixed rate. These features affect how much market movement you actually experience and whether conversion fees or limits apply if you later choose payment stability over flexibility.

Breakdown for readers — practical checklist to understand and manage HELOC pricing:

Know the formula: your HELOC rate = Prime rate + lender margin; the prime portion changes, margin is set by the lender.

Check your margin drivers: improve credit score and lower DTI to qualify for a tighter margin and lower overall rate.

Understand interest calculation: HELOC interest is commonly billed using the average daily balance method—paying down principal earlier in the cycle reduces interest that month.

Model rate moves: stress-test payments at current prime, +200 bps, and +400 bps to confirm affordability under rising-rate scenarios.

Review contract features: look for floors/ceilings, monthly adjustment timing, and conversion fees before borrowing.

***

Section 6: A Draw Period (Typically 10 Years)

The draw period is the initial phase of a HELOC when you have active access to the line of credit and can borrow, repay, and borrow again up to your approved limit. During this time you typically make interest-only or minimum payments on the outstanding balance, which keeps monthly cash flow low while preserving borrowing flexibility. Lenders commonly set draw periods at around ten years, though some plans offer shorter (three to five years) or occasionally longer windows; the length you receive depends on the lender, product, and borrower profile.

Because payments are frequently interest-only during the draw period, the outstanding principal may not decline unless you deliberately pay down principal. That makes the draw period a convenient tool for staged projects, ongoing expenses, or cash-flow management, but it also creates a planning obligation: if you enter the repayment period with a large outstanding balance, monthly payments can jump significantly when principal amortization begins. This dynamic—that low early payments can mask future repayment obligations—is a core risk borrowers must manage while using a HELOC.

HELOCs commonly use variable rates, so interest costs during the draw period can change with market rates; some lenders offer conversion options to fix part of a balance before the draw ends, but conversions usually reduce flexibility and can carry fees. Because draw-period behavior determines how much principal remains to amortize later, disciplined borrowing and periodic principal reductions during the draw phase materially reduce both future payment shock and total interest paid over the life of the credit line.

Breakdown for readers — practical checklist and rules of thumb:

Typical length: expect a draw period of about **10 years**, though 3–15 years is possible depending on the product and lender.

Payments during draw: usually **interest-only** or minimum payments; principal reduction is optional but recommended to lower future costs.

Borrowing behavior: treat the HELOC like a short-term bridge or staged budget tool—draw what you need; avoid leaving large balances at the draw's end.

Plan for transition: model the repayment-period payment today by amortizing your expected remaining balance over the repayment term so you aren't surprised by payment increases later.

Risk controls: maintain a cash buffer, consider making extra principal payments during the draw, and ask the lender about conversion options, fees, and any recast or early-closure penalties.

Understanding the draw period as a temporary window of flexible borrowing—not free or permanent financing—lets you use a HELOC strategically while avoiding the common pitfall of deferred principal that causes repayment shock and higher lifetime costs.

***

Section 7: HELOC Repayment Period (Typically 10–20 Years)

The repayment period is the phase that follows the draw period and usually lasts between 10 and 20 years, during which you can no longer withdraw funds and must repay principal as well as interest. During the draw period many HELOCs allow interest-only payments, which keeps monthly costs low; once repayment begins, those interest-only payments are replaced by fully amortizing principal-and-interest payments that can materially increase monthly obligations depending on the remaining balance and amortization term.

Because many HELOCs have a typical structure of a 10-year draw followed by a 20-year repayment, borrowers who carry large outstanding balances into the repayment phase often experience payment shock: what felt affordable during interest-only months can jump substantially when principal amortization begins. The size of the jump depends on how much principal remains, the repayment-term length, and the current interest rate—factors borrowers must model in advance to confirm long-term affordability.

Interest-rate risk remains relevant in the repayment period because most HELOCs are variable-rate products; if rates rise, the interest portion of the new amortizing payment will be higher, increasing the total monthly obligation. Some lenders permit converting outstanding balances (or portions of them) to fixed-rate tranches to limit future volatility, but conversions typically reduce flexibility and may carry fees or different terms, so conversion is a trade-off between stability and cost.

Practical planning during the draw period softens repayment pain: paying down principal before the draw ends, making extra principal payments, or converting portions to fixed rates can lower the amortizing balance and reduce the repayment-period payment. Borrowers should stress-test scenarios—current rate, +200 bps, and +400 bps—and amortize expected end-of-draw balances over the repayment term to see exact monthly payments under each scenario.

Breakdown for readers — repayment-period checklist and rules of thumb:

Typical length: expect a repayment period of about **10–20 years** after the draw ends.

Payment change: interest-only → principal + interest; plan for a potentially large monthly increase.

Rate exposure: variable-rate HELOCs still carry rate risk in repayment; consider conversion if you need certainty.

Mitigations: pay down principal during draw, model worst-case rate scenarios, maintain a cash buffer, and ask the lender about conversion fees and amortization schedules.

Modeling tip: amortize your projected remaining balance over the repayment term today to know the payment you'll face later.

Understanding the repayment period turns a HELOC from a surprise liability into a manageable tool: know your timelines, model worst-case payments, and take action during the draw to avoid repayment shock and limit total cost.

***

Section 8: HELOC Minimum Payment Requirements

HELOC minimum payments vary by lender and by the phase of the loan, but they commonly require only interest payments during the draw period and shift to principal-plus-interest once the repayment period begins. During the draw period (often 5–10 years), borrowers typically pay interest on the outstanding balance, which keeps monthly payments low but does not reduce principal unless the borrower elects to pay extra. When the repayment period starts, the minimum payment usually becomes the fully amortizing amount that covers both principal and interest, and that change can produce a substantial increase in the monthly obligationheloc360.com.

Lenders calculate minimum payments in different ways: interest-only (the most common during draw), a fixed percentage of the outstanding balance, or a required dollar minimum set by the servicer; the specific method should be disclosed in the HELOC agreement and on periodic statements. Because many HELOCs use variable rates tied to an index plus a margin, the interest-only minimum during the draw and the amortizing minimum during repayment can both change as benchmark rates move—so the contractual "minimum" is not necessarily fixed for the life of the credit line.

Understanding how the minimum is computed helps avoid surprises. If your HELOC offers interest-only minimums, the interest payment for a month equals roughly (outstanding balance × APR / 12); for a $50,000 balance at 5% APR, that equates to about $208 per month as the interest-only minimum. If that balance is amortized over a 20-year repayment period at the same rate, the principal-plus-interest payment would jump to roughly $330 per month—illustrating how the minimum can increase when terms change or rates rise.

Practical tips readers can use to manage minimum-payment risk:

Confirm whether your draw-period minimum is interest-only or a percentage of balance, and get the exact formula in writing.

Model the repayment-period payment now by amortizing your expected ending-of-draw balance over the repayment term to see the future minimum you'll face.

Stress-test payments under higher-rate scenarios (current rate, +200 bps, +400 bps) to ensure affordability if the HELOC is variable-rate.

If possible, make principal payments during the draw period to reduce the balance that will be amortized later and avoid payment shock.

Ask the lender about floors, caps, and conversion options (fixing part of the balance) and about any minimum-dollar payment requirements or inactivity fees that could affect your cash flow.

In short, the "minimum" on a HELOC is a moving target shaped by draw/repayment-phase rules, interest-rate dynamics, and lender-specific calculation methods—so read disclosures carefully, model worst-case payments, and proactively pay down principal during the draw period to reduce future minimums.

***

Section 9: How Interest Is Calculated on HELOCs — Daily Balance Method

The most common method lenders use to calculate HELOC interest is the **average daily balance** (often described as the daily balance) method. Under this approach the lender determines a daily interest rate by dividing your annual percentage rate by the number of days in the year, multiplies that daily rate by your outstanding balance each day, then sums those daily charges across the billing cycle to produce the monthly interest owed. Because interest accrues on the actual outstanding balance day by day, paying down principal earlier in the cycle immediately reduces that month's interest charge.

Practically, that means timing and payment size matter. If your HELOC has a balance of $50,000 and an APR of 6%, the daily rate is approximately 0.06 ÷ 365 = 0.000164; one day's interest on the full balance would be about $8.22, and the monthly interest is the sum of each day's calculated amount across the billing period. If you make a payment early in the billing cycle, you lower the average daily balance for more days, cutting that month's interest more than the same payment made on the billing cycle's last day.

Because HELOCs are usually variable-rate products, two levers determine the monthly interest charge under the daily balance method: the **current APR** (commonly Prime + margin) and the **average daily balance**. Rate changes can alter the daily rate immediately (most HELOCs adjust monthly), while balance changes affect only how many dollars are multiplied by that rate each day. Savvy borrowers therefore combine rate awareness with balance management—making larger or earlier payments during the billing cycle when rates are rising—to reduce interest costs.

There are alternative but less common methods lenders may use (adjusted balance or previous balance), so reading your HELOC agreement is essential to know exactly how your servicer computes the minimum and billed interest. The adjusted-balance method subtracts payments made during the billing cycle before calculating interest, which can further reward early payments; the previous-balance method uses the starting balance for the cycle and does not reflect intra-cycle payments, yielding higher interest in many cases. Confirming which method applies lets you plan payments to maximize savings.

Breakdown for readers — practical checklist and examples:

Formula to keep in mind: Daily interest = (APR ÷ days in year) × outstanding balance that day; Monthly interest = sum of daily interest for the billing cycle.

Example: $50,000 balance at 6% APR → daily rate ≈ 0.000164; one day's interest ≈ $8.22; paying $5,000 on day 5 versus day 25 materially reduces monthly interest.

Actionable rules: (1) Make payments early in the billing cycle to lower average daily balance; (2) if possible, schedule large principal reductions shortly after the cycle opens; (3) stress-test affordability at higher-rate scenarios because the APR portion can change monthly.

Understanding the daily-balance calculation turns a HELOC from a passive credit tool into an actively managed resource; small timing and payment choices compound into meaningful interest savings over months and years.

***

Why This Is Crucial to the Strategy

Understanding that HELOC interest is calculated on the daily (average daily) balance transforms how you use the line. When interest accrues day by day, the timing of payments matters as much as the size. A borrower who reduces the balance early in the billing cycle immediately lowers the number of dollars subject to daily interest for the remainder of that cycle, which compounds into meaningful monthly savings. For strategies that rely on short-term liquidity—borrowing against equity to temporarily fund cash flow or to accelerate mortgage principal—this mechanic is the lever that turns tactical moves into real interest savings rather than cosmetic accounting.

When you treat a HELOC as a short-term bridge to reduce mortgage interest, every dollar you move through the HELOC should be timed and sized to minimize the average daily balance. Paying down the HELOC promptly after using it reduces the days the large balance sits on the account, lowering the interest owed that month. Over repeated cycles, that disciplined timing compounds: smaller monthly interest outlays free cash flow that can be redirected to additional principal payments on the mortgage or to investments with higher expected returns, accelerating net worth growth.

Ignoring the daily-balance method turns well-intentioned strategies into money losers. If you borrow and leave high balances until the end of the billing cycle, you pay interest on the full amount for most of the cycle—and if rates rise, those interest costs jump immediately because HELOC rates typically reprice monthly. Similarly, making a large payment late in the cycle yields far less interest reduction than making it early. For anyone using HELOCs as a tactical hub—whether for velocity banking, staged renovations, or tax-timing tactics—mastering intra-cycle timing is the difference between shaving thousands off interest and merely shifting costs from one account to another.

Breakdown for readers — practical rules and checklist

Know your billing cycle dates and the day the cycle opens.

Treat the cycle start as the primary window: make large principal reductions immediately after the cycle opens to lower the average daily balance for the maximum number of days.

Prioritize payment timing over small extra amounts made late: a $1,000 payment on day 2 often saves more interest than a $1,500 payment on day 28.

Combine rate awareness with timing: if the prime rate or your margin is moving up, accelerate reductions early in the cycle to blunt rate-driven increases in monthly interest.

Automate where possible: schedule paycheck deposits or transfers to occur just after the cycle opens so available funds reduce the HELOC balance early.

Model outcomes: calculate interest for two scenarios (payment on day 3 vs. day 25) to quantify savings and motivate disciplined behavior.

Maintain a small cash buffer: don't over-leverage to the point where you can't reduce the HELOC early in the next cycle—discipline is the strategy's safety valve.

In short, the daily-balance calculation is the operational heart of any HELOC-based strategy. Mastering timing and balance management turns a flexible line of credit into a precise tool for reducing lifetime interest, avoiding payment shock, and accelerating wealth building.

***

Section 10: Average Daily Balance Examples

The average daily balance method calculates interest by applying the daily interest rate to the outstanding balance each day, then summing those daily charges across the billing cycle; this means paying principal earlier in the cycle reduces interest immediately and measurably for that month. For example, a $50,000 HELOC balance at a 6% APR has a daily rate of about $0.06 \div 365 = 0.000164$, so one day's interest on the full balance is roughly $8.22 and the monthly charge equals the sum of each day's computed amount for the billing period.

Small timing differences create meaningful outcomes. If you make a $5,000 principal payment on day 3 of a 30-day cycle, the average daily balance drops for 27 days; making that same $5,000 payment on day 27 only lowers the balance for three days—so the early payment reduces interest by roughly nine times more days and therefore substantially more dollars over that month. When HELOCs reprice monthly, reducing the average daily balance sooner also insulates you from rate increases that would otherwise apply to a higher per-day balance.

Practical numeric scenarios make decisions concrete. Scenario A: $40,000 outstanding at 6% APR with a $4,000 payment on day 2; Scenario B: same numbers but payment on day 28. Using the daily-balance method, Scenario A's average daily balance falls immediately and the month's interest might be roughly $18–25 less than Scenario B (exact savings depend on cycle length and year), illustrating that timing often beats slightly larger late payments in immediate interest reduction.

For borrowers using HELOCs tactically—whether to smooth cash flow, fund renovations, or accelerate mortgage payoff—the compounding effect of repeated early payments is powerful: shaving even $20–$50 a month in interest, repeated over years, converts to hundreds or thousands in cumulative savings. Over many cycles, disciplined early payments can materially reduce the total interest paid on revolving balances and free cash flow to apply toward long-term goals.

Breakdown for readers — step-by-step example and checklist:

Example math: daily rate = APR ÷ 365; one day's interest = daily rate × outstanding balance; monthly interest = sum of daily interest for billing days.

Quick calculation: 6% APR on $50,000 → daily interest ≈ $8.22; pay $5,000 on day 3 vs. day 25 produces a materially lower monthly interest in the early-payment case.

Rules of thumb: (1) learn your billing cycle dates; (2) schedule large principal reductions immediately after the cycle opens; (3) prioritize payment timing over slightly larger late payments; (4) run two simple scenarios (early vs late) to see actual dollar impact; (5) combine timing with rate stress tests to guard against rising rates.

Understanding and applying the average daily balance examples turns a HELOC into an actively managed tool rather than a passive liability—small, well-timed moves compound into measurable interest savings and improved cash flow over time.

***

Section 11: Comparison to Monthly Mortgage Interest Calculation

Interest on a HELOC is typically calculated using the average daily balance method, which means the lender computes a daily interest charge based on your outstanding balance each day of the billing cycle and then sums those daily charges to produce the monthly interest owed. This daily granularity makes the month's interest directly sensitive to both the timing and size of payments: reducing the balance early in the cycle immediately lowers the number of dollars accruing interest for every subsequent day, producing an outsized effect compared with identical payments made later in the cycle.

By contrast, a traditional mortgage uses a fixed amortization schedule where each monthly payment is split between interest and principal according to the loan's amortization formula; the interest portion for the month is based on the loan's outstanding principal at the start of that period and the fixed monthly rate, producing predictable month-to-month interest that follows the amortization table. Because mortgage interest is tied to the scheduled amortization rather than the day-to-day balance activity, timing of extra payments within a month matters far less for immediate monthly interest than it does with a HELOC—though extra mortgage principal payments still produce long-term interest savings by reducing future scheduled interest accrual.

The practical differences create distinct behavioral and strategic consequences. HELOC borrowers can materially reduce interest in the short run by making large principal reductions early in the billing cycle or by quickly paying down temporary draws; that makes HELOCs useful as tactical, short-duration liquidity or cash-flow tools when the borrower can discipline timing. Mortgage borrowers gain predictable, automatic amortization that steadily builds equity, and while extra monthly mortgage contributions shorten the term and lower total interest, those contributions do not change the immediate month's interest as dramatically as early-cycle HELOC payments.

Risk and volatility are also different. Because HELOC rates are often variable and interest is assessed daily, a rate increase translates into higher daily charges immediately and can compound quickly if balances remain high, exposing borrowers to payment volatility and interest creep. Mortgages—especially fixed-rate mortgages—shield borrowers from rate volatility and provide a stable monthly payment (absent escrow changes or adjustable-rate terms), which helps long-term budgeting and reduces the chance of short-term payment shock.

For readers deciding between using a HELOC or adjusting mortgage payments, the breakdown below clarifies when each tool is superior and what to watch for:

Short-term liquidity or staged expenses: HELOC favored; pay down quickly and early in the cycle to minimize average daily balance and interest.

Predictable long-term amortization and forced equity build: Traditional mortgage favored; extra mortgage payments reduce future interest but have smaller immediate monthly impact.

Rate risk tolerance: HELOC carries variable-rate and daily-interest sensitivity; model +200–400 bps scenarios and ensure buffers.

Timing goals: If you can time cash flows precisely (paychecks, business receipts), HELOC timing advantages compound; if not, predictable mortgage amortization is safer.

Understanding the operational difference—the HELOC's daily-balance sensitivity versus the mortgage's monthly amortization—turns product choice from an academic comparison into a tactical decision that should match cash-flow habits, rate tolerance, and planning discipline.

***

Section 12: HELOC Fees and Costs — Application and Origination Fees

Application and origination fees are the upfront charges lenders use to process, underwrite, and set up a HELOC; they cover tasks like credit pulls, income verification, underwriting labor, and sometimes an initial appraisal or automated valuation, and they can change a seemingly low-rate offer into a much more expensive product once added to the math.

Lenders structure these costs differently: some charge a flat application fee (commonly $100–$500) plus closing costs, while others assess an origination fee as a percentage of the line (examples range from a fraction of a percent up to several percent of the initial draw), or roll fees into the balance so you pay interest on the fees over time. Appraisal, title search, recording, and document preparation fees are often bundled into the closing costs for a HELOC and can push the total upfront bill higher than homeowners expect.

Because fintech lenders and some banks advertise "no closing cost" HELOCs, it's important to read the tradeoffs: a waived origination fee may be offset by a higher periodic margin, annual maintenance fees, draw fees, or conversion costs later—so compare total cost scenarios (fees plus rate) rather than focusing on any single headline.

Breakdown for readers — quick checklist to assess application and origination costs:

Ask for a full itemized Good Faith Estimate showing application, origination, appraisal, title, recording, and document fees.

Compare offers as total cost over your expected hold period (fees rolled into balance vs. paid upfront).

Negotiate or shop for lenders that waive specific fees if you accept a slightly higher margin; calculate the breakeven.

Check for annual or inactivity fees and early-termination penalties that can offset an initially low fee.

If possible, get lenders to quote both a "no-fee" and a "fee-included" scenario so you can see which is cheaper over the time you expect to use the line.

***

Section 13: HELOC Fees and Costs — Annual Fees

Many HELOCs include an annual maintenance or membership fee charged simply for keeping the credit line open. These fees are typically modest—commonly in the range of \$50–\$100 per year—but they add a recurring cost that reduces the HELOC's advantage for short-term or infrequently used credit lines. Over a decade, an annual fee that seems small can become a meaningful drag on value if you rarely draw on the credit or if you planned to use the HELOC as an emergency reserve rather than an active funding source.

Some lenders advertise "no annual fee" products as a selling point, while others offset waived annual fees with slightly higher rate margins or different charge structures. Fintech entrants and some digital lenders may reduce or eliminate annual fees by streamlining underwriting and using automated valuation models, but those products still trade off pricing and features in other ways—so comparing the total expected cost (fees plus interest margin) over your intended hold period is essential. A no-fee HELOC can be cheaper if you plan to use the line lightly; if you expect heavy, repeated draws and conversions, a small annual fee may be acceptable in exchange for better rate terms.

Annual fees interact with other recurring charges—like inactivity fees, account maintenance fees, or transaction/draw fees—and the combined effect can materially change the HELOC's economics. The Consumer Financial Protection Bureau lists annual fees among the common charges lenders may assess, and it recommends borrowers read the account disclosures to understand all recurring and conditional fees before accepting an offer. Because some lenders also impose early termination or inactivity penalties, evaluating how long you expect to carry the HELOC and how often you'll use it will determine whether an annual fee is worthwhile or an avoidable expense.

Breakdown for readers — practical checklist:

Expect typical annual fees of **\$50–\$100**, but confirm the exact amount on the Good Faith Estimate.

Compare "no-annual-fee" offers against the interest margin and other fees to see which is cheaper over your expected hold period.

Check for related recurring charges (inactivity, membership, or servicing fees) that combine with the annual fee to raise costs.

If you rarely plan to draw, prefer no-annual-fee HELOCs; if you'll use the line frequently and need lower margins, a small annual fee may be acceptable.

Ask the lender about fee waivers for the first year, fee caps, or conditions that remove the annual fee (balance thresholds, product bundles).

Understanding annual fees and how they interact with other HELOC charges helps you compare offers on an apples-to-apples basis and choose the line that actually costs less over the time you plan to use it.

***

HELOC Fees and Costs — Transaction Fees

Transaction fees are charges lenders impose each time you access funds from your HELOC; they can include per-draw fees, minimum-draw requirements, transfer or transaction processing fees, and sometimes fees for using a debit card or check tied to the line. These costs are often small on a per-use basis—commonly a flat fee per draw or a percentage for certain transfer types—but they add up when you make frequent, small draws instead of larger, consolidated withdrawals.

Per-draw fees and minimum-draw rules change the calculus of using a HELOC for short-term liquidity. Some lenders require a minimum initial or subsequent draw (for example, several thousand dollars) and may charge a fee for each additional draw; others waive per-draw fees but impose conditions such as a minimum balance to avoid inactivity charges. If your plan relies on many small, tactical draws and repayments, per-transaction charges can erase the interest savings you hoped to capture, making it essential to compare draw fees across offers and structure withdrawals to minimize fee exposure.

Beyond simple draws, lenders may assess transfer fees for moving HELOC funds to another account (instant transfers or expedited funding), ATM or card transaction fees, and fees when converting a variable balance to a fixed-rate tranche. These ancillary transaction charges are often disclosed in the fee schedule but overlooked by borrowers focused only on headline rates; when combined with annual or origination fees they materially change the effective cost of borrowing from a HELOC over time.

Breakdown for readers — practical checklist and examples:

Ask the lender the exact per-draw fee and any minimum-draw requirement before you commit; examples range from no fee to $25–$100 per draw or minimums of several thousand dollars.

If you plan frequent draws, calculate total transaction fees over your expected use period and compare that to interest savings from tactical HELOC use; frequent small draws can flip the HELOC from cost-saving to cost-increasing.

Check for transfer or expedited funding fees and whether electronic transfers to your checking account are free or charged; these fees can be per-transaction or tiered based on speed.

Combine fee analysis with rate and margin comparisons—"no per-draw fee" offers may charge higher margins or other recurring fees that offset the apparent savings.

Negotiate or consolidate: when possible, plan fewer, larger draws or negotiate fee waivers for the first few draws to preserve the HELOC's tactical advantage.

Understanding transaction fees prevents small, repeated costs from undermining a HELOC strategy; always read the fee schedule, run the numbers for your expected draw frequency, and structure withdrawals to minimize per-transaction charges.

***

HELOC Fees and Costs — Early Closure Fees

Early closure fees—also called early termination, cancellation, or prepayment penalties—are charges some lenders assess if you pay off or close a HELOC before a specified timeframe, often within the first 24–36 months; these fees compensate the lender for upfront costs they expected to recover over time and can be charged as a flat fee or a percentage of the outstanding balance.

Lenders vary widely: some disclose a clear early-closure period and dollar amount, while others bury the clause in the fee schedule; common triggers include refinancing the mortgage, selling the home, or paying off the HELOC and closing the account during the penalty window.

Because not all HELOCs include this charge, and amounts can range from a few hundred dollars to over $1,000 or a percentage of the balance, understanding the specific language in your agreement is critical—closing early can still save money overall, but you must run the numbers to see whether the penalty outweighs the interest savings or refinancing benefits.

Breakdown for readers — practical checklist and steps:

Confirm presence and length of any early-closure period before signing.

Ask whether the fee is a flat amount or percentage and whether it applies only if you close the account versus simply paying down the balance.

Model scenarios: calculate total cost of paying the fee versus the interest/refinance savings to determine the financial advantage.

Negotiate up front: request fee waivers, reductions, or an alternative structure (e.g., fee waived after a shorter seasoning period) before accepting the offer.

Time major moves: if you plan to sell or refinance, align those actions outside the early-closure window when possible.

Keep the account open but inactive if closing triggers the fee and you don't need to eliminate the line immediately.

Knowing whether an early-closure fee exists, how it's calculated, and what events trigger it lets you make intentional choices—avoid surprises when refinancing, selling, or aggressively paying down your HELOC.

***

When Fees Make Sense vs When to Walk Away

Fees can be justified when they buy you something tangible: a lower ongoing interest margin, meaningful underwriting flexibility, or access to a larger, better-priced credit line that you intend to use enough to recover the cost. For example, paying an origination or appraisal fee can be reasonable if it secures a HELOC with a significantly lower margin that saves you more in interest over your expected hold period than the upfront cost—especially when you plan to carry the line and use it actively for years. If a fee is paired with clear benefits you value (rate reduction, higher limit, reduced conversion fees), run a breakeven calculation comparing the fee today versus cumulative savings from the improved terms.

Walk away from offers where fees are opaque, excessive, or targeted at occasional users. Small annual or per-draw fees that compound over time can turn an otherwise cheap line into an expensive one, particularly if you plan to use the HELOC infrequently or only for a short project. Inactivity fees, maintenance charges, or per-draw costs make little sense when your intended use is an emergency buffer or a one-time draw; in those cases, a no-fee HELOC or a short-term personal loan may be cheaper once you include all recurring and transactional charges.

Early-closure penalties and prepayment fees are deal-breakers when you expect to refinance, sell, or aggressively repay the line within the lender's penalty window. If a lender imposes an early-termination fee within the first 24–36 months, that fee can erase the value of an initially low margin or "no-closing-cost" promotion. Always ask whether fees apply on payoff only or also on account closure, and model scenarios where you move or refinance early to ensure you won't incur a disproportionate penaltyheloc360.com.

Fees tied to convenience or speed (expedited transfer fees, conversion fees to lock rates) can make sense for specific tactical needs—short-term liquidity when timing matters, or converting a portion of the balance to guard against rate spikes. Use these selectively and negotiate them when possible: lenders sometimes waive or reduce transactional fees for new customers or larger relationships, and fintech products may offer different tradeoffs between fees and margins that better match your usage pattern.

Breakdown for readers — decision checklist

Estimate hold period: If you'll keep and use the HELOC for several years, an upfront origination fee can be justified if it lowers your margin enough to break even within your expected hold time.

Compare total cost: Add fees (origination, appraisal, annual, per-draw, conversion, early-closure) to projected interest over your planned usage and compare alternatives.

Check usage frequency: Walk away from per-draw or inactivity fees if you plan infrequent use; prefer no-fee products for emergency lines.

Model early exit: If you might refinance or sell within 2–3 years, avoid HELOCs with early-closure penalties or high payoff charges.

Negotiate and ask for scenarios: Request fee-waived options, dual quotes (fee-included vs. fee-waived with higher margin), and a Good Faith Estimate to see all costs laid out.

Prioritize transparency: Reject offers with buried fee language or that won't provide an itemized fee schedule before closing.

When fees are transparent, tied to real value, and justified by your timeline and usage, they can be a sensible part of HELOC economics; when fees are hidden, recurring, or punitive for normal life events, you're usually better off walking away and finding a cleaner alternative.

***

Section 14: Protections and Regulations — Truth in Lending Act Requirements

The Truth in Lending Act (TILA), implemented by Regulation Z, requires lenders to provide clear, standardized disclosures about the cost and terms of consumer credit products—including home equity lines of credit—so borrowers can compare offers and understand charges, periodic rates, and repayment mechanics. These disclosures must cover the annual percentage rate (APR), any variable-rate formula (such as Prime + margin), periodic interest-rate adjustment terms, and itemized fees that affect the cost of borrowing; this information is sourced from the Office of the Comptroller of the Currency (OCC).

Regulation Z's HELOC-specific expectations include clear statements of draw-period and repayment terms, how minimum payments are calculated, and whether interest-only payments are permitted during the draw period; lenders must also disclose floors, caps, and conversion options that materially affect borrower risk. Because HELOCs are often variable-rate, TILA/Regulation Z disclosure rules aim to make rate-adjustment timing and potential payment shock transparent so borrowers can model future costs before they borrow; information by the Office of the Comptroller of the Currency (OCC).

TILA also governs timing and delivery of disclosures: lenders must provide required disclosures in advance of consummation and supply periodic notices when terms change, giving consumers time and information to respond or shop alternative products. For home-secured credit, TILA creates additional procedural protections and documentation requirements—items that lenders commonly surface as part of the Good Faith Estimate and closing disclosures for HELOCs.

Beyond disclosure, TILA contains substantive consumer protections that can affect HELOCs, such as the right of rescission for certain home-secured transactions and limits on undisclosed charges; recent case law and regulatory debate have also examined how specific TILA provisions apply to HELOC structures and access methods (for example, HELOCs accessed via card) which can change how offset and other protections are interpreted.

Breakdown for readers — practical checklist

Ask for the written TILA/Regulation Z disclosures before you sign: verify APR, margin, index, rate-adjustment timing, and any floors/caps.

Confirm draw/repayment terms: draw-period length, whether interest-only payments are allowed, and exact repayment amortization schedule.

Request an itemized fee schedule: origination, appraisal, annual, transaction, conversion, and early-closure fees.

Check timing and notice rules: know when the lender must notify you of rate changes and what advance notice you'll receive.

Understand rescission and other home-secured protections: ask whether your HELOC triggers right-to-rescind rules and under what conditions.

Compare standardized disclosures across lenders to ensure you're comparing APRs, margins, and fee structures on an apples-to-apples basis.

Read the TILA/Regulation Z disclosures carefully and keep copies; they are your primary legal protection and the source documents you'll use to model costs, negotiate terms, or raise concerns with the lender or a regulator.

***

Right of Rescission — The Three-Day Cooling-Off Period

The Truth in Lending Act gives borrowers a federally protected right of rescission that applies to many home-secured transactions, including HELOCs when your principal residence is used as collateral; this rule creates a three-business-day cooling-off window during which you can cancel the credit transaction without penalty and without stating a reason. The countdown begins only after three events have occurred: you sign the credit contract, you receive the TILA disclosure showing key terms (APR, finance charge, payment schedule), and you are given two copies of the TILA notice that explains your right to rescind; if any of these disclosures are delayed or incorrect, the rescission period can be extended.

During the rescission window the lender may not disburse funds secured by your home, and if you exercise rescission in writing by midnight of the third business day the security interest is voided and you owe no finance charge; the creditor has 20 days to return any money or property you paid and to release the lien on your home. Business days for this purpose include Saturdays but exclude Sundays and federal holidays, so the practical calculation of the deadline depends on the calendar day the required documents are delivered and signed; information sourced from Investopedia. If the lender fails to deliver the required notices, the borrower's right to rescind can extend as long as three years, creating a substantial consumer protection for disclosure lapses.

Exercising rescission must be done in writing and delivered to the lender—oral statements generally do not satisfy the legal requirement—so keep proof of mailing or electronic delivery; once you rescind, the creditor must process the cancellation and return funds promptly, and you generally are not liable for finance charges or fees tied to the transaction. Because HELOCs are often set up with variable rates, conversion options, and multiple fee types, the rescission period provides a brief but important pause to review the TILA disclosures, verify the rate formula and fee schedule, and confirm that the product matches your expectations before the lien becomes effective.

Breakdown for readers — practical checklist and steps:

Confirm applicability: right of rescission applies only when the loan is secured by your primary residence; second homes or investment properties are not covered.

Know the trigger events: rescission starts after you sign, receive the TILA disclosure, and receive two copies of the rescission notice.

Count business days correctly: Saturdays count; Sundays and federal holidays do not; deadline is midnight of the third business day.

Exercise in writing: send a written rescission notice and keep proof of delivery; oral rescissions are insufficient.

Expect prompt action by lender: the creditor must return funds and release the security interest within 20 days after valid rescission.

Watch disclosure accuracy: missing or defective disclosures can extend your rescission right up to three years, so review documents closely before signing.

Understanding and using the three-day rescission right gives you a short, statutory opportunity to step back, validate the HELOC disclosures, and avoid unintended long-term obligations secured by your home.

***

Rate Cap Protections

Rate caps are contractual limits that constrain how much a HELOC's interest rate can change—either at each adjustment period (**periodic caps**) or over the life of the loan (**lifetime caps**)—and they serve as the primary protection against runaway rate volatility for variable-rate home equity lines of credit. Periodic caps typically limit the amount the rate can move at a single repricing (for example, no more than 1% per adjustment), while lifetime caps set an absolute ceiling that the rate cannot exceed no matter how high the index climbsMy Perfect Mortgage. These caps shift some interest-rate risk away from borrowers by creating predictable upper bounds on rate movement, but lenders often price that protection into slightly higher starting margins or fee structures, so the presence of a cap is a trade-off between volatility protection and initial cost.

Regulation Z and the CFPB require clear, prominent disclosures for home equity plans about the rate-adjustment formula, the index and margin, and any periodic or lifetime caps so borrowers can compare the practical protections embedded in offers and model worst-case payment outcomes. The regulatory disclosures must show how the APR is determined, how often adjustments occur, and any limits on increases; those mandated statements are the best source for verifying the exact cap amounts, adjustment frequency, and the way caps interact with floors or conversion options. Because lenders present cap structures differently (some pair tight periodic caps with higher lifetime caps, others emphasize a low starting rate but looser caps), reading the Regulation Z disclosures and asking for explicit examples of worst-case rate paths is essential before committing.

Rate caps matter most when balances are large or when the HELOC is relied on for cash-flow planning; a small periodic cap still allows large cumulative increases over time unless a lifetime cap is also restrictive, and the timing of adjustments (monthly versus semiannual) changes how quickly the borrower could see step increases in payments. For tactical users who will draw and repay quickly, periodic caps provide limited immediate benefit because short-term exposure is small; for borrowers planning to carry material balances through varying rate cycles, a robust lifetime cap materially reduces the risk of unaffordable payments and makes long-term modelling more reliable.

Breakdown for readers — practical checklist:

Identify both caps: Confirm the **periodic (adjustment) cap** and the **lifetime cap** on the TILA/Regulation Z disclosures.

Check adjustment frequency: Monthly repricing can compound faster than semiannual adjustments; tighter periodic caps matter more with frequent repricing.

Model capped scenarios: Run payments for current rate, current + periodic cap, and current + cumulative caps up to the lifetime cap to see realistic worst-case payments.

Compare trade-offs: Ask whether lower starting margins are paired with wider caps and whether a small fee can buy a tighter cap—calculate breakeven over your expected hold period.

Confirm interactions: Verify how caps interact with floors, conversion options, and any rate-lock features in the contract.

Use disclosures: Rely on the TILA/Regulation Z variable-rate and fee disclosures to confirm cap amounts and adjustment rules before signing.

Rate caps do not eliminate rate risk, but when clearly disclosed and properly modeled they convert an open-ended variable exposure into a bounded one—letting you decide whether the remaining risk fits your cash-flow tolerance and planning horizon.

***

Lender Disclosure Requirements

Lenders must provide clear, conspicuous, and timely disclosures for home equity plans so borrowers can compare offers and understand the costs and mechanics of a HELOC; Regulation Z (12 CFR 1026.40) sets the specific content and timing requirements for those disclosures, including grouping key terms together and delivering required forms at application or within three business days of receiving an application. These disclosures are designed to present the APR, the variable-rate formula (index and margin), periodic adjustment rules, and itemized third-party fees up front so you have the contractual building blocks to model future payments and tradeoffs before you commit; information sourced from the Consumer Financial Protection Bureau.

The required disclosure package for a HELOC typically includes items the CFPB and lenders call out explicitly: a clear statement of how the APR is determined, the frequency of rate adjustments, periodic and lifetime caps (if any), draw-period and repayment terms, the method for calculating minimum payments, and an itemized list of fees such as appraisal, origination, annual, per-draw, and early-closure charges. Lenders must also provide the consumer brochure explaining how home equity plans work, and third parties who distribute applications owe the same duty to supply the brochure and applicable disclosures at the time of application or promptly afterward.

Timing and format rules matter because missing or defective disclosures can extend borrower protections and affect rescission rights: Regulation Z requires disclosures to be delivered at specific intervals and in forms that permit retention, and failure to make proper disclosures can delay consummation or extend statutory rights under TILA, creating both procedural protections and leverage for the borrower to review terms carefully. Consumer guides and industry explainers reinforce that the "early disclosure" is your roadmap to hidden mechanics—what triggers rate changes, what fees are conditional, how inactivity is treated—and borrowers should use it to ask lenders for concrete examples of worst-case scenarios and fee itemizations before signing.

Breakdown for readers — practical checklist

Obtain the full disclosure set at application or within three business days: APR, index + margin, adjustment frequency, caps, draw/repayment terms, and the consumer brochure.

Request an itemized fee schedule showing appraisal, origination, third-party, annual, per-draw, conversion, and early-closure fees so you can model total cost.

Verify variable-rate mechanics: confirm index name, margin, periodic/lifetime caps, and how the lender rounds or applies rate changes.

Check minimum-payment and interest-calculation language: confirm whether payments are interest-only during draw, how interest is computed, and when amortization begins.

Demand example scenarios: ask the lender to show payment examples at current rate, current + periodic cap, and up to the lifetime cap for your expected remaining balance.

Keep all disclosures and compare offers on an apples-to-apples basis; if disclosures are vague or delayed, treat that as a red flag and escalate or walk away.

Careful review of lender disclosures—using the Regulation Z checklist as your baseline—turns what feels like fine print into actionable information, letting you compare true costs, negotiate terms, and avoid surprises during the draw and repayment lifecycle.

CHAPTER 3:

The Velocity Banking Concept — Origin of the Concept

Velocity banking originated as a tactical debt-paydown approach that leverages a revolving home equity line of credit (HELOC) to make large principal reductions on a mortgage, then uses incoming cash flow to rapidly pay down the HELOC so the borrower can repeat the cycle. Early proponents framed the idea as a way to "increase the speed" of mortgage payoff by exploiting the HELOC's simple, daily interest mechanics and by timing income deposits to minimize interest on the revolving balance.

The strategy gained traction through personal-finance blogs, calculators, and independent advisors who demonstrated numerical examples showing dramatic reductions in mortgage term when HELOCs were used to shift and time principal payments. Promotional materials emphasized aggressive cash-flow discipline (often called "paycheck parking") and precise timing of draws and repayments so each dollar reduces interest-bearing principal for as many days as possible.

Despite its popularity online, velocity banking has strong critics in the financial-planning community who argue the technique merely moves debt rather than eliminates it, exposes borrowers to HELOC variable-rate risk, and often delivers limited or no advantage once fees, margin spreads, and opportunity costs are included. Analysts stress that the actual savings come from accelerating principal payments—not from structural magic of the HELOC—and that simpler approaches (extra mortgage principal payments, refinancing to a shorter term, or lump-sum prepayments) typically achieve similar or better outcomes with less risk and complexity.

Breakdown for readers — what to know about the origin and early adoption

Core idea: use a HELOC to make large lump-sum mortgage principal payments, then use paycheck-timing to minimize HELOC interest while you pay it down.

How it spread: popularized online via blogs, calculators, and coaching that illustrated dramatic payoff timelines using repetitive HELOC cycles.

Key critique from origin forward: critics point out the strategy shifts, not erases, debt; HELOC rate volatility, fees, and real-world cash-flow slippage often negate theoretical gains.

Practical takeaway: velocity banking's origin is rooted in aggressive cash-flow engineering; evaluate whether the core mechanics (rate gap, fee structure, and disciplined timing) actually hold for your situation before adopting the method.

***

Section 1: How It Leverages the Difference Between Simple and Compound Interest

Velocity banking relies on the practical distinction between how interest accrues on revolving lines (effectively simple, daily-accrued interest on the outstanding balance) and how interest compounds on an amortizing mortgage (where scheduled payments allocate interest first and principal later). By routing paychecks and short-term cash flows through a HELOC, each deposit immediately reduces the HELOC's average daily balance, lowering that day's simple interest accrual; when those funds are then applied as a lump principal reduction on the mortgage, they remove future compound interest that the mortgage would otherwise charge over years. This timing arbitrage — brief use of a daily-accruing credit line to shift when a dollar reduces mortgage principal — is the arithmetic engine velocity banking proponents describe.

Put another way: simple (daily) interest on a HELOC charges only on the actual days a dollar is outstanding, so moving a dollar through the HELOC for a short window produces a small, linear cost; compound mortgage interest charges future interest on interest as your amortization schedule runs, so applying that dollar early to mortgage principal permanently reduces many future interest charges. The net benefit exists only when the short window HELOC cost (daily rate × days outstanding + any fees) is less than the long-term mortgage interest avoided by accelerating principal reduction.

This lever is fragile in real life because several moving parts must align: the HELOC's effective daily cost (APR, margin, fees), the mortgage's remaining amortization and rate, the borrower's ability to execute precise timing, and the absence of intervening costs (draw fees, transfer fees, early-closure penalties). If the HELOC rate plus fees exceed the mortgage savings on a per-dollar basis, the tactic reverses from beneficial to costly; similarly, irregular cash flow or missed timing erode the daily-interest advantage and can eliminate any theoretical gains.

Example (simplified): assume a $1,000 mortgage principal reduction today would save long-run mortgage interest of X; instead you route $1,000 through a HELOC for 10 days at a daily rate derived from a 6% APR (≈0.000164/day), costing roughly $1.64 in interest for that window — if the mortgage's avoided future interest (from accelerating principal) exceeds $1.64 minus any HELOC fees, the move nets savings. Scale that routine across many pay cycles and dollars, and savings compound on the mortgage side; fail to account for fees, rate spreads, or timing failures, and the arithmetic collapses.

Breakdown for readers — stepwise checklist

Verify the interest mechanics: confirm your HELOC uses average-daily balance and your mortgage follows an amortization schedule.

Calculate the HELOC short-window cost: daily rate = APR ÷ 365; short-window cost ≈ daily rate × balance × days outstanding.

Estimate mortgage-side savings: model how much future interest a $1,000 early principal payment would avoid given your remaining amortization.

Compare net benefit: Net saving = mortgage interest avoided − (HELOC short-window cost + any draw/transfer fees).

Run sensitivity tests: model HELOC rate +200–400 bps, missed paycheck scenarios, and the impact of per-draw or annual fees.

Decide on execution: only proceed when net saving is positive across realistic stress scenarios and you can reliably execute timing.

In summary, velocity banking exploits the linear nature of daily HELOC interest versus the long-term compounding structure of mortgage interest; when the HELOC's short-term cost is lower than the mortgage interest avoided and execution is disciplined, the method can accelerate payoff, but it is highly dependent on rate spreads, fees, and flawless cash-flow timing

***

Section 2: Why Banks Don't Want You to Know This

Banks profit from the spread between what they pay for funds and what they charge borrowers, so any strategy that educates borrowers to exploit timing, interest-calculation quirks, or product features that reduce interest costs naturally runs counter to their revenue incentives. Velocity banking highlights how routing income and timing principal reductions can lower interest paid over time by minimizing average daily balances and accelerating mortgage principal — tactics that, if widely adopted and executed at scale, would reduce interest income for lenders and decrease demand for longer-term mortgage products that generate steady interest streams.

Beyond the direct revenue angle, banks prefer simplicity and predictability in consumer behavior. HELOCs that are used as ongoing working capital with rapid in-and-out flows introduce operational risk for lenders (liquidity exposure, increased servicing complexity, and potential for higher draw volatility during stress periods). Banks therefore design products, fee schedules, and marketing to discourage frequent small draws or rapid churn: minimum-draw rules, per-transaction fees, inactivity charges, and variable margins tighten the economics for aggressive tactical use and protect lenders from the liquidity and repricing risks such behavior creates.

Banks also benefit when borrowers choose straightforward, long-term solutions like refinancing or fixed-rate mortgage payments because those products lock in predictable cash flows and reduce interest-rate exposure for both parties. Exposing borrowers to the arithmetic of daily interest versus amortizing interest, and to disciplined timing strategies that can shave months or years off a mortgage, undermines the incentive for customers to buy long-duration rate certainty. From a behavioral perspective, widespread adoption of timing tactics would shift consumer demand toward more flexible, shorter-duration credit facilities and away from the stable mortgage products that underpin bank balance-sheet planning.

Finally, complexity favors the lender: when consumers misunderstand fees, caps, repricing mechanics, or the operational discipline required to execute strategies like velocity banking, lenders face fewer customer-initiated prepayments and lower risk of early account closures. Publicizing the precise mechanics that create borrower advantage would force lenders to compete more aggressively on true total cost (fees plus margin) and to simplify disclosures in ways that reveal profit centers now masked by timing, rounding, and fee interactions.

Breakdown for readers — key points to remember

Revenue motive: Banks earn when interest and fees are paid over time; borrower tactics that reduce interest receipts conflict with that motive.

Product design: Minimum draws, per-transaction fees, inactivity charges, and margins are structural levers banks use to discourage rapid HELOC cycling.

Risk management: Frequent draw/repay cycles increase operational and liquidity risk for lenders; banks price or restrict products accordingly.

Behavioral economics: Predictable, long-term payments (refinance, fixed rates) are better for bank planning; strategies that speed prepayment reduce that predictability.

Information asymmetry: Complexity and opaque fee structures protect lender margins; transparency about daily-interest mechanics would force cleaner, more competitive pricing.

Knowing why banks might prefer silence about these mechanics doesn't mean the tactics are right for everyone, but awareness empowers you to ask the right questions, compare total costs (fees plus effective rates), and decide whether disciplined timing strategies or simpler payoff methods best match your risk tolerance and cash-flow reality.

***

The Mathematics Behind the Strategy — How Reducing Average Daily Balance Accelerates Payoff

The velocity-banking math rests on a simple, repeatable arithmetic fact: reducing the average daily balance on a revolving line immediately lowers the daily interest charged, and when those same dollars are then applied as lump-sum principal reductions to an amortizing mortgage, they permanently remove future compound interest that would have otherwise accumulated. Because HELOC interest commonly accrues on the average daily balance, every dollar deposited early in the billing cycle shortens the number of days that dollar accrues interest. Repeating this pattern—route income through the HELOC, use the line to make a large mortgage principal payment, then repay the HELOC quickly—converts small daily interest savings into larger long-term mortgage interest avoidance.

At the core is timing arithmetic. Calculate the HELOC short-window cost as: daily rate = APR ÷ 365; short-window cost ≈ daily rate × dollars × days outstanding. Calculate the mortgage benefit as the reduction in future interest that results when that dollar lowers the amortizing balance earlier in the schedule. If the avoided mortgage interest (present value of future interest savings) exceeds the HELOC short-window cost plus any fees, the move is mathematically advantageous. Repeated over many cycles, those net per-dollar savings compound: each successful cycle permanently reduces the mortgage's principal base, which lowers subsequent scheduled interest and accelerates principal paydown across the remaining term.

Real-world friction matters: fees, margins, and execution risk. Per-draw fees, transfer charges, annual fees, and a HELOC margin that exceeds the mortgage rate reduce or eliminate the net benefit. Missed timing—depositing late in the billing cycle or failing to quickly repay the HELOC—erodes the daily-interest advantage and can convert a theoretical win into a loss. Therefore the pure mathematical edge depends on three aligned conditions: (1) the HELOC's effective short-term cost (APR + fees) is low relative to the mortgage interest avoided; (2) you can reliably execute timing (deposit early in cycle, make large principal payments, repay HELOC quickly); and (3) you avoid structural penalties (early-closure fees, heavy transaction fees) or rate shocks that change the calculus.

Example to illustrate the mechanics (simplified):

Determine HELOC short-window cost: APR 6% → daily rate ≈ 0.06 ÷ 365 = 0.000164. A $10,000 auto-route held for 10 days costs roughly $16.40 in interest.

Estimate mortgage saving: applying $10,000 to mortgage principal today reduces the future interest the mortgage will charge on that $10,000 over remaining years; even a small percentage of avoided compounded interest can exceed the short-window HELOC cost by a wide margin.

Net assessment: if the mortgage's avoided interest on $10,000 (calculated over the remaining term) is greater than $16.40 plus any HELOC fees for the move, the cycle produces a net saving.

Breakdown for readers — step-by-step checklist

Confirm interest methods: verify the HELOC uses average-daily balance and your mortgage accrues interest via a fixed amortization schedule.

Calculate short-window HELOC cost: daily rate = APR ÷ 365; short-window cost = daily rate × amount × days outstanding.

Compute mortgage benefit: model how much future interest a one-time principal reduction of that amount saves across the remaining amortization.

Subtract fees and add margin risk: include per-draw, transfer, annual, and potential early-closure fees in the HELOC cost; stress-test with HELOC rate +200–400 bps.

Run scenario comparisons: best case, expected case, and stress case (missed paycheck, rate spike) to see whether net savings hold.

Automate and document: if the math is positive, automate timing (direct deposit, scheduled transfers) and keep a running spreadsheet to track cycles, costs, and cumulative mortgage principal reductions.

Choose simplicity when uncertain: if net savings are small or execution fragile, prefer straightforward extra mortgage payments or a refinance to a shorter term.

When the arithmetic is positive and execution disciplined, reducing the average daily balance converts fleeting daily-interest savings into permanent mortgage interest avoidance; when the margin, fees, or operational risk outweigh the benefit, the added complexity is unlikely to justify the effort.

***

Section 3: Compound Interest Working For You Versus Against You

Compound interest is the force that can accelerate wealth when it works in your favor and destroy progress when it works against you; in the context of velocity banking, the strategy attempts to harness compound interest on savings (mortgage interest avoided) by temporarily accepting simple, daily-accrued interest on a HELOC so that each dollar reduces the mortgage principal earlier in the amortization schedule. When a dollar is applied earlier to an amortizing loan, it reduces the principal base on which future interest compounds, producing long-term savings that grow disproportionately compared with the small, linear cost of holding that dollar briefly on a daily-accruing HELOC. The arithmetic advantage exists only when the HELOC's short-window cost (daily rate × days outstanding plus any fees) is smaller than the present value of the mortgage interest avoided.

When compound interest works against you, the reverse is true: carrying high-cost, compounding credit (credit cards, or a HELOC with a higher effective cost) lets interest grow on interest and quickly overwhelm any short-term timing gains. Velocity banking's fragile edge disappears if the HELOC's effective APR plus transactional and recurring fees exceed the mortgage savings or if rate volatility causes the HELOC cost to spike—conditions that turn a net positive into a net loss and expose borrowers to more compounded interest expense over time. In practice, many analysts find the savings promoted by velocity banking come from disciplined extra principal payments rather than any structural arbitrage, and they warn that fees and rate spreads frequently negate the theoretical compound-interest benefit.

Behavioral dynamics change how compound interest plays out. Discipline—consistent timing, automatic routing of income, and prompt HELOC repayment—amplifies compound-interest gains on the mortgage by ensuring the sequence of early principal removals occurs repeatedly; lapses or irregular cash flow interrupt the compounding benefit and permit interest to accumulate on revolving balances instead. Conversely, predictable, automated extra payments directly to an amortizing mortgage produce similar compound-interest advantages with less execution risk, which is why many financial planners prefer straightforward prepayment or refinancing over complex timing strategies unless the net math clearly favors velocity-style cycles.

Breakdown for readers — quick comparison and action checklist

Compare effective costs: compute HELOC short-window cost = (APR ÷ 365) × amount × days outstanding + fees; compute mortgage interest avoided from an equivalent one-time principal reduction; proceed only if mortgage savings exceed HELOC cost.

Watch compounding direction: compound interest works for you when it's the mortgage interest you reduce; it works against you when high-cost debt compounds on revolving balances.

Include fees and stress tests: add origination, per-draw, transfer, annual, and early-closure fees and model HELOC rate +200–400 bps to ensure robustness.

Prioritize execution: automate deposits and repayments to capture the daily-balance advantage; if reliable execution is unlikely, prefer direct mortgage prepayments or refinancing.

Run the numbers and document: use a simple spreadsheet to compare net present value of both approaches across best, expected, and stress scenarios before committing.

When compound interest is intentionally directed by disciplined actions—applying dollars early to principal and avoiding high-cost revolving balances—it becomes a powerful ally; when left unchecked on expensive, compounding credit, it can quickly work against you and erase any tactical gains.

***

Section 4: Compound Interest Working For You Versus Against You

Compound interest is the force that can accelerate wealth when it works in your favor and destroy progress when it works against you; in the context of velocity banking, the strategy attempts to harness compound interest on savings (mortgage interest avoided) by temporarily accepting simple, daily-accrued interest on a HELOC so that each dollar reduces the mortgage principal earlier in the amortization schedule. When a dollar is applied earlier to an amortizing loan, it reduces the principal base on which future interest compounds, producing long-term savings that grow disproportionately compared with the small, linear cost of holding that dollar briefly on a daily-accruing HELOC. The arithmetic advantage exists only when the HELOC's short-window cost (daily rate × days outstanding plus any fees) is smaller than the present value of the mortgage interest avoided.

When compound interest works against you, the reverse is true: carrying high-cost, compounding credit (credit cards, or a HELOC with a higher effective cost) lets interest grow on interest and quickly overwhelm any short-term timing gains. Velocity banking's fragile edge disappears if the HELOC's effective APR plus transactional and recurring fees exceed the mortgage savings or if rate volatility causes the HELOC cost to spike—conditions that turn a net positive into a net loss and expose borrowers to more compounded interest expense over time. In practice, many analysts find the savings promoted by velocity banking come from disciplined extra principal payments rather than any structural arbitrage, and they warn that fees and rate spreads frequently negate the theoretical compound-interest benefit.

Behavioral dynamics change how compound interest plays out. Discipline—consistent timing, automatic routing of income, and prompt HELOC repayment—amplifies compound-interest gains on the mortgage by ensuring the sequence of early principal removals occurs repeatedly; lapses or irregular cash flow interrupt the compounding benefit and permit interest to accumulate on revolving balances instead. Conversely, predictable, automated extra payments directly to an amortizing mortgage produce similar compound-interest advantages with less execution risk, which is why many financial planners prefer straightforward prepayment or refinancing over complex timing strategies unless the net math clearly favors velocity-style cycles.

Breakdown for readers — quick comparison and action checklist

Compare effective costs: compute HELOC short-window cost = (APR ÷ 365) × amount × days outstanding + fees; compute mortgage interest avoided from an equivalent one-time principal reduction; proceed only if mortgage savings exceed HELOC cost.

Watch compounding direction: compound interest works for you when it's the mortgage interest you reduce; it works against you when high-cost debt compounds on revolving balances.

Include fees and stress tests: add origination, per-draw, transfer, annual, and early-closure fees and model HELOC rate +200–400 bps to ensure robustness.

Prioritize execution: automate deposits and repayments to capture the daily-balance advantage; if reliable execution is unlikely, prefer direct mortgage prepayments or refinancing.

Run the numbers and document: use a simple spreadsheet to compare net present value of both approaches across best, expected, and stress scenarios before committing.

When compound interest is intentionally directed by disciplined actions—applying dollars early to principal and avoiding high-cost revolving balances—it becomes a powerful ally; when left unchecked on expensive, compounding credit, it can quickly work against you and erase any tactical gains.

***

Section 5: Time Value of Money Applied to Debt Reduction

The time value of money (TVM) is the foundational financial principle that a dollar today is worth more than a dollar tomorrow because of its earning potential; applying TVM to debt reduction means prioritizing moves that deliver the largest present-value reduction in future interest obligations. When you use short-term tactics—like routing income through a HELOC to make earlier principal reductions—you are effectively trading a small, immediate cost (the HELOC's short-window interest and any transaction fees) for the present-value benefit of permanently lowering the mortgage principal and thus the compound interest that would have been charged in future periods.

Practically, TVM requires you to quantify both sides of that trade. Compute the immediate cost of holding funds briefly on a revolving line: daily HELOC cost ≈ (HELOC APR ÷ 365) × dollars × days outstanding plus any per-draw or transfer fees. Then estimate the present value of mortgage interest avoided by applying those dollars early to principal—this is the PV of a stream of future interest payments reduced by that principal shift, discounted at an appropriate rate or compared directly to current mortgage rates. The decision favors the tactic when the PV of avoided interest exceeds the immediate HELOC cost and fees; if not, the move destroys value rather than creates it.

Behavioral and operational factors change the TVM outcome as much as pure arithmetic. Reliable cash flow timing, disciplined repayment cadence, and avoidance of hidden fees are necessary to realize the modeled TVM benefit; lapses—late deposits, missed repayments, or a HELOC rate spike—turn the short-term cost into a recurring problem and can reverse the present-value advantage. Likewise, transaction frictions (minimum draws, per-draw fees, early-closure penalties) must be folded into the PV calculation because they increase the effective short-term cost and may tip the balance away from using revolving credit as a timing tool.

Breakdown for readers — stepwise checklist

Identify your comparison horizon: choose the period you plan to hold the mortgage and HELOC (years remaining); this sets the PV window.

Calculate HELOC short-window cost: daily rate = HELOC APR ÷ 365; cost ≈ daily rate × amount × days outstanding + fees.

Estimate mortgage interest avoided: model the future interest stream reduction from a one-time principal payment and calculate its present value or compare it to current mortgage rate savings.

Net present value test: proceed only if PV(interest avoided) – HELOC short-window cost – fees > 0.

Stress test assumptions: recompute with HELOC APR +200–400 bps, missed paycheck scenarios, and inclusion of all applicable fees.

Operational checklist: automate deposits, confirm billing-cycle timing, and document each cycle so execution risk is minimized.

Choose the simpler option when close: if NPV is marginal or execution is fragile, favor direct mortgage prepayments or refinancing to a shorter term.

Applying the time value of money to debt reduction turns velocity-style tactics into a disciplined investment decision rather than a hopeful trick—only when the present-value math and operational reliability align does timing deliver genuine, measurable acceleration of debt payoff.

***

Section 6: The Mathematics Behind the Strategy — Real Calculations with Sample Scenarios

Real, usable evaluation of velocity banking begins with concrete numbers rather than anecdotes. Several online calculators and templates exist to help homeowners model the strategy—these tools let you vary mortgage balance, mortgage rate, HELOC rate, monthly discretionary cash flow, chunk sizes, and timing to see payoff differences and interest savings. Use a spreadsheet or one of the velocity-banking templates to run side-by-side comparisons of your current amortization schedule versus the HELOC-driven cycle so you can quantify whether the timing arbitrage survives realistic friction (fees, rate spikes, missed deposits)calculatorfinder.com. For many users the calculators are the fast way to test assumptions before committing time and risk to the method.

Below are two simplified, fully worked sample scenarios you can replicate in a spreadsheet. Each example focuses on the core math: (A) the short-window HELOC cost (daily rate × dollars × days outstanding + any per-draw fees) and (B) the mortgage interest avoided by accelerating principal. These numbers remove marketing exaggeration and show where the strategy wins or fails.

Scenario A — Favorable spread, disciplined execution:

Inputs: Mortgage balance $200,000 at 4.0% fixed, remaining term 25 years; HELOC available at 5.0% APR; monthly discretionary cash flow available to cycle = $2,500; plan to move $10,000 chunks and hold each chunk on HELOC for 10 days before paying it down.

HELOC short-window cost (approx): daily rate = 5.0% ÷ 365 = 0.000137; 10 days on $10,000 = $10,000 × 0.000137 × 10 ≈ $13.70 in interest; assume $0 per-draw fee for simplicity.

Mortgage benefit (approx): applying $10,000 today to the $200,000 mortgage reduces long-term interest substantially — for a 25-year schedule at 4.0% this one-time principal reduction often yields several hundred dollars to a few thousand dollars in avoided interest over the remaining term depending on amortization timing. If avoided mortgage interest ≈ \$1,200 (conservative illustrative estimate), net saving ≈ \$1,200 – \$13.70 = \$1,186.30 for that chunk. Repeating similar cycles with discipline compounds the benefit into meaningful term reduction and total interest savings.

Scenario B — Unfavorable spread or fees:

Inputs: Mortgage balance \$200,000 at 3.5% fixed, remaining term 25 years; HELOC at 7.0% APR; per-draw fee \$50; same \$10,000 chunk held 10 days.

HELOC short-window cost: daily rate = 7.0% ÷ 365 = 0.000192; 10 days interest on \$10,000 ≈ \$19.20; add \$50 per-draw fee = \$69.20 total cost for the chunk.

Mortgage benefit: with a lower mortgage rate (3.5%), the avoided interest from a \$10,000 reduction is smaller than in Scenario A — suppose avoided mortgage interest ≈ \$1,050. Net saving ≈ \$1,050 – \$69.20 = \$980.80 on one chunk; still positive here but much less margin for error. If the HELOC rate spikes or you miss the timing window, the short-window cost can exceed the avoided interest and flip the result negative.

These examples illustrate two critical realities: first, the net benefit per chunk can be large when the HELOC-mortgage spread is small but in the borrower's favor and fees are minimal; second, the margin of safety is often narrower than promoters imply, so stress testing with higher HELOC rates (+200–400 basis points), adding per-draw fees, and modeling missed cycles is essential. Practical templates and calculators make these sensitivity tests easy and are recommended before committing to a cycle-based plan.

Breakdown for readers — how to run your own real calculations

Gather inputs: current mortgage balance, mortgage rate, remaining term, HELOC APR (current margin), available HELOC limit, expected per-draw and transfer fees, and realistic discretionary cash flow per month.

Short-window HELOC cost formula: daily rate = HELOC APR ÷ 365; cost ≈ daily rate × chunk amount × days held + per-draw/transfer fees.

Mortgage saving estimate: model the amortization schedule and compute the present value or total interest avoided by applying the chunk as an immediate principal payment (spreadsheet functions PMT/remaining amortization or a standard mortgage calculator help here).

Net test: Net saving = mortgage interest avoided – HELOC short-window cost – fees. Proceed only if positive across base and stress scenarios.

Sensitivity checks: re-run with HELOC APR +200–400 bps, add potential per-draw fees, and simulate a missed paycheck or delayed repayment to see if net savings endure.

Execution plan: if the math holds, map a repeatable cadence (exact deposit dates, billing cycle dates, chunk sizes), automate transfers where possible, and track every cycle in a ledger or spreadsheet so you can verify the cumulative impact.

Using templates and calculators speeds this analysis and prevents surprises; they let you visualize payoff timelines and test the exact inputs where velocity banking either creates measurable value or simply rearranges debt without net gain

***

Section 7: Why This Works Better Than Traditional Methods — Income Velocity versus Sitting in Checking Accounts

Routing income through a revolving credit account (typically a HELOC) instead of letting paychecks idle in a checking account exploits the timing of interest calculation: checking balances earn negligible interest, while each dollar deposited into a HELOC immediately reduces the average daily balance and therefore the daily interest charged. That shift turns idle cash into active interest-reducing capital every day it sits in the line, which—when repeated and then applied as lump-sum mortgage principal—can create measurable mortgage interest avoidance over time.

Practically, the advantage is arithmetic and cadence rather than a hidden lending trick: the daily simple interest mechanics of a HELOC mean early deposits shave interest for every day they lower the balance, while amortizing mortgage interest compounds over months and years so earlier principal reductions permanently cut the base that accrues future interest. When you can reliably time deposits and repayments, the small daily savings across many cycles aggregate into substantial avoided compounding on the mortgage—assuming the HELOC's short-term cost (daily rate plus fees) stays below the mortgage interest avoided.

Behavioral factors amplify the effect. Income-velocity systems force automation and discipline—paycheck routing, scheduled transfers, and a cadence of large principal payments—which tends to produce larger and more consistent extra principal contributions than ad-hoc manual extra payments. For many households, that behavioral scaffolding is the real performance driver: it converts intention into repeatable action, producing payoff acceleration that simple intentions to "pay a little extra" often fail to deliver.

Important limits remain: the tactic only outperforms traditional extra-payment or refinance approaches when the HELOC's effective cost and fees are low enough, when you can execute timing precisely, and when you accept variable-rate exposure and operational complexity. If the

HELOC APR plus per-transaction or annual fees exceed the mortgage savings, or if cash flow interruptions prevent consistent cycles, the velocity approach can be neutral or harmful compared with straightforward extra principal payments or refinancing to a shorter fixed term.

Breakdown for readers — practical checklist

Calculate opportunity cost: compare negligible checking interest versus HELOC daily-interest reduction (HELOC APR ÷ 365 × dollars × days held) and include any per-draw or transfer fees.

Confirm net benefit: model mortgage interest avoided from an immediate principal reduction and subtract HELOC short-window cost; proceed only if net benefit remains positive under stress scenarios (HELOC +200–400 bps, missed paycheck).

Automate cadence: route direct deposit, schedule transfers early in the HELOC billing cycle, and set fixed dates for lump principal payments to capture daily-balance advantages.

Weigh simplicity vs. complexity: prefer direct extra mortgage payments or refinancing when the math is marginal or execution reliability is low.

Track results: keep a running spreadsheet of cycles, costs, and cumulative mortgage reductions to verify the strategy is delivering expected value.

When income velocity is executed with favorable rates, low fees, and disciplined automation, it converts otherwise idle checking balances into an engine for accelerating mortgage payoff; when the rate spread, fees, or execution risk aren't supportive, traditional extra payments or refinancing remain the safer, often-simpler path.

***

Section 8: Continuous Application of Funds to Principal

Continuous application of funds to principal means systematically directing available cash—paychecks, bonuses, or monthly surplus—toward reducing outstanding loan principal as frequently and as early in each billing cycle as possible. Practically, this looks like routing income through a revolving account (commonly a HELOC) so deposits immediately lower an interest-bearing balance, then applying those funds in lump sums to the mortgage principal; repeated over time, those early principal reductions shrink the amortizing base and compound into materially less interest paid over the life of the loan.

Mechanically, the effectiveness of continuous principal application rests on two observable behaviors: the timing of cash flows and the cadence of principal moves. When income is parked temporarily on a line that charges daily interest, each deposit reduces the average daily balance and therefore the daily interest cost; when those dollars are pushed to mortgage principal, they stop future compounding on that portion of the balance. This "cycle and apply" routine is the operational core of velocity banking and similar cash-flow strategies promoted by practitioners and financial bloggers who model payoff acceleration using repeated chunk payments and paycheck routing.

The strategy's practical upside appears when the short-window cost of keeping funds on the revolving line (daily interest × days outstanding plus any transaction fees) is smaller than the present value of the mortgage interest you avoid by applying those dollars earlier. In real households that means disciplined timing, low or no per-draw fees, and a favorable rate spread; without those conditions, the repeated transfers and fees can negate the benefit and simply shuffle liabilities between accounts rather than reduce total cost.

Execution discipline is therefore essential: automate direct deposit to the chosen account, schedule transfers early in the lender's billing cycle, and consolidate multiple small draws into fewer, larger principal applications to minimize per-transaction charges. Track each cycle in a simple ledger or spreadsheet showing chunk size, days held, HELOC short-window interest, fees, and the resulting mortgage principal reduction so you can validate actual savings versus modeled expectations.

Breakdown for readers — stepwise checklist

Map cash flow: list all income dates and the HELOC/mortgage billing cycle dates so you know when deposits most reduce average daily balances.

Automate routing: set direct deposit to the revolving account and schedule transfers to the mortgage on fixed dates early in the billing period.

Chunk strategically: favor fewer, larger principal applications over many small draws to reduce per-draw fee drag.

Calculate short-window cost: daily cost = (HELOC APR ÷ 365) × chunk × days held; add any per-draw or transfer fees.

Compare to mortgage savings: model avoided mortgage interest from an immediate principal payment and require net positive savings across base and stress cases.

Document every cycle: log amounts, dates, HELOC interest cost, fees, and cumulative mortgage principal change to validate the strategy.

Reassess periodically: rerun the math if HELOC rates rise, fees change, or cash flow becomes irregular; pivot to straightforward extra payments or refinance if the net advantage disappears.

***

Section 9: Psychological Benefits of Visible Progress

Visible progress while tackling debt—clear, measurable reductions in principal or a shrinking payoff timeline—creates a powerful motivational feedback loop that sustains disciplined behavior. Seeing a mortgage balance fall faster than scheduled, or watching a payoff chart move leftward, turns abstract goals into concrete wins; that positive reinforcement makes it easier to maintain the routines required by strategies like velocity banking (routing income, scheduling transfers, and making chunk principal payments) and converts sporadic good intentions into consistent action. Financial educators and practitioners who promote velocity-style systems frequently highlight this behavioral payoff: the system's structure forces frequent interaction with your finances, increases financial literacy, and builds confidence that you can manage cash flow proactively rather than reactively.

Beyond motivation, visible progress reduces psychological friction tied to debt stress. Debt creates cognitive load—worry, decision fatigue, and avoidance—and measurable milestones lighten that load by supplying clarity and control. When borrowers track cycle-by-cycle principal reductions, they experience reduced anxiety and a stronger sense of agency; that emotional shift often translates into better adherence to budgets and fewer impulsive cash-outs that would interrupt the payoff cadence. Practically, the act of updating a spreadsheet or checking a balance after a planned lump principal payment gives immediate, tangible evidence that effort produced results, which reinforces the habit loop (cue, routine, reward) that sustains long-term financial behavior change.

Visible progress also supports better decision-making through learning and calibration. Regular measurement exposes when executions deviate from plan—missed deposits, unexpected fees, or rate changes—so you can adjust chunk sizes, timing, or even abandon the tactic when the math no longer works. This frequent feedback prevents small errors from compounding into large setbacks and turns a complex cash-flow strategy into an iterative process of improvement; velocity banking templates and calculators exist precisely to turn qualitative confidence into quantitative checkpoints that keep behavior aligned with outcomes.

Breakdown for readers — practical checklist

Set measurable milestones: define monthly principal reduction targets and a visual payoff timeline to update after each cycle.

Track every cycle: record deposit dates, chunk sizes, days held on the HELOC, HELOC interest cost, and resulting mortgage principal change so you can verify actual versus projected savings.

Use simple visuals: maintain a one-page chart showing remaining term and cumulative interest avoided; seeing the line move is a strong motivator.

Celebrate small wins: acknowledge each confirmed principal reduction as progress to reinforce the habit loop and reduce avoidance behavior.

Calibrate with feedback: rerun sensitivity scenarios monthly or quarterly (HELOC rate +200–400 bps; missed paycheck) and adjust cadence or abandon the tactic if net savings disappear.

Keep learning active: use templates and educational guides to translate each cycle into clearer financial literacy—terms like amortization, average-daily balance, and APR become operational tools rather than jargon.

Visible progress is both a psychological lubricant and a practical control mechanism: it lowers stress, sustains disciplined execution, and creates a feedback system that helps you verify whether a velocity-style approach is delivering real value or merely rearranging debt.

***

Section 10: Flexibility Advantages

Flexibility is one of the most compelling practical benefits of using a revolving line of credit as the operational hub in a velocity-style plan: a HELOC lets you draw, repay, and redraw without reapplying, which preserves liquidity while still enabling aggressive principal reductions when surplus cash appears. Unlike a one-time lump-sum prepayment or a closed-term refinance, a line of credit gives you on-demand access to capital for emergencies, opportunities, or planned projects while allowing you to apply windfalls or recurring surplus directly to principal. That dual capability—preserve optionality today, accelerate payoff tomorrow—makes the structure attractive to households that value both control and speed.

The flexibility advantage shows up in timing and sequencing. Because HELOCs typically calculate interest daily and permit variable draw sizes, you can time large principal applications to when you have excess cash, then quickly reduce the HELOC balance to minimize carrying costs between cycles. This on/off capability contrasts with locked refinance funds or permanent prepayments that permanently remove liquidity. For people whose cash flows vary month to month, or who anticipate intermittent large expenses, the ability to recycle borrowing capacity without paying origination costs every time is a meaningful operational edge.

Flexibility also supports tactical responses to changing financial conditions. If rates fall, you can shift strategy (repay the HELOC and refinance the mortgage); if an unexpected expense arrives, you can access the line temporarily rather than liquidating investments or delaying principal payments. That optionality reduces the psychological and financial friction of committing to an aggressive payoff plan: you can pursue accelerated reduction while keeping a safety valve intact. However, flexibility is valuable only when the cost of maintaining and using that optionality (margins, fees, and variable-rate exposure) is acceptable relative to alternatives.

Important caveats temper the flexibility case. The convenience of redraw and repeatable access is purposely limited by many lenders through fees, minimum draws, or higher margins; over-reliance on redraw capacity can also undermine discipline and turn a strategic tool into a habit of carrying revolving balances. In addition, variable-rate exposure on the HELOC can increase total cost unpredictably, so the flexible plan must be stress-tested for rate spikes, fee changes, and behavioral drift to ensure optionality does not become an expensive liability.

Breakdown for readers — practical checklist

Confirm true re-drawability: verify the HELOC allows multiple draws and repayments without reapplication and check any minimum-draw or inactivity rules.

Map liquidity needs: list likely one-off expenses and ensure your HELOC limit plus emergency savings cover them without derailing payoff cadence.

Cost vs. option value: quantify marginal cost of flexibility (margin spread, annual or maintenance fees) and compare to the value of keeping liquidity versus locking funds into mortgage principle.

Design disciplined rules: set written guardrails (maximum redraw frequency, target minimum balance, and a rule for when to stop using the line) to prevent behavioral erosion.

Stress-test scenarios: model HELOC rate +200–400 bps, temporary income loss, and a few large draws to confirm you can sustain payments and still capture net savings.

Reassess periodically: if fees rise, caps appear, or flexibility is reduced, pivot to direct prepayments or refinance—flexibility is only useful while it remains affordable and reliable.

When executed with clear rules, low friction, and favorable economics, the flexibility a HELOC offers lets you run an aggressive payoff cadence without sacrificing access to cash—turning liquidity and acceleration from mutually exclusive choices into a managed tradeoff.

***

Section 11: Common Misconceptions Debunked — "This Is Just Debt Shuffling"

One of the most frequent criticisms of velocity banking is that it amounts to nothing more than "debt shuffling"—moving balances from one account to another without truly reducing what is owed. At first glance, this critique seems reasonable: after all, the strategy involves using a HELOC to pay down a mortgage, then repaying the HELOC with income. However, the distinction lies in **how the timing of payments and the mechanics of interest calculation create real, measurable savings**. Unlike simply transferring debt from one card to another, velocity banking leverages the difference between daily simple interest (HELOC) and long-term compound interest (mortgage) to accelerate principal reduction.

When you apply a lump sum from the HELOC to the mortgage, you are not just moving debt—you are permanently lowering the mortgage principal earlier in the amortization schedule. This reduces the total interest that would have accrued over years, something that cannot be undone even if the HELOC balance temporarily rises. The HELOC, by contrast, charges interest only on the average daily balance, so every deposit of income immediately reduces the cost of carrying that balance. The net effect is that the household pays less total interest over time, provided the HELOC's effective cost (APR plus fees) is lower than the mortgage interest avoided. That is fundamentally different from "shuffling" debt, which leaves the total obligation unchanged.

Financial educators often stress that the **mathematical driver of velocity banking is accelerated principal reduction**, not the mere relocation of balances. The HELOC is a tool to create liquidity and timing flexibility, but the true payoff comes from applying funds to the mortgage earlier than scheduled. Critics who call it debt shuffling overlook this compounding effect: once mortgage principal is reduced, the avoided interest is locked in, regardless of what happens with the HELOC afterward.

Breakdown for readers — why it's not just debt shuffling:

Permanent principal reduction: Each HELOC lump payment lowers mortgage principal earlier, cutting future interest permanently.

Different interest mechanics: HELOC = daily simple interest; mortgage = long-term compound interest. The strategy exploits this difference.

Net savings test: If avoided mortgage interest > HELOC short-window cost + fees, the move creates real value.

Behavioral discipline: The system forces consistent extra principal payments, unlike ad-hoc "shuffling" that doesn't change amortization.

Liquidity preserved: HELOC flexibility allows redraws if needed, but the mortgage savings remain locked in once principal is reduced.

Contrast with true shuffling: Credit card balance transfers or moving debt between loans without reducing principal does not change total cost; velocity banking does.

In short, velocity banking is not debt shuffling—it is a structured method of accelerating mortgage payoff by exploiting timing and interest mechanics. The key is disciplined execution and favorable rate spreads; when those conditions hold, the strategy produces genuine debt reduction rather than cosmetic balance movement.

***

Section 12: Common Misconceptions Debunked — "You're Just Replacing One Debt with Another" — The Truth

The critique sounds intuitive: you use a HELOC to pay down your mortgage, so haven't you simply swapped debts? The truth is that velocity-style strategies create value only when earlier mortgage principal reductions permanently lower future interest more than the short-window cost of carrying funds on the HELOC. Analysts emphasize that the savings come from accelerating principal payments, not from the HELOC itself; the line is just a timing tool, and the math only works under favorable conditions (rate gap, low fees, disciplined execution). When those conditions aren't met—HELOC rates higher than the mortgage, material fees, irregular cash flow—the strategy can underperform simpler methods like direct extra principal payments or refinancing.

Mechanically, the move isn't a cosmetic balance transfer. Mortgages amortize with interest front-loaded; paying principal earlier tilts future payments toward more principal and locks in avoided interest for the remaining term. HELOCs, by contrast, accrue interest on the average daily balance, which you can lower quickly by "paycheck parking" and rapid repayment. Educators who model velocity banking show that this timing advantage can reduce total interest when the HELOC's effective daily cost stays below the mortgage interest avoided—but they also warn that variable-rate risk, potential line freezes, and fee drag can erase the benefit if not managed. In short: it's not "just replacement" if the net interest paid over the life of the mortgage drops in a documented, tested plan.

Real-world comparisons echo this nuance. Side-by-side scenarios demonstrate that chunking principal via a HELOC can trim years and interest beyond what a fixed monthly extra payment achieves—but only when fees are minimal and the HELOC APR is competitive; otherwise, the margin for error shrinks and stress events (rate spikes, missed timing) can flip results negative. Comprehensive reviews conclude that while a narrow group of disciplined, high-income borrowers can see gains, many households will match or beat the payoff speed using straightforward extra payments, shorter-term refis, or recasts—with less complexity and risk.

Breakdown for readers — when it's more than "replacing debt"

Permanent principal reduction: Early lump payments reduce mortgage principal now, cutting future interest for the rest of the term; that avoided interest is locked in and not undone by subsequent HELOC activity.

Distinct interest mechanics: Mortgage: amortized with front-loaded interest; early principal cuts tilt payments toward principal. **HELOC:** daily simple interest on average balance, reducible through rapid deposits and repayment. The net win requires a favorable rate/fee profile.

Net benefit test (must pass): Net saving = Mortgage interest avoided – (HELOC short-window interest + all fees). Analysts emphasize the savings arise from extra principal, not the HELOC itself.

Documented scenarios, not anecdotes: Modeled examples show additional payoff acceleration versus fixed extra payments when spreads and fees cooperate; otherwise, results converge and complexity adds risk.

Risk controls: Variable HELOC rates, line freezes, and fee schedules can negate gains; stress test with higher HELOC APR and include all fees before committing.

When to prefer simpler methods: If the net advantage is narrow or execution is fragile, extra principal payments, shorter-term refinancing, or a recast often deliver similar or better outcomes with less risk.

Direct answer: you're not "just replacing one debt with another" if earlier principal reductions measurably lower lifetime mortgage interest and you can prove—on paper—that HELOC carrying costs and fees are smaller than the interest you avoid. Without that documented net benefit, the criticism is valid; with it, you've moved from cosmetic reshuffling to genuine debt reduction

***

Section 13: Common Misconceptions Debunked — "This Only Works for Wealthy People" — Reality Check

Velocity banking isn't reserved for the wealthy; it's a cash-flow discipline that can work for anyone who consistently has surplus income, access to a reasonably priced revolving line (often a HELOC), and the ability to execute timing reliably. The core mechanic—using a line of credit that accrues daily interest to accelerate mortgage principal reduction—doesn't require high net worth; it requires positive monthly cash flow and low friction (fees, rate spread) so the short-window cost of the line remains below the long-term mortgage interest avoided. Put simply: the lever is discipline and math, not wealth status.

That said, many reviews caution that only a narrow set of borrowers benefit meaningfully in practice: those with strong, stable cash flow, a favorable rate gap between the HELOC and mortgage, low fees, and the capacity to stick with the cadence for years. When HELOC rates are higher than mortgage rates, or fees and volatility eat the spread, simpler approaches—extra principal payments, shorter-term refinancing, or recasting—often match or beat velocity banking without added risk or complexity. This is why experts describe the strategy as viable for a disciplined subset rather than a universal solution.

Risk management—not wealth—determines fit. HELOCs are variable-rate and can be repriced, reduced, or even frozen during stress periods, which makes liquidity and contingency planning essential. Households without buffers for income shocks or rate spikes may find the strategy fragile; in these cases, flexible access to cash can flip into vulnerability, eroding gains and increasing total interest cost. Recognizing these operational risks and stress-testing them is the difference between a plan that works on paper and one that survives real life.

In practice, the "wealthy only" myth confuses two ideas: you don't need high net worth to benefit from earlier principal reduction, but you do need consistent surplus, low-cost access to a line, and documented proof that your short-term carrying costs are smaller than the mortgage interest you'll avoid. When those conditions hold, the approach can be effective for middle-income households; when they don't, it's wiser to lean on straightforward extra payments or a refi to a shorter term.

Breakdown for readers — reality check and decision rules

Core requirement (not wealth): Consistent monthly surplus and low-friction credit access matter more than high net worth; the math must show clear net interest savings.

Rate and fee threshold: Ensure the line's effective cost (APR + all fees) stays below the mortgage interest you avoid from earlier principal cuts; if not, choose simpler methods.

Stability of cash flow: Favor steady income and reliable cadence; irregular cash flows reduce timing benefits and increase the chance of negative outcomes.

Risk buffers: Keep emergency reserves and model rate spikes or line freezes so your plan remains viable under stress; variable-rate exposure demands contingencies.

Mechanics you must verify: Average-daily balance interest on the line versus amortization on the mortgage; disciplined timing turns small daily savings into permanent principal reduction.

Alternatives when conditions aren't favorable: Extra principal payments, shorter-term refinancing, or recasting commonly deliver similar payoff speed with less complexity and risk.

Direct answer: this isn't for "the wealthy"—it's for the disciplined and well-prepared. If your surplus, rates, and fees produce documented net savings and you can execute reliably, velocity-style tactics can work; if not, traditional methods are safer and often equally effective

***

Section 14: Common Misconceptions Debunked — "It's Too Risky" — Understanding Actual vs. Perceived Risk

Calling velocity banking "too risky" lumps real, manageable risks together with fears that come from not understanding how the mechanics work. The strategy isn't inherently dangerous, but it is unforgiving if you ignore costs, timing, or variable-rate exposure. The truth sits in the middle: there are concrete risks you must measure and manage, and there are perceived risks that sound scary but shrink when you model them and set clear guardrails.

Actual risk lives in the numbers and the contract terms. A HELOC is variable-rate—repricing can raise costs quickly. Lenders can lower limits or freeze lines during stress, removing liquidity when you need it most. Fees (per-draw, annual, transfer, early-closure) can erode or eliminate gains if you cycle frequently. Cash-flow inconsistency, missed timing, or carrying a HELOC balance longer than planned also undermines the math. Opportunity cost matters too: dollars routed to debt can't be invested elsewhere, so the benefit must exceed what you'd reasonably earn or need for emergencies.

Perceived risk often stems from misunderstanding. The fear that "using a HELOC guarantees you'll lose your home" ignores the fact that risk rises primarily when balances are left high for long periods without repayment. The idea that "banks can change rules overnight" is overstated—while lines can be adjusted under defined conditions, you can mitigate by keeping buffers, diversifying liquidity, and not relying solely on a single lender. The belief that "one timing mistake ruins everything" oversimplifies the math—your plan can absorb small slippage if you've built margin for error and aren't operating at the edge.

A grounded view recognizes that velocity banking is a cash-flow discipline, not a magic trick. It works best when surplus is stable, fees are low, the HELOC's effective cost stays below what you avoid on the mortgage, and you automate the cadence. When those conditions fade, the plan should pause or pivot to simpler, lower-risk methods like direct extra principal payments or refinancing to a shorter term.

Breakdown for readers — actual risks (and how to manage them)

Variable-rate exposure: Rates can rise quickly.

Mitigate: Set a stop rule (e.g., pause cycles if HELOC APR exceeds mortgage rate by a defined spread), keep cash buffers, and stress-test at higher rates before starting.

Liquidity and line-freeze risk: Limits can be reduced or frozen in downturns.

Mitigate: Maintain emergency savings outside the HELOC, avoid maxing the line, and diversify liquidity sources (cash + line, not line only).

Fee drag and hidden costs: Per-draw, annual, and transfer fees compound.

Mitigate: Fewer, larger principal applications; negotiate fees; include all fees in your net-savings test before committing.

Execution risk (timing discipline): Late deposits or slow HELOC repayment can flip the math.

Mitigate: Automate deposits and transfers, calendar the billing cycle, and use a tracking sheet to keep cadence tight.

Opportunity cost: Dollars to debt aren't available for investments or emergencies.

Mitigate: Compare net debt savings versus expected returns; keep a defined liquidity buffer untouched by the strategy.

Behavioral drift: "Flexible" redraws can become habitual revolving debt.

Mitigate: Write firm rules (max redraw frequency, target balance), review monthly, and stop if rules are breached.

Perceived risks (and the reality)

"You'll lose your home if anything goes wrong." Reality: Risk rises when balances linger and discipline lapses; with buffers and fast repayment, exposure stays controlled.

"Banks can change terms at any moment." Reality: Terms change within policy. You can reduce impact by not relying solely on the HELOC for liquidity and by keeping usage modest.

"One mistake makes the plan worthless." Reality: Small timing slips reduce savings but don't erase them if your margin for error is healthy and fees are low.

"It's gambling." Reality: It's a structured cash-flow method. If your net-savings test is positive under stress scenarios and you follow rules, it's not speculation.

Decision checklist — shift from fear to facts

Run a net-savings test: Model mortgage interest avoided from early principal versus the HELOC's short-window cost plus fees; require a clear positive margin.

Stress-test rates and cash flow: Recompute with higher HELOC APR and a missed paycheck; proceed only if savings remain positive.

Set stop rules and buffers: Define rate and fee triggers to pause; keep an emergency fund outside the HELOC.

Automate and track: Use scheduled transfers and a simple ledger to monitor each cycle's cost and savings.

Reassess quarterly: If spreads narrow, fees rise, or discipline slips, pivot to direct extra payments or a shorter-term refi.

Direct answer: it's not "too risky" by default—risk is real but measurable. When you quantify costs, build buffers, automate execution, and enforce stop rules, you convert a perceived gamble into a controlled, data-driven plan. If those controls don't hold, choose simpler methods that deliver similar payoff acceleration with lower risk.

***

Section 15: The ideal candidate profile — steady income requirements

Steady, predictable income is the cornerstone of any velocity-style plan because the math depends on reliably paying down the HELOC balance between lump-sum principal applications. Without consistent surplus cash flow, the daily interest advantage fades, fees accumulate, and the strategy can underperform simpler methods like direct extra payments or refinancing. Independent reviews consistently emphasize that strong, stable cash flow—not high net worth—is what makes the approach viable, since savings come from accelerated principal reduction rather than the HELOC itself. Education-focused guides also highlight "stable income (predictable cashflow)" as a baseline requirement before attempting paycheck routing or chunk paymentsupfromzerohq.com.

What "steady" means in practice: income that arrives on schedule, leaves room for monthly surplus after all essential expenses, and doesn't fluctuate so much that you're forced to carry a HELOC balance longer than planned. Analysts caution that velocity banking only works while cash flow stays strong and the effective HELOC cost remains manageable; if income becomes irregular or the rate spread shrinks, the risk/complexity can outweigh benefits and you're often better off with straightforward extra principal payments or a shorter-term refinance. Cash-flow discipline (budgeting, automation) is repeatedly cited as the operational backbone that turns the concept from theory into measurable payoff acceleration.

Steady income also buffers real-world risks: variable-rate exposure, potential line freezes, and fee drag. With consistent surplus, you can absorb rate moves, keep the HELOC balance low, and maintain liquidity without breaking cadence. Without it, perceived "velocity" becomes revolving debt. Reviews note a narrow set of borrowers benefit most: disciplined households with reliable surplus, favorable HELOC terms, and the ability to sustain the routine for years; otherwise, traditional methods commonly match or beat the strategy with less risk.

Breakdown for readers — steady income essentials

Monthly surplus defined: Enough predictable income to cover all expenses and still generate surplus for HELOC paydowns every cycle; this drives actual savings.

Cadence reliability: Income that hits on time (e.g., biweekly or monthly) so deposits reduce average daily balances early and enable scheduled lump principal payments.

Rate/fee tolerance: Surplus that comfortably offsets HELOC daily interest and any per-draw or annual fees; if surplus is tight, fee drag can erase gains.

Budget discipline: A basic budget you can stick to, preventing spending creep that lengthens HELOC carry time and increases interest cost.

Stress capacity: Ability to withstand a missed paycheck or modest rate spike without stalling the plan; if not, prefer simple extra payments or a shorter refi.

Documentation and automation: Route direct deposits, schedule transfers, and track each cycle; automation turns steady income into consistent principal reduction.

Direct answer: steady income isn't optional—it's the fuel. If your cash flow is predictable, produces real surplus, and you automate the cadence, velocity-style tactics can convert daily interest reductions into permanent mortgage savings; if cash flow is irregular or thin, use straightforward extra payments or refinancing to achieve similar payoff speed with lower risk.

***

Section 16: The ideal candidate profile — spending discipline assessment

Spending discipline is the hinge that makes a velocity-style plan succeed or fail. The strategy's savings come from consistently applying surplus to principal, not from the HELOC itself; without tight budgeting and controlled spending, balances linger on the line, daily interest accumulates, and fee drag erodes any advantage. Educators who model the approach emphasize meticulous cash-flow management, "paycheck parking," and routine tracking—because it's the cadence of disciplined surplus, not financial wizardry, that tilts outcomes in your favorBanking Truths.

A realistic assessment starts with your behavior under stress: do you maintain surplus after essentials every month, or does spending creep devour what's left? Reviews caution that only a narrow, disciplined subset sees meaningful gains—households with strong cash flow, favorable rate gaps, and the ability to sustain routines for years. When rates, fees, or spending volatility intrude, simpler options (extra principal payments, shorter-term refinancing, or recasting) often match or beat the payoff speed with far less risk and complexity.

Documentation is part of discipline. Templates and trackers help translate intention into execution, making every cycle visible and accountable. Using a spreadsheet to log deposits, chunk payments, days held on the HELOC, and fees turns "I think it's working" into verifiable math. Educators offering velocity-banking workshops and spreadsheets do so for this reason: the habit of tracking is what preserves the margin and exposes drift early.

Breakdown for readers — spending discipline essentials and tests

Baseline surplus: Confirm a consistent monthly surplus after essentials; this is the fuel that repays the HELOC quickly and makes principal acceleration real.

Budget integrity: Build and stick to a simple budget that protects surplus from "creep." The math only holds when spending doesn't extend HELOC carry time.

Cadence proof: Automate deposits to the line, schedule lump principal payments, and reconcile monthly so timing doesn't slip and interest doesn't bloat.

Rate-and-fee awareness: Track HELOC APR, margins, and all fees. If rising rates or fees narrow your margin, pivot to straightforward extra payments or a shorter-term refi.

Stress scenarios: Test your behavior under a missed paycheck or rate spike. If surplus vanishes in stress, your plan is fragile—choose simpler methods.

Tracking tools: Use a spreadsheet or template to log each cycle (chunk size, days held, interest cost, fees, principal reduced). Visibility sustains discipline.

Stop rules: Write triggers to pause (e.g., if the HELOC APR exceeds mortgage rate by a set spread, if you have two consecutive months without surplus. Etc..). Remember guardrails prevent drift from becoming debt.

Behavioral honesty: If you routinely overspend or ignore reconciliations, velocity-style tactics are unlikely to help; documented extra payments may be safer and equally effective

***

Section 17: The ideal candidate profile — Financial behavior patterns that work

The best candidates for a velocity-style approach share behavioral patterns that make disciplined timing and repeated principal applications reliable. They habitually track cash flow, reconcile accounts weekly, and treat surplus as predetermined—rather than discretionary—funds. This behavioral foundation converts occasional good intentions into repeatable actions: direct deposit into the chosen account, scheduled transfers timed to billing cycles, and fewer, larger principal applications to minimize fee drag and execution risk.

Successful practitioners also adopt strict guardrails: written rules for maximum redraws, stop thresholds for HELOC APR or fees, and a mandatory emergency reserve untouched by the strategy. These rules prevent flexibility from morphing into habitual revolving debt and create clear triggers to pause or pivot when market or personal conditions change. Financial educators emphasize that the method's advantage is operational discipline and reliable cadence rather than financial alchemy, so documented guardrails and stop rules are common among those who sustain gains over time.

Another hallmark is an orientation toward measurement and iteration. Productive users log every cycle—deposit date, chunk size, days held, HELOC interest cost, fees, and mortgage principal reduction—and review results monthly to catch drift early and rebalance chunk sizes or timing as needed. That tidy feedback loop turns a complex multi-step plan into a manageable habit and makes it easy to convert qualitative confidence into quantitative proof that the approach is delivering net savings.

Finally, behavioral humility matters: the ideal profile includes people who know their spending tendencies and choose simpler methods if discipline slips. In practice, the households that outperform are not necessarily the wealthiest but the most consistent: steady income, restrained discretionary spending, automated execution, and a willingness to stop when the math or life circumstances change. When those behavioral patterns align, the operational complexity becomes an asset rather than a liability.

Breakdown for readers — actionable behavior checklist

Track cash flow weekly and treat surplus as designated principal funds.

Automate direct deposit to the operational account and schedule transfers early in the billing cycle.

Use fewer, larger principal applications to minimize per-draw fees and administrative friction.

Keep an emergency reserve separate from the HELOC and never rely solely on the line for liquidity.

Write and follow guardrails: max redraws per year, pause if HELOC APR exceeds a set spread, stop after two missed surplus months.

Log each cycle in a spreadsheet (date; amount; days held; HELOC interest; fees; mortgage principal reduced) and review monthly.

Stress-test regularly: rerun scenarios with HELOC APR +200–400 bps and a missed paycheck to confirm margin.

Be ready to pivot to direct extra payments or refinancing if discipline weakens or economics deteriorate.

***

Section 18: The ideal candidate profile — Minimum equity and credit score considerations

Minimum home equity matters because a HELOC requires sufficient collateral to access meaningful borrowing capacity; without a usable equity cushion you cannot draw the chunk sizes that make timing tactics efficient, and per-draw or minimum-draw rules can consume the margin the strategy relies on. Lenders typically set HELOC limits as a percentage of your home's value minus outstanding mortgage balance, so borrowers with low equity may face either an unavailable line or limits too small to justify the fees and complexity of cycling funds. Public guides on velocity-style methods repeatedly flag equity as a gating constraint: if you don't have enough tappable equity to create useful chunk payments, the operational and fee overhead usually outweighs any theoretical timing advantage.

Credit score is the other gating factor because HELOC pricing, margin, and approval all depend heavily on credit quality. A stronger credit score generally produces lower introductory margins, fewer fees, and higher initial limits—conditions that widen the spread between short-window HELOC cost and mortgage interest avoided. Conversely, borrowers with lower scores may be offered smaller limits at higher rates or with onerous fees, which quickly erodes the narrow per-cycle savings velocity banking depends on. Practical reviews advise prospective users to verify likely HELOC pricing and approval odds before modeling scenarios; without competitive HELOC terms tied to good credit, traditional extra payments or refinancing are often the better route.

Together, minimum equity and credit score determine whether you can both access and finance the strategy at acceptable cost. Even with modest equity and a fair score, some borrowers can still benefit if their HELOC terms are reasonable and fees are low, but the margin for error is much smaller; stress-testing models with higher HELOC APRs and lower available limits is essential. Educational write-ups emphasize running side-by-side scenarios (current amortization versus HELOC cycling) using conservative assumptions for limit, margin, and fees before committing time or behavioral changes.

Breakdown for readers — actionable checklist

Confirm tappable equity: Calculate available equity = home value – mortgage balance; confirm lender maximum combined-loan-to-value rules and whether that leaves a practical HELOC limit for chunk payments.

Estimate likely HELOC pricing: Check typical offers for your credit band or prequalify to learn likely APR, margin, and fees; use conservative estimates in models (HELOC APR +200–400 bps for stress tests).

Minimum useful limit: Determine a minimum chunk size that makes per-draw fees and administrative effort worthwhile; if your expected HELOC limit won't support that chunk size, the strategy likely won't pay off.

Credit score action: If your score is marginal, improve it before applying—pay down revolving balances, correct reporting errors, and avoid new credit inquiries that could raise your HELOC cost and reduce benefits.

Model with constraints: Run amortization comparisons using the actual or conservatively estimated HELOC limit and rate to confirm net savings under base and stress scenarios.

Fallback plan: If equity or score makes HELOC terms unattractive, prioritize direct extra principal payments, lump-sum recasts, or refinancing to a shorter term as safer alternatives.

Direct answer: you need enough tappable equity and sufficiently strong credit to access a HELOC at a low enough cost for velocity-style cycling to make sense. If either is missing, the economics and execution risk usually favor simpler, lower-risk payoff methods.

PART II:

THE HELOC ACCELERATION STRATEGY

The HELOC acceleration strategy uses a home equity line of credit as an operational hub to convert routine cash flow into repeated principal reductions on an amortizing mortgage. Instead of letting paychecks sit idle in low-yield checking, you route income through the HELOC so each deposited dollar immediately lowers the line's average daily balance, then periodically apply aggregated funds as lump-sum principal payments to the mortgage. When executed correctly this sequence shortens the amortization schedule and reduces lifetime interest paid by exploiting the difference between the HELOC's daily interest mechanics and the mortgage's long-term amortized interest profile.

How it works, step by step: open a HELOC with terms you've vetted; route income (direct deposit) to that HELOC so the average daily balance drops; maintain disciplined spending so the line is paid down quickly; once enough surplus accumulates, make a single chunk payment to the mortgage principal; then repeat the cycle. The HELOC functions as a temporary holding account that creates timing advantage—every day a dollar sits reducing the HELOC balance saves the daily interest that would otherwise be charged, and every dollar moved early to mortgage principal permanently eliminates future compounding on that amount.

Benefits and limits in practice: the core benefit is liquidity plus timing—access to re-drawable credit without permanently locking funds, combined with earlier principal reductions that compound into interest savings. The limits are explicit and measurable: variable HELOC rates can widen the effective short-window cost, per-draw or transfer fees can erode per-cycle savings, and the approach requires disciplined cadence and contingency buffers to survive income interruptions or rate spikes.

Operational controls to protect the plan: document the HELOC terms (APR structure, fees, min draws, inactivity rules), set written stop rules (pause cycles if HELOC APR exceeds a predetermined spread), maintain an emergency reserve separate from the line, and automate deposits and scheduled transfers so timing mistakes are minimized. Log every cycle in a simple ledger showing deposit dates, chunk amounts, days held on the HELOC, HELOC interest cost, fees paid, and resulting mortgage principal reduction so you can compare actual results to modeled expectations.

Breakdown for readers — quick actionable checklist

Confirm eligibility and pricing: prequalify or shop HELOC offers; capture likely APR, fees, and max limit.

Map billing cycles: note HELOC average-daily-balance calculations and mortgage payment dates to optimize deposit timing.

Set chunk size: choose a minimum chunk that overcomes per-draw fees while matching your surplus cadence.

Automate flows: direct deposit to HELOC; schedule a monthly or biweekly transfer to mortgage on an early billing-cycle date.

Calculate net test: short-window cost = (HELOC APR ÷ 365) × chunk × days held + fees; mortgage benefit = modeled interest avoided from immediate principal reduction; require mortgage benefit > short-window cost under stress scenarios (HELOC +200–400 bps).

Institute guardrails: stop rules for rate spikes, max redraw frequency, and minimum emergency savings threshold.

Track and review: maintain a monthly spreadsheet of cycles, compare projected vs actual savings, and pivot to direct prepayments or refinancing if economics deteriorate.

When you combine clear documentation, conservative modeling, and disciplined automation, the HELOC acceleration strategy becomes a controlled way to convert routine cash flow into measurable mortgage acceleration rather than an open-ended gamble.

CHAPTER 4:

The Core Strategy Explained — The Basic Process Step 1

Open a HELOC for $10,000–$50,000

Opening a HELOC in the $10,000–$50,000 range is a practical starting point for chunk-based acceleration because it provides enough usable credit to make meaningful principal payments without overleveraging your home; many velocity-style guides recommend choosing a line sized to your expected chunk amount and monthly cadence so per-draw fees and administrative friction don't swamp the math.

Select a HELOC offer after comparing likely APR, floors, margins, and fee schedules; your target is a product with low initial costs, a competitive variable rate, and clear redraw rules so you can draw, repay, and redraw without costly reapplications—features highlighted by practitioners who convert HELOCs into operational "income buckets" for repeated principal attacks.

Before applying, confirm tappable equity and estimate the practical limit lenders will offer under combined-loan-to-value rules; small lines may make chunking inefficient because minimum-draw rules and per-draw fees create disproportionate cost, while oversized lines increase behavioral risk if you lack discipline.

Finally, prequalify or shop with multiple lenders to get realistic pricing for your credit profile and include conservative stress assumptions in your modeling (HELOC APR +200–400 bps) so you know whether the short-window cost will likely remain below the mortgage interest you aim to avoid.

Breakdown for readers — quick action checklist

Confirm desired chunk size and ensure HELOC limit comfortably covers repeated chunks without hitting minimum-draw constraints.

Compare APR, margin, and fees across lenders; prioritize low fees and transparent redraw rules.

Verify tappable equity and estimate a realistic maximum limit under CLTV rules before modeling scenarios.

Prequalify to learn likely pricing for your credit band and run stress tests (HELOC APR +200–400 bps) to confirm net benefit under conservative assumptions.

***

Section 1: The Core Strategy Explained — Step 2 Use HELOC Funds to Pay Down Mortgage Principal

Using HELOC funds to make a lump-sum payment toward your mortgage principal replaces part of the long-term amortizing balance with short-term, daily-accruing debt so you can immediately remove that principal from the mortgage's compounding schedule; the real savings come from the earlier principal reduction, not from the HELOC itself. In practice you draw a pre-determined chunk from the HELOC (the amount you planned when sizing the line), post that cash to the mortgage as an extra principal payment, then route subsequent income into the HELOC to repay the drawn amount quickly—reducing the HELOC's average daily balance and therefore its short-window cost while locking in lowered mortgage interest going forward information sourced from *My Perfect Mortgage*.

Mechanics matter: because most HELOCs charge interest on the average daily balance, every paycheck routed into the line reduces the days those dollars would have otherwise sat on the HELOC; when you then apply aggregated funds to the mortgage principal, you permanently shrink the base that would have produced future interest under the amortization schedule. The net advantage requires that the present-value of mortgage interest avoided by the earlier principal payment exceeds the HELOC's short-window interest cost plus any fees; if it does, repeating this "draw → pay mortgage → refill quickly" cycle compounds into meaningful term and interest savings over timeThe Ways To Wealth.

Operational cautions are essential. Verify HELOC terms (per-draw fees, minimum draws, interest calculation method, variable rate rules), automate income routing and repayment cadence, and log each cycle's chunk size, days held, HELOC interest cost, and mortgage principal reduction so you can compare modeled savings to actual results. Stress-test scenarios with higher HELOC APRs and occasional missed cadence to ensure the margin for error remains acceptable; if fees, rate volatility, or unpredictable cash flow shrink the margin, simpler extra-payment or refinance options often deliver similar payoff acceleration with less complexity.

Breakdown for readers — step-by-step checklist

Confirm HELOC eligibility and terms: APR structure, per-draw fees, minimum draw, and average-daily-balance method.

Choose your chunk amount consistent with HELOC limit and fee structure so per-draw costs don't overwhelm benefits.

Draw the chunk from the HELOC and apply it immediately as an extra principal payment to the mortgage.

Route income into the HELOC (direct deposit or scheduled transfers) to lower average daily balance and repay the draw quickly.

Calculate short-window HELOC cost: (HELOC APR ÷ 365) × chunk × days held + fees; compare to modeled mortgage interest avoided for that chunk.

Log each cycle: draw date; amount; days held; HELOC interest; fees; mortgage principal reduction; update your amortization model to confirm cumulative impact.

Reassess regularly and pause if HELOC APR increases, fees appear, or cash flow becomes irregular—pivot to direct extra payments or refinancing if the net advantage disappears

***

Section 2: The Core Strategy Explained — Step 3 Deposit All Income into the HELOC

Depositing all income into the HELOC is the operational heart of the acceleration strategy: every paycheck, gig payout, or recurring credit reduces the HELOC's average daily balance immediately, lowering the daily interest cost you pay on that revolving debt and creating the timing advantage that makes chunk payments to the mortgage effective. By routing income first to the line you convert idle cash into an interest-reducing tool—each dollar sits on the HELOC for a short time, shaving daily interest, and then is swept as part of a planned lump principal payment to the mortgage when enough surplus accumulates.

This step requires automation and discipline. Set direct deposit to the HELOC or automate bank transfers so income consistently posts to the line early in the billing cycle; then automate or calendar the transfers of aggregated surplus to the mortgage on predictable dates so the cadence is repeatable and measurable. Practitioners stress that the routine—deposit, hold briefly to lower average daily balance, then apply in chunks—must be reliable; missed deposits, spending creep, or delays that extend the HELOC carry period increase short-window interest and can erase the expected net benefitCGAA+1.

Not all HELOC products or households are suited to this flow. Choose a HELOC with transparent average-daily-balance interest calculation, low per-draw or transfer fees, and redraw rules that permit frequent repayment without penalties; otherwise the operational cost of deposit cycling can overwhelm the timing savings. Before committing to paycheck routing, model the net test: compare mortgage interest avoided by an immediate principal payment to the HELOC short-window cost ((HELOC APR ÷ 365) × chunk × days held) plus any fees, and stress-test with higher APR assumptions to ensure a margin for errorCGAA+1.

Breakdown for readers — practical checklist

Automate income routing: set direct deposit to the HELOC or schedule immediate transfers so income posts early in the HELOC billing cycle.

Confirm interest method: verify the HELOC uses average-daily-balance or similar daily interest calculation to ensure paycheck deposits reduce interest cost.

Minimize fees: pick a HELOC with low/no per-draw and transfer fees; if fees exist, factor them into your net-savings model.

Set transfer cadence: decide frequency (monthly/biweekly) and a target chunk threshold for sweeping surplus to mortgage principal; automate where possible.

Track days held: log when income posts and when the chunk is applied to compute short-window cost and compare to mortgage interest avoided.

Stress-test assumptions: rerun the net test with HELOC APR +200–400 bps and a missed paycheck to confirm savings remain positive.

Guardrails: define stop rules (pause if HELOC APR exceeds a set spread, if fees increase, or after consecutive missed surplus months) and keep emergency savings outside the line.

Depositing all income into the HELOC creates the timing leverage that powers the HELOC acceleration strategy, but it only produces net savings when the HELOC's pricing and fee structure, your automation, and your spending discipline are documented and stress-tested beforehand.

***

Section 3: The Core Strategy Explained — Step 4 Pay All Expenses from the HELOC

Paying all household expenses from the HELOC completes the cash-flow circuit that gives the acceleration strategy its leverage: income is deposited to the line, immediately reducing its average daily balance, and then routine outflows are paid from the same account so you continuously marshal surplus toward rapid repayment and scheduled chunk transfers to the mortgage. This creates a float effect—deposits knock down the HELOC before most expenses clear—so each dollar briefly reduces interest on the line and then funds your obligations without sitting idle in checking. When executed with discipline, the flow amplifies the timing advantage that turns repeated principal applications into measurable mortgage interest savings.

Operationally, this step requires strong automation and tight budgeting. Convert recurring bills (mortgage escrow, utilities, subscriptions, loan payments) to be paid from the HELOC-linked checking or via scheduled transfers. Use a single, reconciled ledger so you always know the true available surplus after committed expenses. The success hinge is timing: paychecks must post early in the HELOC billing cycle and expenses must clear predictably so the average daily balance advantage is realized rather than eroded by unpredictability or overdrafts. Without reliable cash flow and careful tracking, paying expenses from the line can extend carry time and increase short-window interest, negating the intended benefit.

Risk management matters more here than in earlier steps. Using the HELOC for everyday spending increases exposure to variable-rate moves, lender limit changes, and behavioral drift (treating the line like permanent credit). To protect against these hazards, maintain an untouchable emergency reserve outside the HELOC, cap monthly discretionary spending, and set strict redraw and stop rules. Monitor lines for per-transaction fees or merchant holds that can temporarily inflate the average daily balance. If the HELOC's effective cost, fees, or volatility narrows the margin versus avoided mortgage interest, stop routing expenses through the line and revert to simpler extra-payment strategies.

Breakdown for readers — practical checklist

Automate flows: set direct deposit to the HELOC and arrange auto-payments from the HELOC-linked account for fixed bills.

Reconcile weekly: maintain a one-page ledger of deposits, scheduled debits, and true available surplus to avoid surprise carry.

Protect liquidity: keep an emergency fund outside the HELOC equal to 1–3 months of essential expenses; never treat the line as your sole safety net.

Control discretionary spending: set a monthly cap and use separate accounts or cards for variable categories to prevent creep.

Watch timing: schedule large debits after planned chunk transfers and align bill dates with HELOC billing cycles to preserve average-daily-balance benefits.

Account for fees and holds: include transfer fees, merchant authorization holds, and per-transaction costs in your net-savings model.

Enforce stop rules: pause expense routing if HELOC APR exceeds a predefined spread, if the line is partially frozen or limits reduced, or after consecutive missed surplus months.

Track and review monthly: log days-held, short-window interest, fees, and mortgage principal reductions to confirm net savings and pivot if economics deteriorate.

Paying expenses from the HELOC can magnify the timing leverage that accelerates mortgage payoff, but it also concentrates operational and interest-rate risk—so only adopt this step after automating flows, stress-testing the math, and establishing firm guardrails.

***

Section 4: The Core Strategy Explained — Net Positive Cash Flow Reduces HELOC Balance

Net positive cash flow is the engine that drives the HELOC acceleration strategy: when your income consistently exceeds your expenses each pay period, the surplus becomes the mechanism that rapidly repays the HELOC draw used to make mortgage chunk payments. Each paycheck deposited to the line immediately lowers its average daily balance, reducing daily interest accrual; as you apply surplus to the HELOC between chunk events, the outstanding line shrinks and your available credit regenerates for the next principal attack. Over repeated cycles, a steady positive cash flow converts short-term borrowing into quick repayment, and the cumulative effect is both a falling HELOC balance and permanently reduced mortgage principal that shortens the amortization timeline.

Mechanically, the relationship is straightforward but timing-sensitive. HELOC interest is typically calculated on the average daily balance, so every dollar that sits on the line for fewer days cuts the interest charged for that period. If your household produces net positive cash flow each cycle and you automate deposits to the HELOC, the borrowed chunk gets repaid faster than it would with sporadic cash injections. Faster repayment reduces the days a chunk accrues interest on the line, improving the net savings picture when compared to leaving the same dollars in the mortgage longer. The strategy therefore depends less on borrowing and more on converting recurring surplus into disciplined, repeatable principal repayment.

Two practical realities determine whether net positive cash flow produces meaningful gains: magnitude and reliability. Magnitude matters because small, inconsistent surpluses may be eaten by per-draw fees or variability in interest; you need surplus large enough to repay draws quickly and cover any transaction costs. Reliability matters because missed paychecks, seasonal income swings, or creeping discretionary spending extend HELOC carry time and can flip the math from positive to negative. Successful implementations treat surplus as pre-allocated principal funds—automated, tracked, and protected by a separate emergency reserve—so behavioral drift or short-term crises do not derail cadence.

Operational controls strengthen the link between net positive cash flow and shrinking HELOC balances. Automate direct deposit to the HELOC and schedule fixed transfers from the line to the mortgage on early billing-cycle dates; reconcile weekly so you can see true surplus; and set stop rules (pause chunking if HELOC APR exceeds a set spread or if two consecutive months show zero surplus). Logging each cycle—deposit date, surplus amount, days held, HELOC interest cost, and mortgage principal reduction—turns intuition into verifiable results and makes it simple to adjust chunk size or cadence when economics shift.

Breakdown for readers — actionable checklist

Treat surplus as non-discretionary: designate every net positive dollar for HELOC repayment until the draw is cleared.

Automate deposits and transfers: direct deposit to HELOC; schedule a sweep of accumulated surplus to the mortgage on set dates.

Size surplus appropriately: confirm monthly surplus is large enough that per-draw fees and short-window interest don't overwhelm savings.

Track days held: log when surplus posts and when it's applied to calculate short-window cost precisely.

Maintain a buffer: keep an emergency fund outside the HELOC equal to 1–3 months of essentials to avoid using the line for true emergencies.

Stress-test cash flow: model a missed paycheck and HELOC APR +200–400 bps; proceed only if the net savings remain positive.

Enforce stop rules: pause chunking if fees rise, the HELOC APR widens beyond your tolerance, or surplus disappears for consecutive months.

Review monthly: compare actual HELOC interest paid and mortgage principal reduced to your model; tighten spending or adjust chunk sizes if margins shrink.

Net positive cash flow is not an abstract advantage—it's the practical currency of the strategy. When surplus is reliable, sufficiently large, and managed with automation and guardrails, it converts borrowed chunks into rapid repayment and real mortgage acceleration; without it, the HELOC simply becomes another long-term liability.

***

Section 5: The Core Strategy Explained — Step 6 Repeat When HELOC Is Paid Off

Repeating the cycle once the HELOC draw is repaid is how the acceleration strategy compounds its benefit: after you draw a chunk, apply it to mortgage principal, and then repay that HELOC draw quickly with routed income and surplus, you restore available credit to launch the next chunk attack. Treating each completed cycle as one iteration in a repeatable process turns isolated principal reductions into cumulative mortgage acceleration. The power of repetition is simple arithmetic plus timing: each chunk permanently removes principal from the amortization schedule, and repeating that removal multiple times multiplies the interest avoided and shortens the remaining term.

Operational discipline determines whether repetition creates real value. Before initiating the next draw, confirm that the HELOC balance is meaningfully paid down (or zero), your monthly surplus is intact, and the HELOC's pricing and fee environment remain favorable. Repeating without checking these conditions converts a disciplined strategy into risky leverage: a rate spike, new fees, or an unexpected drop in cash flow between cycles can quickly reduce or erase the margin that made the prior iteration worthwhile. Good operators pause between cycles to reconcile the ledger, compare actual short-window interest paid to projected savings, and adjust chunk size or cadence based on results.

Timing choices govern effectiveness when repeating cycles. You can repeat on a fixed cadence (monthly, biweekly, or quarterly) or adaptively—waiting until a target surplus threshold is reached. Fixed cadence favors predictability and easier automation; adaptive cadence can improve efficiency by allowing larger chunks that minimize per-draw fee drag. Whichever approach you choose, document the rule and follow it consistently so behavioral drift doesn't turn redraw flexibility into permanent revolving debt.

Repetition also invites continuous improvement through measurement. After each completed cycle, log the chunk amount, days the HELOC held that chunk, HELOC interest cost and fees, and the mortgage interest avoided. Use those results to refine your net-savings model and stress tests. If repeated cycles show diminishing returns because margins narrowed or fees accumulated, pause and compare alternatives (direct extra principal payments, recast, or refinance) rather than continuing by habit.

Breakdown for readers — repeat-cycle checklist

Confirm zero or acceptably low HELOC balance before the next draw.

Verify monthly surplus remains consistent and that no major cash-flow changes occurred since the last cycle.

Recheck HELOC terms: current APR, per-draw or transfer fees, and any new lender notices.

Choose cadence: fixed schedule (automated) or adaptive (wait for target surplus); document the rule.

Size the next chunk to balance fewer draws (lower fee drag) with available credit and emergency buffer needs.

Log the previous cycle: draw amount; days held; HELOC interest; fees; mortgage principal reduction; compare actual vs modeled savings.

Stress-test the plan periodically with HELOC APR +200–400 bps and a missed paycheck to confirm margins remain positive.

Enforce stop rules: pause repeating if HELOC APR widens beyond your threshold, fees rise, or you miss surplus targets for consecutive cycles.

If net savings shrink, pivot to simpler payoff methods rather than continuing cycles by inertia.

Repeating the HELOC→mortgage chunk cycle is the mechanism that compounds acceleration, but it must be treated as a disciplined, measured practice: validate the math, preserve liquidity, automate what you can, and stop when the documented advantage no longer exists.

***

Section 6: Chunk Strategy vs Full Replacement — Small Chunk Method ($10K–$30K) Safer, Slower

The small chunk method uses repeated, modest HELOC draws—commonly in the $10,000–$30,000 range—to make periodic lump principal payments against the mortgage, trading rapid compression for lower operational and behavioral risk. By keeping chunk sizes modest you reduce the chance of overleveraging the home, lower the per-cycle exposure to variable-rate swings, and make the cadence easier to sustain for households with steady but not excessive surplus; practitioners often present chunking as a disciplined alternative to one-time full replacement because it preserves optionality while still delivering measurable principal reduction.

Mechanically, smaller chunks create a gentler cycle: each draw reduces mortgage principal by a meaningful but manageable amount, subsequent payback is quicker given typical household surplus levels, and fewer large draws means lower sensitivity to per-draw fees and lender minimum-draw rules. Because the strategy relies on timing advantages (HELOC average-daily-balance reduction followed by mortgage principal application), small, frequent iterations that your cash flow comfortably repays keep average daily HELOC balances low and limit the days a chunk accrues interest—improving the chance that the mortgage interest avoided exceeds the HELOC short-window cost.

The safety tradeoffs are practical: smaller chunks reduce the behavioral temptation to treat the HELOC as permanent credit, lower psychological stress from larger temporary borrowings, and make emergency-reserve sizing more realistic. They also make it easier to document outcomes cycle-by-cycle using spreadsheets or calculators so you can validate net savings and adjust cadence—tools and templates exist to compare chunking scenarios against traditional extra-payment or refinance options so borrowers can see when the small chunk route is actually advantageous.

Breakdown for readers — small chunk checklist

Chunk size rule: target $10K–$30K per draw so repayments align with typical monthly surplus and minimize fee drag.

Limit exposure: verify HELOC limit covers multiple chunks without maxing out; avoid using more than a modest share of available credit.

Repayment cadence: set a repayment window (e.g., 1–3 pay periods) so chunk days-held remain short and HELOC short-window interest stays small.

Fee accounting: include per-draw and transfer fees in every cycle's net-savings test; if fees approach savings, increase chunk size or stop.

Automation and tracking: automate deposits and scheduled sweeps; log draw date, days held, HELOC interest, fees, and mortgage principal reduced.

Stress tests: rerun models with HELOC APR +200–400 bps and a missed paycheck to confirm margins remain positive.

Behavioral guardrails: set a max redraw frequency, maintain emergency savings outside the line, and pause chunking if discipline weakens.

The small chunk method is intentionally conservative: it sacrifices some speed for greater resilience, clearer documentation of savings, and lower probability of catastrophic mistakes—making it the safer entry point for most households considering HELOC-driven acceleration

***

Section 7: Chunk Strategy vs Full Replacement — Large Chunk Method ($50K+) Faster, Requires More Discipline

The large chunk method accelerates payoff by using bigger HELOC draws—typically $50,000 or more—to make substantial one-time principal reductions on your mortgage. Because each large chunk immediately removes a significant portion of the amortizing balance, the mortgage interest avoided per cycle is much larger, so fewer iterations are required to cut years off the term. When the rate and fee math lines up, a handful of well-timed large chunks can compress a 30-year amortization dramatically faster than many small-chunk programs, making speed the primary attraction of this approach.

But speed brings concentrated exposures. Larger draws increase your short-term leverage and magnify sensitivity to variable HELOC rates, lender limit changes, and per-draw costs. A $50K+ draw held even a few extra days at a higher HELOC APR can erode a large portion of the avoided mortgage interest, so repayment cadence, automation, and contingency planning must be airtight. Borrowers using this method need clear stop rules, a robust emergency reserve outside the line, and capacity to absorb rate shocks without extending carry time. In practice, the large chunk approach rewards disciplined households with steady surplus and high confidence in their cash-flow forecasts; it punishes households that rely on optimistic timing or flexible spending.

Operational choices differ from small-chunk strategies. You'll want to negotiate the lowest possible per-draw fees, verify redraw and minimum-balance rules, and often prefer fewer, larger draws to keep per-draw fees proportionally small. Timing matters more: align the draw, deposit cadence, and mortgage-payment sweep precisely to minimize days-held, and verify the HELOC's interest calculation method (average daily balance) so paycheck routing actually reduces cost. Because the stakes are larger, conservatively stress-test every scenario—raise the HELOC APR by 200–400 basis points and simulate missed pay periods—before initiating a large chunk.

Behaviorally, the large chunk method demands stricter discipline and stronger psychological readiness. The visible size of a large draw can tempt overspending or give rise to worry; both outcomes undermine execution. Successful large-chunk users pre-commit to guardrails: a fixed maximum redraw frequency, a written emergency reserve that is never touched, automated repayment flows, and a rule to pause cycles if the HELOC APR widens beyond a set spread. When those controls are in place, large chunks deliver rapid, verifiable mortgage acceleration; without them, the method magnifies risks and can convert a promising plan into a costly juggling act.

Breakdown for readers — large chunk checklist

Chunk sizing: target $50K+ per draw to maximize per-cycle mortgage interest avoided and reduce number of cycles.

Eligibility: confirm HELOC limit comfortably supports desired chunk and leaves breathing room for emergency liquidity.

Pricing priorities: negotiate low margin and low per-draw fees; factor any annual or transfer charges into net savings.

Timing precision: align draw, direct-deposit cadence, and mortgage sweep dates to minimize days held on the HELOC.

Repayment cadence: plan rapid payoff windows (days to a few pay periods) and automate transfers to ensure fast repayment.

Stress tests: rerun net-savings models with HELOC APR +200–400 bps and simulate missed paychecks; require positive margins under stress.

Guardrails: set stop rules for rate spikes, reduced limits, or consecutive missed surplus months; maintain an emergency fund outside the HELOC.

Behavior rules: limit redraw frequency, avoid discretionary use of the line, and require monthly reconciliation of each cycle.

When to prefer large chunks: you have steady, sizable surplus; favorable HELOC pricing; ample tappable equity; and strong tolerance for operational complexity.

When to avoid: uncertain cash flow, thin emergency reserves, high fees, or HELOC pricing that closes the margin versus avoided mortgage interest.

Large chunks accelerate results but demand more precise execution and stronger safeguards. Treat the method as a high-leverage operational plan—use conservative modeling, automate aggressively, and stop if the documented net benefit narrows.

***

Section 8: Chunk Strategy vs Full Replacement — Full Replacement Method Advanced Strategy

The full replacement method is an advanced, high-leverage variation of HELOC acceleration that replaces a large portion—or the entirety—of the mortgage principal with a single or small number of HELOC draws, then repays the line rapidly using disciplined cash flow and repeat cycles. Rather than repeated moderate chunks, full replacement shifts most mortgage debt into a more flexible, daily-interest vehicle so you can exploit timing and cash-flow effects at scale. Proponents argue this compresses amortization fastest when HELOC pricing, tappable equity, and borrower discipline all line up.

This strategy magnifies both potential savings and risks. Because the moved principal is much larger, the mortgage interest avoided per cycle is materially higher; but days-held and any unexpected rate movement on the HELOC also carry much larger dollar consequences. Advisors who analyze velocity methods point out that full replacement only makes sense when the HELOC's effective short-window cost (including stress-tested APRs and all fees) consistently stays below the mortgage interest avoided and when the borrower maintains airtight repayment cadence and robust contingency reserves.

Operational complexity rises with scale. Full replacement demands precise timing (direct deposit, bill timing, and mortgage sweeps), negotiated fee structures (minimal per-draw and transfer costs), and strict behavioral controls to prevent the line from turning into permanent revolving debt. It's also important to consider alternatives: in many market environments, refinancing directly into a shorter-term mortgage or performing a partial recast may deliver comparable term compression with lower variable-rate and liquidity risk—so run side-by-side models before committing to full replacement.

Because the full replacement approach amplifies sensitivity to assumptions, conservative stress-testing is essential. Simulate HELOC APR increases of several hundred basis points, missed pay periods, and temporary line limit reductions; require the net-savings margin to remain positive under these scenarios before proceeding. If the margin holds, document written stop rules, maintain an emergency fund outside the line, automate every transfer, and log cycle results to ensure actual outcomes track modeled expectations.

Breakdown for readers — practical checklist

Confirm suitability: ample tappable equity, strong credit, and HELOC offers with low margins and fees.

Size decision: determine the replacement amount and verify HELOC limit comfortably covers it while preserving contingency capacity.

Pricing test: compare mortgage interest avoided vs HELOC short-window cost + fees under base and stress scenarios (HELOC APR +200–400 bps).

Operational readiness: automate direct deposit, schedule mortgage sweeps, and align billing cycles to minimize days-held.

Negotiation priorities: secure low per-draw/transfer fees and clear redraw rules before drawing large sums.

Guardrails: set stop rules for rate spikes, reduced limits, or missed surplus months; keep an emergency reserve outside the line.

Alternatives check: model refinancing or recast outcomes side-by-side—choose the option with the best risk-adjusted payoff.

Continuous monitoring: log each cycle (draw, days held, HELOC interest, fees, principal reduced) and reassess quarterly; pause if documented advantage narrows.

***

Section 9: Chunk Strategy vs Full Replacement — Which Approach Fits Your Situation

Deciding between small chunks, large chunks, or full replacement starts with your cash-flow reality and risk tolerance. If you prefer lower operational risk and can only reliably generate modest surplus each month, the small chunk method—repeated $10K–$30K draws—usually fits better because it matches repayment speed to typical household surpluses and reduces sensitivity to variable HELOC swings. Tools like velocity-banking spreadsheets help you run side-by-side scenarios so you can see whether modest, repeatable chunks actually deliver net savings after fees and stress-testing assumptions.

If you have larger, stable surplus, ample tappable equity, and high confidence in sticking to tight automation and guardrails, the large chunk route (commonly $50K+) shortens the calendar faster but concentrates exposure to rate moves and timing mistakes—making precise timing, low fees, and fast repayment essential to preserve the margin versus avoided mortgage interest. Critics and CFPs stress that the HELOC itself doesn't create savings—the savings come from earlier principal reduction—so when HELOC APRs and fees approach or exceed your mortgage rate, refinancing or straightforward extra payments typically win on risk-adjusted grounds; this information is sourced from *The Ways To Wealth*.

Full replacement is an advanced, high-leverage option that only suits borrowers who can secure a competitively priced HELOC, tolerate large swings in daily interest exposure, and maintain large emergency reserves and ironclad discipline; because it replaces a substantial portion of mortgage principal with daily-accruing debt, the dollar impact of any rate spike, line limit change, or missed cadence is amplified, so run conservative stress tests and compare outcomes against partial recast or a term refinance before proceeding. Financial educators recommend modeling worst-case spreads (HELOC APR +200–400 bps) and requiring a positive margin under those scenarios before committing to a scaled or full replacement.

Practical fit comes from matching three constraints: (1) surplus magnitude and reliability, (2) HELOC pricing/fees and available limit, and (3) behavioral discipline with documented guardrails. If any one of those is weak—irregular income, tight or expensive HELOC, or unreliable spending control—favor the smaller-chunk or simple extra-payment/refinance paths. Use a spreadsheet to quantify net savings per cycle (mortgage interest avoided minus HELOC short-window cost and fees) and require that advantage to remain positive in stress scenarios before you scale up.

Breakdown for readers — decision checklist

Confirm cash-flow profile: small, steady surplus favors small chunks; large, reliable surplus may justify large chunks or scaled replacement.

Verify HELOC economics: prequalify to learn realistic APR, margins, and fees; if HELOC cost approaches mortgage rate, pause.

Estimate needed limit: ensure tappable equity supports your chunk plan without maxing the line or removing emergency liquidity.

Run net-savings model: require mortgage interest avoided > (HELOC short-window interest + all fees) under stress (HELOC APR +200–400 bps).

Assess behavior: only pursue larger or full-replacement strategies if you reliably automate deposits, reconcile monthly, and maintain a separate emergency reserve.

Start conservative: pilot with one small chunk and log actual days-held, HELOC interest, and mortgage reduction; scale only when documented results match modeled expectations.

Fallback options: if margins shrink, switch to extra principal payments, recast, or refinance to a shorter term rather than persisting out of habit.

***

Section 10: Chunk Strategy vs Full Replacement — The Power of Income Flow

Why depositing income immediately matters

Depositing income directly into the HELOC is the mechanical core of the acceleration strategy because it converts each paycheck from idle cash into an immediate reduction of the HELOC's average daily balance, which lowers the line's daily interest accrual and creates the timing advantage that makes lump principal payments effective. In practice this "paycheck parking" or direct-deposit routing is what allows borrowers to extract value from the sequencing—income reduces the daily interest charge on the HELOC first, then aggregated surplus is swept as a chunk to the mortgage where it permanently reduces amortizing principal. Educational overviews of velocity-style methods underline that the savings come from earlier principal reduction enabled by this flow, not from the HELOC itself, so routing matters because it enables repeatable, measurable principal attacks.

Immediate deposit also enforces behavioral structure: when income is treated as designated principal-repayment funds (not discretionary cash), it reduces the temptation to spend surplus and makes automation feasible. Practitioners advise automating direct deposit and scheduled mortgage sweeps, so timing is consistent and human error is minimized; this discipline is what preserves the small per-cycle margins that the strategy relies on, because delays or spending creep lengthen days-held on the HELOC and inflate short-window interest costs. In short, the flow converts good intentions into repeatable mechanics—without automation and habit, the average-daily-balance benefit dissolves into noise and fees.

From a testing and modeling perspective, immediate deposit makes the net-savings calculation tractable and auditable: you can measure days-held, compute short-window HELOC cost ((HELOC APR ÷ 365) × chunk × days held), and compare it to the mortgage interest avoided by the earlier principal reduction. That visibility is critical—practical guides recommend piloting a single cycle, logging actual deposit times, days held, HELOC interest, and subsequent mortgage reduction, then comparing real outcomes to model expectations before scaling up. If the documented net benefit holds under conservative assumptions (stress tested HELOC APR +200–400 bps and a missed paycheck), the income-flow choreography is likely delivering value; if not, simpler extra payments or refinancing usually win on risk-adjusted grounds.

Breakdown for readers — practical checklist

Automate direct deposit to the HELOC so income posts early in the billing cycle.

Confirm the HELOC charges daily/average-daily-balance interest so deposits reduce cost immediately.

Set a sweep rule and cadence (monthly/biweekly) that triggers when surplus reaches your chunk threshold.

Log each cycle: deposit date; chunk amount; date swept to mortgage; days held; HELOC interest paid; fees; mortgage principal reduction.

Calculate net test: mortgage interest avoided > (HELOC short-window cost + fees) under base and stress scenarios.

Pilot one cycle, review actual vs modeled results, then scale only if documented margins remain positive.

Maintain guardrails: emergency fund outside the line, stop rules for HELOC APR spikes, and limits on redraw frequency.

***

Section 11: Chunk Strategy vs Full Replacement — Daily Balance Reduction Impact

Reducing the HELOC's average daily balance is the mechanical lever that produces the timing advantage in HELOC-based acceleration: every dollar deposited to the line on day one reduces the base on which daily interest is calculated, so routing paychecks into the HELOC temporarily lowers interest owed and creates a window where aggregated surplus can be swept to mortgage principal for permanent interest savings. Practical analyses of velocity-style approaches emphasize that the savings are not created by the HELOC but by paying down amortizing principal earlier; thus the measurable benefit tracks directly to how many dollars and how many days you successfully remove from the HELOC before making the chunk payment back to the mortgage.

The dollar math is straightforward but sensitive: short-window HELOC cost ≈ (HELOC APR ÷ 365) × chunk × days held, while mortgage benefit equals the interest avoided over the remaining amortization on that principal reduction. Because the HELOC interest accrues daily, shaving days held—even by a few pay periods—can materially change the net result, which is why advocates recommend automation, careful billing-cycle alignment, and trial cycles to compare modeled vs actual outcomes. At the same time, published reviews caution that variable HELOC rates, per-draw fees, and inconsistent timing can quickly erode the thin margins this strategy relies on, so rigorous tracking and conservative stress-testing are essential before scaling up.

Breakdown for readers — how daily balance reduction affects outcomes

Mechanic: each deposited dollar immediately reduces average daily balance and daily interest; more dollars and earlier deposits = larger short-window savings.

Short-window cost formula: (HELOC APR ÷ 365) × chunk × days held (add any fees).

Mortgage benefit: modeled interest avoided from immediate principal reduction over remaining loan term.

Margin test: require mortgage benefit > (short-window cost + fees) under base and stress scenarios.

Timing levers: deposit timing, sweep date, and billing-cycle alignment control days held.

Operational controls: automate deposits, schedule mortgage sweeps early in the HELOC cycle, and log actual deposit/sweep dates to compute real days held.

Risk mitigators: include per-draw fees and possible APR increases in models; pilot one cycle and compare actual data to projections before repeating.

***

Section 12: Chunk Strategy vs Full Replacement — How Every Dollar Counts

Every dollar matters because the measurable savings in HELOC-driven acceleration come from paying down amortizing principal earlier, not from the existence of a HELOC itself. Routing income through a line converts each paycheck into a temporary reduction in the HELOC's average daily balance, which lowers daily interest accrual; when aggregated and swept to the mortgage as a chunk, those dollars permanently reduce future mortgage interest. Practitioners and evaluators stress that the strategy only produces net gains when the avoided mortgage interest from earlier principal reductions exceeds the HELOC's short-window interest and fees.

Mechanically the math is precise and sensitive. Short-window HELOC cost is approximately (HELOC APR ÷ 365) × chunk × days held, plus any per-draw or transfer fees; the mortgage benefit is the interest avoided on that principal over the remaining amortization. Because HELOC interest accrues daily, shaving even a few days off the days-held materially changes net outcome—so deposit timing, billing-cycle alignment, and rapid repayment cadence determine whether each dollar produces net savings or net cost. Clear logging of deposit dates, days-held, interest paid, and mortgage principal reduction turns intuition into verifiable results and makes the strategy auditable cycle by cycleupfromzerohq.com+1.

Behavior and automation convert theory into practice. Treating income as "designated principal funds" (automating direct deposit to the HELOC and scheduling sweeps to the mortgage) reduces discretionary drift and preserves per-cycle margins; conversely, delays, spending creep, or missed transfers extend HELOC carry time and can erase the thin margins the approach depends on. Evaluators caution that only disciplined households with predictable surplus, low fees, and favorable HELOC pricing reliably extract value—otherwise simpler extra-payment or refinancing approaches typically win on risk-adjusted grounds.

Testing and conservative stress-testing are nonnegotiable. Pilot a single cycle, log real deposit and sweep times, compute the actual short-window cost, and compare that to modeled mortgage interest avoided; then rerun the model with higher HELOC APR assumptions (e.g., +200–400 basis points) and simulate missed pay periods. If the documented net benefit holds under conservative assumptions, scaling is reasonable; if not, stop and compare extra-payment, recast, or refinance alternatives before increasing leverage.

Breakdown for readers — practical checklist

Understand the engine: every deposited dollar reduces HELOC average daily balance and thus daily interest; aggregated dollars swept to mortgage permanently lower future interest.

Short-window cost formula: (HELOC APR ÷ 365) × chunk × days held + per-draw/transfer fees.

Mortgage benefit: interest avoided from immediate principal reduction over remaining term; compute per-chunk and cumulatively.

Timing levers: automate direct deposit to the HELOC, schedule sweeps early in the HELOC billing cycle, and align bill dates to minimize days held.

Pilot and log: run one full cycle; record deposit date, sweep date, days held, HELOC interest paid, fees, and mortgage principal reduction.

Stress-test: rerun models with HELOC APR +200–400 bps and a missed paycheck; require a positive margin under stress.

Behavioral rule: treat surplus as non-discretionary until each chunk is repaid; maintain an emergency fund outside the HELOC.

Stop rules: pause chunking if HELOC APR widens beyond your threshold, fees grow, or documented margins turn negative.

***

Section 13: Chunk Strategy vs Full Replacement — Time Value Optimization

Time value optimization in HELOC-driven acceleration is the deliberate choreography of deposits, draws, and sweeps to maximize the amount of principal removed from an amortizing mortgage as early as possible. The core idea is simple: a dollar that reduces mortgage principal today prevents more future interest than the same dollar applied later, so sequencing income to briefly lower the HELOC average daily balance and then sweeping aggregated surplus into the mortgage captures that time value. Practical guides show the gains come from earlier principal reduction rather than the HELOC itself, which means the optimization problem is one of timing and days-held rather than of finding a permanently cheaper loan.

Mechanics: minimize days held and maximize dollars shifted early. Because HELOC interest accrues on an average daily balance, every paycheck routed into the line reduces interest immediately; when those dollars are later swept to the mortgage, they permanently lower the amortizing base. The net test compares short-window HELOC cost ≈ (HELOC APR ÷ 365) × chunk × days held plus fees, against the mortgage interest avoided by immediate principal application. Optimization therefore focuses on shortening days held (through fast repayment cadence and billing-cycle alignment), increasing the size of dollars swept when per-draw fees permit, and automating flows so human delays don't erode the thin margins the strategy relies on.

Timing levers that matter most are deposit timing, sweep timing, and cadence. Deposit income as early in the HELOC billing cycle as possible so more days of the cycle benefit from lower average daily balance; schedule mortgage sweeps on a date that maximizes days the deposited dollars reduce the HELOC but still meets your repayment-speed target; and choose a cadence (biweekly, monthly, or adaptive by surplus threshold) that balances fewer draws (lower fee drag) against keeping days-held short. Modeling and pilot cycles are essential: run a single iteration, log actual deposit and sweep timestamps, compute real days held and the short-window cost, then compare to modeled mortgage benefit before scaling up.

Risk and opportunity costs are central to optimization decisions. Because HELOCs are typically variable rate and may include per-draw or transfer fees, any optimization that increases days held or frequency of draws can quickly reverse expected savings; therefore, **conservative stress tests (HELOC APR +200–400 basis points, missed paycheck scenarios)** and side-by-side comparisons with simple extra payments or refinancing are standard practice for prudent operators. In many markets, advisors warn that the HELOC's added complexity and variable exposure mean simpler strategies often match or beat HELOC cycling on a risk-adjusted basis unless timing and pricing assumptions hold for years.

Breakdown for readers — time value optimization checklist

Automate deposits: route direct deposit to the HELOC so income posts early in the billing cycle.

Minimize days held: schedule sweeps to mortgage at the fastest practical cadence consistent with your surplus; log actual deposit and sweep dates.

Size for fees: choose chunk sizes large enough to keep per-draw and transfer fees small relative to expected savings.

Align billing cycles: map HELOC interest cycle and mortgage payment dates; pick sweep dates that maximize average-daily-balance benefit without lengthening days held unnecessarily.

Pilot and measure: run one full cycle, record deposit/sweep timestamps, compute HELOC short-window cost and mortgage interest avoided, and compare results to model.

Stress-test: rerun your net test with HELOC APR increased by 200–400 bps and simulate a missed paycheck; require a positive margin under stress.

Compare alternatives: model straightforward extra payments, recast, or refinance alongside HELOC cycling to ensure the time-value gain justifies complexity and risk

***

Visual Walkthrough - Month-by-Month Example

Starting position: a $250,000 mortgage sets a clear baseline for measuring impact. Assume a 30-year amortization and a conventional mortgage rate; the goal is to compare the standard amortization path to one accelerated by HELOC chunking. For this walkthrough we'll model a conservative, common scenario: open a HELOC with a usable limit that supports a $25,000 chunk, maintain disciplined cash flow that produces predictable surplus each month, and automate deposits so paychecks hit the HELOC early in its billing cycle—this is the practical setup many velocity-banking overviews use when demonstrating real-world results.

Month 1: HELOC draw and mortgage chunk. Draw $25,000 from the HELOC and apply it immediately as a principal-only payment to the mortgage. This single action reduces the amortizing balance and the mortgage interest that would have accrued on that $25,000 going forward; the HELOC balance now shows the $25,000 draw and begins accruing daily interest. The key operational step this month is to route all incoming deposits into the HELOC and freeze discretionary spending so the line can be repaid quickly. Practical guides stress that the net benefit depends on whether the avoided mortgage interest on the $25,000 exceeds the HELOC's short-window cost (daily interest on the draw plus any fees).

Months 2–12: income deposits and expense tracking. Throughout the next 11 months, deposit every paycheck into the HELOC so the average daily balance drops as income posts, then pay household expenses from the HELOC so the cash-flow loop is continuous. Use a one-page ledger or simple spreadsheet to record deposit dates, sweep amounts, days each dollar sat on the HELOC, interest charged on the line, and the remaining mortgage balance after the chunk payment. If your monthly surplus is, for example, $1,200, that surplus goes entirely to repaying the HELOC draw until the $25,000 is cleared; this cadence is consistent with published case studies that show repeatable repayment windows of under a year for similar chunk sizes and surplus levels.

HELOC payoff and results. When the HELOC draw is fully repaid (for a $25,000 chunk repaid at $1,200/month plus normal expense routing, this can occur in roughly 18–24 months depending on exact surplus and HELOC interest), you will have permanently removed that $25,000 from the mortgage's amortization base and reduced future interest accrual accordingly. Log the total short-window interest paid on the HELOC during the hold period and compare it to the modeled mortgage interest avoided on that $25,000 over the remaining term; if the mortgage interest avoided exceeds the HELOC cost plus fees under conservative assumptions, the iteration produced net savings.

Repeat cycle demonstration. With the HELOC balance cleared, restore available credit and repeat: draw another $25,000, apply to mortgage principal, then route income to the HELOC and repay quickly. Repeating this cycle several times compounds the effect—each chunk permanently reduces the mortgage base, and multiple iterations can compress years from the schedule. Practical examples show that repeating modest chunks at sustainable cadence is how households transform routine surplus into measurable mortgage acceleration without permanently refinancing, provided automation and guardrails remain in place.

Total time to mortgage freedom (**illustrative estimate**). Exact timing depends on mortgage rate, HELOC APR, surplus magnitude, chunk size, and fees. As a rough illustrative scenario: a $250,000 mortgage where you apply four $25,000 chunks over time (totaling $100,000 of principal removed) and aggressively continue surplus-driven extra payments could shorten a 30-year schedule by many years—often by a decade or more in optimistic but realistic cases—while saving substantial interest, assuming HELOC pricing and execution remain favorable. Always model side-by-side with straightforward extra-payment and refinance scenarios and stress-test HELOC APR by several hundred basis points to ensure the plan holds under adverse moves.

Breakdown for readers — month-by-month action checklist

Month 0 (setup): confirm tappable equity, open HELOC, automate direct deposit to HELOC, and build a 1–3 month emergency buffer outside the line.

Month 1: draw chunk (e.g., $25,000); apply immediately as a principal-only mortgage payment; route all income to HELOC and pause nonessential spending.

Months 2–N (repayment window): deposit every paycheck to HELOC; pay recurring expenses from HELOC; sweep accumulated surplus toward HELOC repayment on fixed dates; log deposit/sweep timestamps and interest costs.

At payoff: compute total HELOC short-window cost = sum of daily interest on the draw + fees; compute mortgage interest avoided from the principal reduction; confirm net savings under stress scenarios (HELOC APR +200–400 bps).

Repeat: only initiate the next chunk after HELOC balance is acceptably low or zero, surplus remains stable, and HELOC pricing/fees are still favorable.

Monitor and pivot: review actual vs modeled results quarterly; if margins shrink, favor direct extra payments or refinancing rather than continuing cycles.

Sources: practical velocity-banking guides and case studies that walk through HELOC chunk examples and month-by-month cycles.

***

Comparison Charts

Comparison charts crystallize the decision between a traditional payoff path and a HELOC-driven method by turning complex cash-flow dynamics into side-by-side visuals that highlight timeline, cumulative interest, and end-state wealth differences. A well-constructed chart places the traditional amortization curve next to projected balances under a HELOC chunking plan so readers can instantly see when principal diverges, how much interest accumulates under each path, and when the HELOC approach recoups its own short-window costs—this visual framing is how many practitioners demonstrate the practical advantage (or disadvantage) of velocity-style tactics.

Interest-paid comparison charts must show cumulative interest over time for both strategies and isolate the HELOC short-window costs (daily interest on draws plus fees) so viewers can see net interest saved, not just mortgage interest avoided. Present the mortgage interest curve, the HELOC interest additions per cycle, and the net gap between them; annotations should call out key assumptions (mortgage rate, HELOC APR, chunk sizes, days held, and fees) because small changes to these inputs materially shift the interest crossover point—reviews and how-to guides stress that transparent assumptions are essential for honest comparisons.

Years-saved analysis converts interest and principal divergence into calendar impact: plot the point where cumulative principal reductions under the HELOC plan result in reaching a target payoff date earlier than the baseline amortization. Use multiple scenario lines (base case, HELOC APR +200 bps, missed-income case) so readers can see robust and stressed outcomes; many HELOC/velocity explainers recommend side-by-side scenario modeling because it reveals whether the strategy's theoretical speed survives realistic rate or cash-flow shocks.

Net-wealth difference at the end is the most decision-relevant chart for many readers: it shows the borrower's eventual equity position and cumulative interest cost under each path, and it should include alternative uses of any freed cash (e.g., investing interest savings). Display final net worth (home equity minus remaining debt plus investment value of saved interest) under each scenario and annotate assumptions for investment returns or tax treatment if you include them. Because HELOC methods trade variable-rate exposure for timing benefits, the net-wealth chart must be honest about risk-adjusted outcomes and include stress cases so readers can judge whether incremental speed justifies added complexity and rate risk.

Breakdown for readers — charting checklist

Define baseline assumptions: mortgage balance, mortgage rate, amortization years, HELOC APR (base and stress), chunk sizes, days held, and per-draw/transfer fees.

Build four core charts: balance timeline (mortgage vs HELOC method); cumulative interest paid; payoff date lines (years saved); and end-state net-wealth comparison.

Include scenario overlays: base case, HELOC APR +200 bps, HELOC APR +400 bps, and a missed-income disruption to show sensitivity.

Isolate HELOC short-window cost: compute (HELOC APR ÷ 365) × chunk × days held + fees and plot it separately so net savings are transparent.

Annotate assumptions visibly on each chart and provide a one-line summary of the conclusion (e.g., "Net savings positive under stress up to +200 bps; pause if APR > X").

Pilot and validate: run the model with one real cycle of your cash flow and compare actuals to projections before relying on long-term charts.

Use conservative presentations: favor stress scenarios and require a positive margin under them before recommending scale-up.

Sources: practical velocity/HELOC guides and comparative analyses that model chunking outcomes and emphasize transparent, stress-tested charting for decision making

CHAPTER 5:

The Numbers Does It Really Work Case Study 1

The Conservative Approach

Profile and baseline assumptions: this case study begins with a $300,000 mortgage, household gross income of $8,000 per month, and monthly expenses of $6,500—leaving a modest documented surplus of $1,500 to deploy into acceleration tactics each month. For clarity we assume a conventional 30-year amortization on the mortgage and a HELOC priced competitively but variable; the comparison below measures outcomes by cumulative interest paid, years to payoff, and net interest savings versus the traditional path.

Traditional payoff outcome: on the 30-year amortization path the mortgage's front-loaded interest produces a cumulative interest burden in the low-to-mid hundreds of thousands (illustratively $347,000 in this scenario), because monthly payments in the early years primarily cover interest rather than principal—a structural fact of amortizing loans that underlies why accelerating principal matters.

HELOC strategy outcome and how the compression is achieved: using a conservative chunking program that applies available surplus aggressively to a HELOC cycle (depositing income to the line, sweeping surplus as periodic chunks to the mortgage, and repeating) compresses the amortization materially in the modeled result—paying the mortgage in roughly 11 years with cumulative interest around $127,000 in this illustrative case—because each chunk permanently removes principal early, which reduces future interest compounding on the mortgage balance. The incremental savings derive from timing and earlier principal reduction rather than any magical lower cost in the HELOC itself.

Mechanics that produce the 19-year / $220K delta: the program converts the $1,500 monthly surplus into rapid HELOC repayment cadence and sizes chunks so per-draw fees and short-window HELOC interest remain materially below the mortgage interest avoided on each chunk. Each chunk's net test is the short-window cost ≈ (HELOC APR ÷ 365) × chunk × days held + fees, compared to the mortgage interest avoided on that principal over the remaining term; when repeated and automated, these cycles compound into the multi-decade time savings shown here.

Risks, stress tests, and documented guardrails: conservative implementations require documented stress testing (increase HELOC APR by several hundred basis points, simulate missed paychecks, and include all per-draw/transfer fees) and concrete stop rules—pause chunking if the HELOC APR closes the gap to mortgage rate, if monthly surplus evaporates, or if the lender alters terms—because HELOCs are variable and add liquidity and rate risk that can erase thin margins quickly. Practitioners emphasize piloting a single cycle, logging deposit/sweep timestamps, days held, HELOC interest paid, and actual mortgage reduction to verify the modeled outcome before scaling.

Breakdown for readers practical checklist

Confirm documented surplus: verify take-home income minus essential expenses equals the surplus you'll commit to HELOC cycles.

Run the net-savings test for a single chunk: mortgage interest avoided > (HELOC APR ÷ 365) × chunk × days held + all fees.

Pilot one cycle: automate direct deposit to HELOC, sweep accumulated surplus to the mortgage once chunk threshold met, and log actual days held and interest costs.

Stress-test: rerun models with HELOC APR +200–400 bps and simulate a missed paycheck; require positive margin.

Establish guardrails: emergency fund outside HELOC (1–3 months), stop rules for rate spikes or lost surplus, and maximum redraw frequency.

Validate and scale: only repeat if pilot actuals closely match or beat modeled expectations; otherwise prefer extra principal payments, recast, or refinance.

Sources: consumer-facing velocity/HELOC analyses and conservative evaluations of HELOC acceleration methods that stress the importance of early principal reduction and rigorous stress testing.

***

Section 1: The Numbers — Does It Really Work?

Case Study #2: The Aggressive Approach

Profile: In this scenario, the household begins with a $450,000 mortgage. Monthly income is $12,000, while expenses total $9,000, leaving a surplus of $3,000 each month. This surplus is significantly larger than in the conservative case study, which allows for more aggressive use of the HELOC strategy. With greater cash flow, the household can sustain larger HELOC draws and repay them faster, creating a compounding effect on mortgage reduction.

Larger HELOC chunks used: Instead of modest $20K–$30K chunks, this household applies larger draws of $50K–$75K directly to the mortgage principal. Each chunk immediately reduces the amortizing balance, cutting years of scheduled interest. Because the surplus is strong, repayment of these larger HELOC draws can occur within 18–24 months, keeping short-window HELOC interest manageable. The larger chunks magnify the savings per cycle, but they also require stricter discipline and careful monitoring of HELOC terms to ensure the net benefit remains positive.

Timeline and interest savings: With repeated large chunks, the mortgage payoff timeline compresses dramatically. Instead of the standard 30-year payoff, the aggressive approach can reduce the mortgage to approximately 7–9 years, depending on HELOC APR stability and repayment cadence. Cumulative interest drops from what would have been well over $500,000 in a traditional amortization to roughly $180,000–$200,000 in this aggressive model. That represents hundreds of thousands in avoided interest and more than two decades of time saved. The key driver is the early removal of principal, which prevents compounding interest from accumulating over decades.

Risks managed: Aggressive strategies magnify exposure to variable HELOC rates, lender limit changes, and behavioral drift. To manage these risks, the household must:

Maintain a robust emergency fund outside the HELOC (at least 3–6 months of expenses).

Stress-test the plan with HELOC APR increases of +200–400 basis points to ensure savings remain positive.

Automate deposits and sweeps to avoid timing errors that extend days-held.

Set stop rules: pause chunking if surplus drops below $2,000/month, if HELOC APR exceeds mortgage rate by more than a set spread, or if lender fees increase.

Track each cycle with a ledger: log draw date, repayment period, HELOC interest paid, fees, and mortgage principal reduced.

Breakdown for Readers — Aggressive Approach Checklist

Surplus strength: Confirm monthly surplus ($3,000+) can sustain larger HELOC draws without extending repayment windows.

Chunk sizing: Target $50K–$75K chunks to maximize mortgage interest avoided per cycle.

Repayment cadence: Plan repayment windows of 18–24 months; automate deposits and sweeps to keep days-held short.

Stress-test assumptions: Run models with HELOC APR +200–400 bps and simulate missed paychecks; require positive margins.

Emergency reserves: Keep 3–6 months of expenses outside the HELOC to avoid using the line for crises.

Fee awareness: Negotiate low per-draw and transfer fees; include them in every net-savings calculation.

Stop rules: Pause chunking if surplus shrinks, HELOC APR spikes, or lender terms change unfavorably.

Documentation: Track each cycle's actual HELOC cost vs mortgage interest avoided; adjust chunk size or cadence if margins narrow.

Conclusion: The aggressive approach demonstrates how larger HELOC chunks, supported by strong surplus and disciplined repayment, can slash decades off a mortgage and save hundreds of thousands in interest. But the same leverage that creates speed also magnifies risk, making automation, stress-testing, and strict guardrails essential for success.

***

Case Study #3: The Modest Income Family

Profile: This household begins with a $200,000 mortgage, a monthly income of $6,000, and monthly expenses of $5,200. That leaves a surplus of $800 per month—smaller than in the conservative or aggressive case studies, but still meaningful when applied consistently. The modest surplus means the family cannot sustain large HELOC draws, but they can use smaller, carefully timed chunks to accelerate payoff without overextending themselves.

Small chunks, disciplined approach: With limited surplus, the family applies smaller HELOC draws—typically $10,000–$15,000 at a time—toward mortgage principal. Each chunk reduces the amortizing balance and prevents years of future interest accrual. Because repayment capacity is modest, the HELOC draw is repaid over a longer window (often 12–18 months), but discipline ensures that every surplus dollar is directed toward clearing the line. This approach emphasizes sustainability: the family avoids the risks of overleveraging while still capturing the benefits of earlier principal reduction.

Realistic timeline: Instead of compressing a 30-year mortgage into under a decade, the modest-income family's disciplined chunking strategy shortens the payoff horizon to roughly 15–18 years. While slower than aggressive approaches, this still represents a significant improvement over the traditional path. The key is consistency—each cycle of small chunks builds on the last, gradually reducing the mortgage balance and compounding the interest savings. By documenting each cycle and stress-testing assumptions, the family ensures that their plan remains viable even if HELOC rates rise or income fluctuates.

Modest but meaningful savings: Over the life of the loan, this disciplined approach can save the family well over $100,000 in interest compared to the traditional 30-year amortization. While the savings are smaller than in higher-income or aggressive scenarios, they are still transformative: the family gains financial freedom more than a decade earlier, reduces exposure to long-term interest costs, and creates margin for other goals such as retirement savings or education funding. The lesson is clear—velocity banking principles can be adapted to modest incomes, provided the household maintains discipline, tracks results, and avoids overextension.

Breakdown for Readers — Modest Income Strategy Checklist

Surplus calculation: Confirm monthly surplus ($800 in this case) is stable and available for HELOC repayment.

Chunk sizing: Target $10K–$15K draws so repayment windows remain manageable (12–18 months).

Automation: Route income directly into the HELOC and schedule sweeps to the mortgage once surplus reaches chunk threshold.

Tracking: Log deposit dates, days held, HELOC interest paid, fees, and mortgage principal reduced for each cycle.

Stress-test: Model HELOC APR increases (+200–400 bps) and simulate missed paychecks; require positive margins under stress.

Guardrails: Maintain an emergency fund outside the HELOC (2–3 months of expenses) and pause chunking if surplus disappears.

Timeline expectation: Plan for 15–18 years to payoff, not instant acceleration; celebrate steady progress.

Savings impact: Recognize that even modest surpluses can save $100K+ in interest and free up years of financial life.

Conclusion: For families with modest income and limited surplus, the HELOC chunking strategy is not about speed but about sustainability. Small, disciplined chunks applied consistently can still deliver meaningful savings and shorten the mortgage timeline by more than a decade, proving that every household—regardless of income level—can adapt the principles of velocity banking to their situation.

***

Section 2: The Break-Even Analysis

At what point does the strategy payoff: The break-even point in a HELOC acceleration strategy occurs when the mortgage interest avoided by earlier principal reduction exceeds the cumulative HELOC interest and fees incurred during the short-window borrowing period. In practice, this means the strategy begins to "pay off" once the household has repaid the HELOC draw quickly enough that the cost of carrying the line is smaller than the long-term interest savings from the mortgage chunk. For example, if a $20,000 HELOC draw costs $600 in short-window interest and fees but avoids $3,000 in mortgage interest over the remaining term, the net savings is positive, and the strategy has crossed its break-even threshold.

How much discipline is required: Discipline is the defining factor in whether the break-even point is reached consistently. The household must route all income into the HELOC, pay expenses from the line, and commit every surplus dollar to repayment until the draw is cleared. This requires automation (direct deposit, scheduled sweeps) and behavioral guardrails (emergency fund outside the HELOC, strict spending caps). Without discipline, surplus leaks into discretionary spending, repayment windows lengthen, and HELOC interest costs rise—erasing the margin that makes the strategy viable.

Variables that affect success: Several variables determine whether the strategy produces net savings:

HELOC APR and fees: Higher rates or per-draw charges narrow or eliminate the margin.

Surplus size and reliability: Larger, predictable surplus accelerates repayment and improves net savings.

Chunk size and cadence: Smaller chunks reduce risk but slow payoff; larger chunks magnify both savings and exposure.

Timing of deposits and sweeps: Days-held on the HELOC directly affect short-window costs.

Market conditions: Rising interest rates or lender policy changes can quickly alter the economics.

Warning signs to abort strategy: Abort the strategy if documented results show negative margins or if risk factors increase beyond tolerance. Warning signs include:

HELOC APR rising close to or above the mortgage rate.

Surplus disappearing for consecutive months due to income loss or expense creep.

HELOC fees increasing to the point they consume most of the savings.

Repayment windows extending beyond planned cadence, causing days-held to inflate.

Emergency reserves being depleted, forcing reliance on the HELOC for crises.

Breakdown for Readers — Practical Checklist

Calculate break-even: Compare mortgage interest avoided vs HELOC short-window cost + fees for each chunk.

Automate flows: Direct deposit to HELOC and scheduled sweeps to mortgage ensure discipline.

Track surplus: Log monthly income, expenses, and repayment progress; confirm surplus is stable.

Stress-test variables: Model HELOC APR +200–400 bps and simulate missed paychecks; require positive margins.

Monitor fees: Include per-draw, transfer, and annual fees in every cycle's net-savings test.

Set stop rules: Abort if HELOC APR exceeds mortgage rate, surplus disappears, or fees overwhelm savings.

Maintain reserves: Keep 2–3 months of expenses outside the HELOC to avoid dependency.

Review quarterly: Compare actual vs modeled results; pivot to extra payments or refinance if margins shrink.

Conclusion: Break-even analysis is the safeguard that ensures HELOC acceleration is not just theoretically effective but practically profitable. By calculating the point where savings outweigh costs, enforcing discipline, monitoring key variables, and recognizing warning signs early, households can determine whether to continue, adjust, or abort the strategy—protecting themselves from unnecessary risk while pursuing financial freedom.

***

Section 3: Sensitivity Analysis

What if interest rates rise? Because HELOCs are typically variable-rate instruments, rising interest rates are the most immediate threat to the strategy's net savings. If the HELOC APR increases by 200–400 basis points, the short-window cost of carrying a chunk rises significantly. For example, a $25,000 draw held for 12 months at 6% APR costs about $1,500 in interest; at 10% APR, the cost jumps to over $2,500. If the avoided mortgage interest is less than this higher HELOC cost, the strategy no longer produces net savings. This is why practitioners recommend stress-testing with higher APR assumptions before committing to repeated cycles.

What if income decreases? A reduction in income directly impacts surplus—the fuel that repays the HELOC draw. If monthly surplus shrinks or disappears, repayment windows lengthen, days-held increase, and HELOC interest costs rise. For example, if surplus falls from $1,500 to $500, a $25,000 draw that was planned to be repaid in 18 months could stretch to 50 months, eroding the margin and potentially turning the HELOC into long-term debt. Households must model income shocks (job loss, reduced hours, seasonal variability) and set stop rules to pause chunking if surplus drops below a safe threshold.

What if expenses increase? Expense creep has the same effect as income reduction: it reduces surplus available for HELOC repayment. Rising costs from inflation, medical bills, or lifestyle upgrades can silently extend repayment windows. Because HELOC interest accrues daily, even modest increases in expenses can push days-held beyond the break-even point. Documenting expenses monthly and reconciling against surplus is essential. If expenses rise consistently, households should reduce chunk size or pause the strategy until surplus stabilizes.

Stress testing your personal scenario Stress testing is the safeguard that ensures the strategy remains viable under adverse conditions. A proper stress test includes: (1) modeling HELOC APR increases of +200–400 basis points, (2) simulating a missed paycheck or temporary income reduction, and (3) adding 10–20% to monthly expenses. If the strategy still shows positive net savings under these conditions, it is robust; if not, households should pivot to simpler extra-payment or refinancing strategies. Documenting these tests in a spreadsheet and reviewing quarterly ensures that the plan remains aligned with reality rather than optimistic assumptions.

Breakdown for Readers — Sensitivity Analysis Checklist

Interest rate stress test: Model HELOC APR +200–400 bps; confirm net savings remain positive.

Income shock test: Simulate one missed paycheck or a 25% income reduction; check repayment window impact.

Expense creep test: Add 10–20% to monthly expenses; verify surplus still covers HELOC repayment.

Break-even check: Require mortgage interest avoided > HELOC short-window cost + fees under stress scenarios.

Stop rules: Pause chunking if surplus disappears, HELOC APR exceeds mortgage rate, or repayment window doubles.

Emergency reserves: Maintain 2–3 months of expenses outside the HELOC to absorb shocks without relying on the line.

Quarterly review: Compare actual vs modeled results; rerun stress tests regularly to ensure ongoing viability.

Conclusion: Sensitivity analysis is the discipline that separates hopeful projections from resilient financial strategies. By stress-testing interest rates, income, and expenses, households can identify the break-even point, enforce guardrails, and know when to pause or pivot. This ensures that HELOC acceleration remains a tool for freedom rather than a hidden liability.

***

Section 4: Online Calculator Introduction

How to access the companion calculator To make the HELOC acceleration strategy practical and transparent, a companion online calculator is provided. This tool allows you to model your own mortgage, income, expenses, and HELOC terms without guesswork. Access is typically through a secure web link or embedded resource in the book's digital companion materials. The calculator is designed to be user-friendly, requiring only basic financial inputs, and it provides immediate feedback on payoff timelines, interest savings, and break-even points. Using the calculator ensures that you are not relying on generic examples but are tailoring the strategy to your exact household situation.

Inputting your specific numbers The first step is to enter your current mortgage balance, interest rate, and term. Next, input your monthly income and expenses to calculate surplus cash flow. Finally, add HELOC details such as available limit, APR, and any fees. These inputs allow the calculator to simulate chunk sizes, repayment cadence, and short-window HELOC costs. By entering your own numbers, you create a personalized model that reflects your reality rather than theoretical averages. This step is critical because the viability of the strategy depends entirely on your unique surplus and HELOC pricing.

Interpreting results Once inputs are entered, the calculator generates outputs such as projected payoff timeline, cumulative interest paid under both traditional and HELOC methods, and net savings. It also highlights the break-even point—the moment when avoided mortgage interest exceeds HELOC costs. Charts and tables show how many years are saved, how much interest is avoided, and how repayment cycles progress month by month. Interpreting these results requires attention to assumptions: if the calculator shows positive savings only under base APR but negative under stress scenarios, that signals caution. The tool is not just about showing optimistic outcomes but about documenting whether the strategy holds under realistic conditions.

Adjusting variables for your situation The calculator allows you to adjust variables such as chunk size, repayment cadence, HELOC APR, and surplus levels. This flexibility lets you run "what-if" scenarios: What if interest rates rise by 2%? What if expenses increase by $500/month? What if you choose smaller chunks instead of larger ones? Adjusting variables helps you stress-test your personal scenario and identify safe guardrails. For example, if savings disappear when HELOC APR rises above a certain threshold, you can set that as a stop rule. By experimenting with different inputs, you gain clarity on which version of the strategy fits your household best.

Breakdown for Readers — Calculator Use Checklist

Access: Use the secure link or digital companion resource to open the calculator.

Inputs: Enter mortgage balance, rate, term, monthly income, expenses, HELOC limit, APR, and fees.

Outputs: Review payoff timeline, cumulative interest, break-even point, and net savings.

Interpretation: Compare traditional vs HELOC outcomes; check whether savings hold under stress scenarios.

Adjustments: Test different chunk sizes, repayment cadences, APR increases, and expense changes.

Stress-test: Require positive margins under HELOC APR +200–400 bps and simulated income/expense shocks.

Decision: Use results to set guardrails, stop rules, and choose the strategy (small chunk, large chunk, or full replacement) that fits your situation.

Conclusion: The online calculator transforms abstract strategy into documented, personalized numbers. By inputting your own data, interpreting results carefully, and adjusting variables to stress-test scenarios, you can determine whether HELOC acceleration truly works for you. This ensures the plan is not based on optimism but on verifiable, adaptable financial modeling.

CHAPTER 6:

Setting Up Your HELOC for Success

Preparing to Apply

To successfully prepare for a HELOC application, you'll need to meet minimum credit score thresholds, maintain a manageable debt-to-income ratio, demonstrate sufficient home equity, and provide standard financial documentation. These factors determine both your eligibility and the terms you'll be offered.

Credit score requirements (typically 680+) Most lenders require a minimum credit score of **680 or higher** to qualify for a HELOC, though some may accept scores as low as 620 depending on other strengths in your profile. A higher score (700+) generally secures better interest rates and more favorable terms. Because HELOCs are considered second liens, lenders are more cautious than with first mortgages, making credit history and payment reliability critical.

Debt-to-income ratio considerations Your **debt-to-income (DTI) ratio** measures monthly debt obligations against gross monthly income. Lenders typically want to see a DTI below **43%**, though some may allow up to 50% for borrowers with excellent credit. For example, if you earn $8,000 per month and your total debts (including the projected HELOC payment) are $2,950, your DTI would be 36.9%, which falls within most lenders' comfort zone. Keeping your DTI low signals that you can responsibly manage additional debt.

Home equity calculation To qualify, you must have at least **15–20% equity** in your home. Equity is calculated as the difference between your home's appraised value and your current mortgage balance. Lenders use the **combined loan-to-value (CLTV) ratio**, which includes your mortgage plus the HELOC amount, divided by the home's value. Most lenders cap CLTV at **85%**, meaning you can borrow up to 85% of your home's value minus what you already owe. For example, if your home is worth $400,000 and your mortgage balance is $250,000, you could qualify for a HELOC up to $90,000.

Documentation you'll need Applying for a HELOC requires proof of income and assets. Common documents include:

W-2s and recent pay stubs for employed borrowers.

Tax returns for self-employed applicants.

Benefit verification letters for retirees or those receiving Social Security.

Mortgage statements and property tax records to confirm current obligations.

Home appraisal or automated valuation to establish property value.

Breakdown for Readers — HELOC Application Checklist

Credit score: Aim for 680+, with 700+ for best rates.

DTI ratio: Keep below 43%; lower is better.

Equity: Ensure at least 15–20% equity; CLTV must stay under 85%.

Documentation: Prepare W-2s, pay stubs, tax returns, mortgage statements, and property valuation.

Income stability: Demonstrate steady employment or reliable benefits.

Payment history: Maintain on-time payments to strengthen approval odds.

Conclusion: Preparing to apply for a HELOC means aligning your financial profile with lender expectations. By maintaining strong credit, managing debt responsibly, calculating equity accurately, and organizing documentation ahead of time, you set yourself up for success and improve your chances of securing favorable terms.

***

Section 1: Choosing the Right HELOC

Banks vs. Credit Unions vs. Online Lenders

To choose the right HELOC, compare lenders across banks, credit unions, and online platforms, evaluate interest rates and fees carefully, and use a checklist to review terms and conditions before committing.

Banks: Traditional banks often provide nationwide availability, established reputations, and bundled services. They may offer higher limits but can be slower in processing applications. For example, Bank of America and Citizens Bank are known for broad accessibility.

Credit Unions: Credit unions are member-owned, not-for-profit institutions. They often provide lower fees, more personalized service, and competitive rates. Many borrowers find them more flexible with underwriting, especially for local members.

Online Lenders: Digital HELOC providers like Figure streamline the process with fast approvals (sometimes within 5 days), fewer documentation requirements, and transparent terms. They are ideal for borrowers who value speed and convenience, though they may lack the in-person support of banks.

Interest Rate Comparison Shopping HELOCs are variable-rate products, so comparing APRs is critical. Rates can vary widely depending on credit score, loan-to-value ratio, and lender type. For example, in 2025, starting APRs among top lenders ranged from about **8.5% to 9.5%**, with credit unions sometimes offering lower rates than banks. Always request quotes from multiple lenders and consider promotional "introductory rates" that may reset higher after 6–12 months.

Fee Structure Evaluation Beyond interest rates, fees can erode savings. Common charges include:

Annual fees (often $50–$100).

Origination or application fees (varies by lender).

Per-draw or transfer fees (important if you plan frequent draws).

Closing costs (banks may charge, online lenders often minimize). Credit unions frequently waive or reduce fees, while online lenders emphasize transparency with fewer hidden charges.

Terms and Conditions Checklist Before signing, review:

Credit score requirement (typically 680+, though some lenders accept lower).

Debt-to-income ratio limits (usually under 43%).

Combined loan-to-value (CLTV) cap (often 85%).

Repayment flexibility (interest-only vs. principal + interest).

Rate adjustment terms (frequency and caps on variable rate changes).

Draw period and repayment period length (commonly 10 years draw, 20 years repayment).

Prepayment penalties or restrictions (ensure you can pay down early without fees).

Breakdown for Readers — HELOC Selection Checklist

Compare **banks** (availability, higher limits), **credit unions** (lower fees, personalized service), and **online lenders** (speed, transparency).

Shop APRs across multiple lenders; watch for **introductory rates** that reset higher.

Evaluate fees: annual, origination, per-draw, and closing costs.

Confirm terms: credit score, DTI, CLTV, repayment flexibility, rate caps, draw/repayment periods, and prepayment rules.

Stress-test your scenario: model rate increases and repayment obligations to ensure affordability.

Conclusion: Choosing the right HELOC requires balancing lender type, rate competitiveness, fee transparency, and contract terms. Banks provide reach, credit unions offer affordability, and online lenders deliver speed. By comparison shopping and using a structured checklist, you can secure a HELOC that aligns with your financial strategy and risk tolerance.

***

Section 2: Setting Up Your HELOC for Success

Application Process

Step-by-step application guide Applying for a Home Equity Line of Credit (HELOC) follows a structured process similar to a mortgage application but with a few unique steps. First, you'll complete an application with your chosen lender, providing personal information, income details, and your property address. Next, the lender will run a credit check and request supporting documents such as pay stubs, tax returns, and mortgage statements. After initial review, the lender orders a home appraisal to confirm property value and equity. Once underwriting is complete, you'll receive approval terms, sign closing documents, and gain access to your HELOC account.

What lenders will review Lenders evaluate several key factors before granting approval. Your **credit score** (typically 680+ for favorable terms) demonstrates repayment reliability. Your **debt-to-income (DTI) ratio** must generally remain below 43%, showing you can manage additional debt. Lenders also assess **loan-to-value (LTV)** or combined loan-to-value (CLTV), ensuring your total mortgage plus HELOC does not exceed 80–85% of your home's appraised value. Finally, they review employment stability and income consistency to confirm you can repay the line responsibly.

Home appraisal process The appraisal is a critical step because it determines how much equity you can borrow against. A licensed appraiser evaluates your home's current market value by comparing it to similar properties in your area, inspecting condition, and factoring in upgrades or repairs. The lender uses this appraisal to calculate available equity: home value minus outstanding mortgage balance. For example, if your home is valued at $400,000 and your mortgage balance is $250,000, you may qualify for a HELOC up to $90,000, assuming an 85% CLTV cap.

Timeline expectations (typically 2–6 weeks) From application to funding, the HELOC process usually takes **2–6 weeks**, depending on lender efficiency, appraisal scheduling, and document readiness. Online lenders may process applications faster (sometimes within 5–10 days), while traditional banks and credit unions often take longer due to manual underwriting. Delays often occur if documentation is incomplete or if appraisal appointments are backlogged. Preparing documents in advance and responding quickly to lender requests can shorten the timeline significantly.

Breakdown for Readers — HELOC Application Checklist

Step 1: Complete lender application with personal, income, and property details.

Step 2: Provide documentation (pay stubs, tax returns, mortgage statements).

Step 3: Lender reviews credit score, DTI ratio, and CLTV.

Step 4: Home appraisal ordered to confirm property value and equity.

Step 5: Underwriting finalizes approval terms.

Step 6: Sign closing documents and access HELOC account.

Timeline: Expect 2–6 weeks; faster with online lenders, slower with banks/credit unions.

Preparation tip: Organize documents early and maintain strong credit to secure favorable terms.

Conclusion: The HELOC application process is straightforward but requires preparation. By understanding what lenders review, anticipating the appraisal, and preparing documents ahead of time, you can streamline approval and secure terms that align with your financial strategy.

***

Section 3: Setting Up Your HELOC for Success

Negotiation Tactics

To set up your HELOC for success, negotiation is just as important as qualification. By strategically approaching rates, fees, terms, and lender competition, you can save thousands over the life of the line.

Rate negotiation strategies Interest rates on HELOCs are typically variable, tied to the prime rate plus a margin. As of mid-2025, national averages hover around **8–9% APR**. Lenders often provide discounts for automatic payments, loyalty programs, or bundled accounts. Before applying, improve your credit score and debt-to-income ratio, as these directly influence the margin added to primeYahoo Finance. Always request quotes from multiple lenders and ask about rate-match guarantees. Even a 0.25% reduction can save thousands over the repayment period.

Fee waiver requests HELOCs often carry **origination fees (1–5% of the credit limit), annual fees ($50–$100), and closing costs**. Many lenders will waive or reduce these if asked, especially if you have strong credit or existing accounts. Online lenders frequently advertise "no-closing-cost" HELOCs, but may impose cancellation fees if the line is closed earlyheloc360.com. When negotiating, request a full fee breakdown and ask for waivers on annual or inactivity fees. Credit unions are often more flexible than banks in granting fee concessions.

Term negotiation points HELOCs typically have a **draw period of 5–10 years** followed by a **repayment period of 10–20 years**. Negotiating term length can align the HELOC with your financial goals. For example, a shorter draw period may reduce temptation to overborrow, while a longer repayment period lowers monthly obligations. Clarify whether interest-only payments are allowed during the draw period and whether rate-lock options are available. These features can provide stability in volatile rate environments.

Using competition to your advantage Shopping around is essential. Experts recommend comparing at least **three lenders** before committing. Use competing offers to negotiate better terms—banks may match credit union rates, and online lenders may reduce fees to stay competitive. Presenting multiple quotes demonstrates you are an informed borrower and increases leverage. Timing also matters: applying when your finances are strong and rates are stable improves bargaining powerLendEDU.

Breakdown for Readers — HELOC Negotiation Checklist

Rates: Improve credit score, ask about loyalty/auto-pay discounts, and request rate-match guarantees.

Fees: Request waivers for origination, annual, or inactivity fees; confirm no hidden cancellation charges.

Terms: Negotiate draw and repayment periods; ask about interest-only options and rate-lock features.

Competition: Collect at least three quotes; use them to leverage better rates and fee concessions.

Documentation: Prepare income, debt, and property records to strengthen your negotiating position.

Conclusion: Negotiating your HELOC is not optional—it's a critical step in maximizing savings and minimizing risk. By pressing for lower rates, fee waivers, favorable terms, and leveraging competition, you transform the HELOC from a simple borrowing tool into a strategic financial instrument.

***

Section 4: Setting Up Your HELOC for Success

Red Flags to Avoid

Balloon payment clauses A balloon payment clause requires a large lump-sum repayment at the end of the loan term. While uncommon in standard HELOCs, some lenders include this feature in hybrid products. The danger is that borrowers may not anticipate the sudden obligation, leaving them vulnerable to refinancing risk or forced liquidation. Always confirm whether your HELOC converts to amortized repayment or demands a balloon payment at maturity. If a balloon clause exists, negotiate its removal or choose another lender.

Excessive fees HELOCs can carry hidden costs beyond interest rates. Common fees include annual maintenance charges, origination fees, appraisal costs, and per-draw transaction fees. Excessive or layered fees erode the savings you expect from the strategy. For example, a $75 annual fee plus $25 per draw can quickly offset interest savings if you use multiple small chunks. Request a full fee schedule upfront and ask for waivers—credit unions and online lenders often provide lower-fee structures than large banks.

Rate caps that are too high Because HELOCs are variable-rate products, lenders set a maximum cap on how high the interest rate can rise. Caps that are too high (e.g., prime + 12%) expose borrowers to extreme payment shocks if rates climb. A reasonable cap provides protection while still allowing lenders flexibility. Review the margin and lifetime cap carefully; if the cap is significantly above current market rates, consider it a red flag. Stress-test your scenario by modeling payments at the cap to ensure affordability.

Unfavorable draw period terms Most HELOCs have a draw period of 5–10 years, during which you can borrow and repay. Some lenders restrict repayment flexibility by requiring interest-only payments during the draw period, which delays principal reduction and increases long-term costs. Others shorten the draw period excessively, limiting your ability to use the line strategically. Favor HELOCs that allow principal + interest payments during the draw period and provide a reasonable window for borrowing.

Prepayment penalties Prepayment penalties undermine the flexibility that makes HELOCs attractive. Some lenders impose fees if you pay off the line early or close the account within a few years. These penalties can trap borrowers in unfavorable terms and reduce the effectiveness of chunking strategies. Always confirm whether prepayment penalties exist and negotiate their removal. A HELOC should empower you to accelerate debt reduction, not punish you for doing so.

Breakdown for Readers — HELOC Red Flags Checklist

Balloon clauses: Avoid HELOCs requiring lump-sum repayment at maturity.

Fees: Watch for annual, origination, appraisal, and per-draw charges; request waivers or reductions.

Rate caps: Ensure lifetime caps are reasonable; stress-test payments at maximum possible APR.

Draw terms: Favor HELOCs with principal + interest repayment options and balanced draw periods.

Prepayment penalties: Reject HELOCs that penalize early payoff or account closure.

Action step: Request a full disclosure of terms and run side-by-side comparisons before signing.

Conclusion: Spotting red flags early protects you from hidden costs and unfavorable terms. Balloon payments, excessive fees, high rate caps, restrictive draw periods, and prepayment penalties can all erode the benefits of a HELOC strategy. By reviewing contracts carefully, negotiating terms, and stress-testing scenarios, you ensure your HELOC remains a tool for financial freedom rather than a liability.

***

Section 5: Setting Up Your HELOC for Success

Setting Up Access

Online banking setup Once your HELOC is approved, the first step is to establish online banking access. Most lenders provide secure portals where you can view balances, track draws, and monitor repayment progress. Setting up online access ensures you can immediately verify transactions, confirm interest accrual, and schedule transfers to your mortgage. Documented financial guides emphasize that online visibility reduces errors and helps borrowers maintain discipline by keeping repayment activity transparent and accessible.

Bill pay configuration Configuring bill pay through your HELOC account allows you to route income deposits into the line and pay expenses directly from it. This setup is central to velocity banking strategies because it ensures every dollar temporarily reduces the HELOC balance before being spent. By automating recurring bills—utilities, insurance, or loan payments—you minimize manual errors and maintain consistent repayment cadence. Lenders typically allow bill pay setup within their online portals, and many waive transaction fees for electronic payments.

Mobile app familiarization Most banks and credit unions now provide mobile apps that mirror online banking functionality. Familiarizing yourself with the app is critical for day-to-day management: you can deposit checks, transfer funds, and monitor balances in real time. Mobile alerts can be configured to notify you of draws, payments, or unusual activity, which adds a layer of security. Documented case studies show that borrowers who actively use mobile apps are more likely to maintain repayment discipline and avoid costly delays.

Check writing privileges Some HELOCs include check-writing privileges, allowing you to access funds directly by writing a check against your line of credit. While convenient, this feature should be used sparingly and strategically—primarily for large, planned expenses or mortgage chunk payments. Because checks bypass digital tracking, it's important to log each transaction manually to maintain accurate records. Lenders may charge per-check fees, so confirm terms before relying on this option.

Debit card options and considerations Many HELOCs also provide debit card access, enabling you to draw funds directly at point of sale. While this offers flexibility, it can also undermine discipline if used for discretionary spending. Experts caution that debit card use should be limited to essential expenses already budgeted in your repayment plan. Review whether your lender charges transaction fees or imposes daily limits, and disable overdraft features to avoid accidental overuse. Treat the debit card as a tool for structured cash flow, not as a source of convenience spending.

Breakdown for Readers — HELOC Access Checklist

Online banking: Set up secure portal access; monitor balances, draws, and repayments regularly.

Bill pay: Automate recurring expenses through HELOC to maximize daily balance reduction.

Mobile app: Download and configure alerts; use for deposits, transfers, and real-time monitoring.

Check writing: Use only for planned large expenses; log transactions manually; confirm per-check fees.

Debit card: Limit use to essential expenses; review transaction fees and disable overdraft features.

Documentation: Keep a ledger of all draws, payments, and fees to verify strategy effectiveness.

Conclusion: Setting up access to your HELOC is more than convenience—it's the infrastructure that makes the strategy work. Online banking, bill pay, mobile apps, and controlled use of checks or debit cards ensure that every dollar is routed efficiently, tracked accurately, and applied with discipline. By configuring these tools upfront, you create a system that supports financial freedom rather than undermines it.

CHAPTER 7:

Implementing the Strategy

Month 1: The Launch

Drawing your first chunk The launch begins with drawing your first HELOC chunk. This is the pivotal step where theory becomes practice. For example, if your HELOC limit allows, you might draw $20,000–$25,000 and immediately apply it toward your mortgage principal. This action reduces the amortizing balance and prevents years of future interest accrual. Documented financial guides emphasize that the benefit comes not from the HELOC itself but from the earlier removal of mortgage principal, which changes the interest curve permanently.

Making the mortgage principal payment Once the chunk is drawn, apply it directly as a principal-only payment to your mortgage. This is critical—do not use the funds for regular monthly payments or discretionary spending. By targeting principal, you accelerate amortization and reduce the interest base. For example, a $25,000 principal payment on a $250,000 mortgage immediately lowers the balance to $225,000, saving thousands in long-term interest. Lenders typically allow principal-only payments through online portals or by contacting customer service, so confirm the process in advance.

Redirecting your income deposits To manage the HELOC draw efficiently, redirect all income deposits into the HELOC account. Each paycheck temporarily lowers the average daily balance, reducing short-window interest costs. Expenses are then paid from the HELOC, ensuring every dollar works twice—first to reduce HELOC interest, then to cover living costs. This routing is the engine of velocity banking, and documented case studies show that households who automate deposits maintain discipline and maximize savings.

Setting up automatic expense payments Automation is essential to prevent errors and maintain cadence. Configure bill pay through your HELOC account so recurring expenses—utilities, insurance, loan payments—are automatically deducted. This ensures consistency and reduces the risk of missed payments or late fees. By automating expenses, you also eliminate manual delays that could extend HELOC days-held and increase interest costs. Financial educators stress that automation transforms the strategy from a manual juggling act into a reliable system.

Breakdown for Readers — Month 1 Launch Checklist

Draw chunk: Select a manageable amount (e.g., $20K–$25K); apply immediately to mortgage principal.

Principal payment: Confirm lender allows principal-only payments; execute through online portal or direct request.

Redirect income: Route all paychecks into HELOC; pay expenses from HELOC to reduce average daily balance.

Automate bills: Set up bill pay for recurring expenses; minimize manual handling and timing errors.

Document cycle: Log draw date, repayment progress, HELOC interest paid, and mortgage balance reduction.

Guardrails: Maintain emergency fund outside HELOC; pause chunking if surplus shrinks or HELOC APR rises.

Conclusion: Month 1 sets the foundation for success. By drawing your first chunk, applying it to principal, redirecting income, and automating expenses, you establish the rhythm that drives mortgage acceleration. Discipline and documentation in this launch phase ensure the strategy produces measurable results and positions you for repeatable cycles in the months ahead.

***

Section 1: Tracking Systems to Implement

Why tracking matters Implementing a HELOC strategy requires precision. Every draw, deposit, expense, and repayment affects the balance and determines whether the plan produces savings or hidden costs. Without a tracking system, it's easy to lose sight of repayment cadence, interest accrual, and surplus allocation. Documented financial guides emphasize that tracking transforms the HELOC from a risky variable-rate tool into a disciplined system for mortgage acceleration.

Digital spreadsheets and ledgers A simple spreadsheet (Excel, Google Sheets) is one of the most effective tracking tools. Create columns for:

Date of HELOC draw

Amount drawn

Mortgage principal payment applied

Income deposits (with dates)

Expenses paid from HELOC

Monthly surplus applied to repayment

HELOC interest charged

Remaining HELOC balance and mortgage balance

This ledger provides a month-by-month snapshot of progress and allows you to calculate whether the avoided mortgage interest exceeds HELOC costs.

Bank and lender dashboards Most banks and credit unions provide online dashboards that show HELOC balances, transactions, and interest accrual. Use these dashboards to cross-verify your spreadsheet entries. Many lenders also allow you to download transaction histories, which can be imported into your tracking sheet for accuracy.

Budgeting apps and automation Apps like YNAB (You Need A Budget), Mint, or Quicken can integrate with your HELOC account to automatically categorize deposits and expenses. Automation reduces manual entry errors and ensures every surplus dollar is accounted for. Set alerts for HELOC balance thresholds or unusual transactions to maintain discipline.

Quarterly review reports Beyond monthly tracking, generate quarterly reports that summarize:

Total HELOC interest paid

Total mortgage principal reduced

Net savings compared to traditional amortization

Stress-test scenarios (e.g., HELOC APR +200 bps)

These reports provide documented evidence of whether the strategy is working and whether adjustments are needed.

Breakdown for Readers — Tracking System Checklist

Spreadsheet ledger: Track draws, deposits, expenses, interest, and balances monthly.

Bank dashboard: Cross-verify balances and download transaction histories.

Budgeting apps: Automate categorization of deposits and expenses; set alerts for discipline.

Quarterly reports: Summarize net savings, interest avoided, and stress-test outcomes.

Documentation habit: Log every transaction; reconcile monthly to ensure accuracy.

Stop rules: Use tracking data to identify warning signs (surplus shrinkage, rising HELOC costs).

Conclusion: Tracking systems are the backbone of a successful HELOC strategy. By combining spreadsheets, bank dashboards, budgeting apps, and quarterly reviews, you create a transparent, documented process that ensures every dollar is working toward mortgage freedom. Without tracking, the strategy risks becoming guesswork; with it, you gain clarity, control, and confidence.

***

Section 2: Implementing the Strategy

Months 2–12: The Rhythm

Daily/weekly monitoring routine After the initial launch, success depends on developing a rhythm of monitoring and adjustment. Daily check-ins ensure deposits are posted correctly and balances reflect expected activity. Weekly reviews allow you to reconcile expenses, confirm surplus allocation, and verify that HELOC interest charges align with projections. Documented financial planning guides emphasize that consistent monitoring prevents small errors—like missed payments or delayed deposits—from compounding into costly setbacks.

Income deposit protocol Every paycheck should be routed directly into the HELOC account. This reduces the average daily balance, lowering short-window interest costs. The protocol is simple: deposit income into the HELOC, then pay expenses from it. This cycle ensures every dollar temporarily reduces debt before being spent. Case studies of velocity banking show that households who automate deposits maintain discipline and maximize savings, while those who skip this step often lose the compounding benefit.

Expense management Expenses must be managed with precision. Paying bills directly from the HELOC ensures the cash-flow loop remains intact, but discipline is required to avoid discretionary spending that extends repayment windows. Document your monthly expenses and reconcile them against surplus to confirm that repayment capacity remains intact. Financial educators stress that expense creep—small increases in lifestyle spending—can silently erode the margin that makes the strategy viable.

HELOC balance tracking Tracking the HELOC balance is essential to measure progress and confirm repayment cadence. Use a spreadsheet or budgeting app to log draws, deposits, expenses, and interest charges. Compare actual HELOC costs against projected mortgage interest avoided to verify net savings. Quarterly reviews should include stress-tests: model HELOC APR increases of +200–400 basis points and confirm the strategy remains positive. This documented tracking ensures transparency and accountability.

Staying motivated through the process The rhythm of months 2–12 can feel repetitive, but motivation comes from documenting progress. Celebrate milestones such as clearing a HELOC draw or reducing the mortgage balance by $50,000. Visual aids—charts showing declining balances or cumulative interest saved—reinforce the impact of discipline. Many households find motivation in quarterly reports that show years shaved off the mortgage timeline. Staying motivated is not just emotional; it's a practical safeguard against complacency.

Breakdown for Readers — Months 2–12 Checklist

Daily routine: Verify deposits and balances; confirm bills are processed correctly.

Weekly routine: Reconcile expenses, surplus, and HELOC interest charges.

Income protocol: Route all paychecks into HELOC; pay expenses from HELOC to maximize balance reduction.

Expense management: Track monthly spending; prevent lifestyle creep; maintain surplus discipline.

Balance tracking: Log draws, deposits, expenses, and interest; run quarterly stress-tests.

Motivation: Celebrate milestones; use charts and reports to visualize progress; reinforce discipline.

Conclusion: Months 2–12 are where the HELOC strategy becomes a lifestyle. By establishing monitoring routines, enforcing income and expense protocols, tracking balances, and celebrating progress, households create a sustainable rhythm that drives mortgage acceleration. Discipline and documentation transform the strategy from theory into measurable results, ensuring long-term success.

***

Section 3: Implementing the Strategy

Optimizing Your Cash Flow

Timing large expenses strategically One of the most important aspects of cash-flow optimization is the timing of large expenses. When using a HELOC strategy, every dollar deposited into the line temporarily reduces the balance and lowers interest costs. Paying large expenses immediately after income deposits minimizes the number of days those funds sit unused. For example, if you know a $3,000 insurance premium is due, schedule it right after a paycheck hits the HELOC so the balance benefits from the deposit before the expense is withdrawn. Documented financial planning guides emphasize that aligning expense timing with deposit cycles can reduce average daily balances and improve net savings.

Paycheck timing considerations The cadence of your paychecks directly influences HELOC efficiency. Weekly or biweekly pay schedules create more frequent balance reductions, while monthly paychecks require careful planning to avoid extended float periods. If you are paid biweekly, routing deposits immediately into the HELOC ensures that balances drop twice per month, reducing interest accrual. Households with monthly paychecks should consider splitting deposits or scheduling bill payments strategically to avoid long gaps where balances remain high. The key is to maximize the number of days income sits in the HELOC before being spent.

Bonus and tax refund allocation Windfalls such as work bonuses or tax refunds provide powerful opportunities to accelerate repayment. Instead of treating these funds as discretionary spending, apply them directly to the HELOC balance or as a mortgage chunk. A $5,000 tax refund, for example, can shorten repayment windows by months and save thousands in interest. Documented case studies show that households who consistently allocate windfalls to debt reduction achieve faster mortgage freedom than those who divert them to lifestyle upgrades. The discipline of treating bonuses and refunds as strategic accelerators is a cornerstone of successful cash-flow management.

Minimizing float time Float time refers to the period between when income is deposited and when expenses are paid. The longer funds remain idle, the less efficient the HELOC strategy becomes. Minimizing float time means aligning deposits and withdrawals so that money reduces debt for as many days as possible. For example, if your paycheck posts on the 1st, schedule major bills for the 3rd or 4th, allowing two days of balance reduction before expenses are deducted. Using online banking and bill pay automation helps reduce float time by ensuring transactions occur promptly and consistently.

Breakdown for Readers — Cash Flow Optimization Checklist

Large expenses: Schedule payments right after deposits to maximize debt reduction before funds are spent.

Paycheck cadence: Route deposits immediately into HELOC; adjust bill timing for monthly paychecks to avoid gaps.

Windfalls: Apply bonuses and tax refunds directly to HELOC or mortgage principal for accelerated payoff.

Float time: Minimize idle days by aligning deposits and expenses; use automation to ensure consistency.

Quarterly review: Track how timing adjustments affect HELOC interest costs and mortgage balance reduction.

Conclusion: Optimizing cash flow is about precision and discipline. By timing expenses strategically, leveraging paycheck schedules, allocating windfalls, and minimizing float time, households can maximize the efficiency of every dollar. Documented financial strategies show that these small adjustments compound into significant savings, turning routine cash flow into a powerful engine for mortgage acceleration.

***

Section 4: Implementing the Strategy

The Payoff Moment

When to make the next mortgage chunk payment The payoff moment is the culmination of disciplined cash-flow management. Once your HELOC draw has been repaid or reduced to a manageable balance, it's time to make the next mortgage chunk payment. The timing of this step is critical: you should only initiate a new chunk when the HELOC balance is near zero or comfortably within your repayment capacity. Documented financial guides emphasize that premature draws can lead to extended repayment windows and higher interest costs, undermining the strategy's effectiveness.

Calculating optimal timing Optimal timing depends on surplus stability, HELOC interest rates, and repayment cadence. A practical formula is to calculate the number of months required to repay the last draw, then confirm that your surplus can sustain another cycle without extending beyond 12–18 months. For example, if you repaid a $20,000 draw in 14 months with a $1,500 surplus, you can confidently initiate another chunk of similar size. Stress-test the timing by modeling HELOC APR increases or expense creep to ensure the margin remains positive. This documented approach ensures each cycle produces net savings rather than hidden costs.

Celebrating milestones Every payoff moment is also a milestone worth celebrating. Whether you've reduced your mortgage balance by $25,000 or shaved two years off your timeline, acknowledging progress reinforces discipline and motivation. Many households use visual aids—charts showing declining balances or cumulative interest avoided—to make the savings tangible. Celebrating milestones is not just emotional; it's a practical safeguard against burnout, reminding you that the strategy is producing measurable results.

Resetting for the next cycle After celebrating, reset the system for the next cycle. This means verifying surplus stability, confirming HELOC terms remain favorable, and preparing documentation for the next draw. Resetting also involves reviewing lessons learned from the previous cycle: Was repayment faster than expected? Did expenses creep upward? Did HELOC interest costs remain manageable? By resetting with documented insights, you refine the strategy and ensure each cycle builds on the last.

Breakdown for Readers — Payoff Moment Checklist

Mortgage chunk timing: Initiate next chunk only when HELOC balance is near zero or repayment capacity is stable.

Optimal timing calculation: Use surplus and repayment cadence to size chunks; stress-test with higher APRs and expenses.

Celebrate milestones: Track mortgage reduction, interest avoided, and years saved; use charts to visualize progress.

Reset cycle: Review surplus, HELOC terms, and lessons learned; prepare for next draw with refined strategy.

Guardrails: Pause chunking if surplus shrinks, HELOC APR rises significantly, or repayment windows extend beyond 18 months.

Conclusion: The payoff moment is both a financial and psychological turning point. By timing mortgage chunk payments carefully, calculating optimal repayment windows, celebrating progress, and resetting for the next cycle, households transform disciplined cash flow into long-term mortgage freedom. Documented strategies show that repeating this cycle consistently is what turns incremental savings into decades of accelerated payoff.

***

Section 5: Implementing the Strategy

Record Keeping Best Practices

Spreadsheet templates provided Accurate record keeping is the backbone of a successful HELOC strategy. Spreadsheet templates offer a structured way to log draws, deposits, expenses, and repayment progress. A well-designed template should include columns for HELOC balance, mortgage principal payments, interest charges, and surplus allocation. By documenting each transaction, you create a transparent record that allows you to calculate whether the avoided mortgage interest exceeds HELOC costs. Financial educators consistently recommend spreadsheets because they provide flexibility, transparency, and the ability to run "what-if" scenarios with your own numbers.

App recommendations Beyond spreadsheets, budgeting and financial apps can automate much of the tracking process. Tools like **YNAB (You Need A Budget)**, **Mint**, or **Quicken** integrate with bank accounts to categorize deposits and expenses automatically. Many HELOC lenders also provide proprietary apps or dashboards that show balances and interest accrual in real time. Using apps reduces manual entry errors and provides alerts for unusual activity or balance thresholds. Documented case studies show that households who actively use apps maintain stronger repayment discipline and avoid costly mistakes compared to those relying solely on memory.

Monthly review checklist A monthly review ensures your strategy stays on track. The checklist should include:

Confirming all income deposits were routed into the HELOC.

Reconciling expenses against surplus to verify repayment capacity.

Logging HELOC interest charges and comparing them to projected costs.

Updating mortgage balance and calculating cumulative interest avoided.

Stress-testing with updated variables (e.g., HELOC APR changes).

This monthly rhythm prevents small errors from compounding and provides documented evidence of progress. Financial planning resources emphasize that consistent reviews are critical for catching expense creep or repayment delays early.

Annual progress assessment At the end of each year, conduct a comprehensive progress assessment. This involves comparing your actual results against projections: total HELOC interest paid, total mortgage principal reduced, and net savings achieved. Annual assessments should also include stress-tests for future cycles, ensuring the strategy remains viable under higher interest rates or income fluctuations. By documenting annual progress, you create a clear picture of how many years have been shaved off your mortgage timeline and how much interest has been avoided. This assessment not only validates the strategy but also provides motivation to continue.

Breakdown for Readers — Record Keeping Checklist

Spreadsheets: Use templates to log draws, deposits, expenses, interest, and balances.

Apps: Integrate budgeting tools (YNAB, Mint, Quicken) or lender dashboards for automation and alerts.

Monthly review: Verify deposits, reconcile expenses, log interest, update balances, and stress-test assumptions.

Annual assessment: Compare actual vs projected results; calculate years saved and interest avoided; refine strategy.

Documentation habit: Keep records consistent and transparent to ensure accountability and motivation.

Conclusion: Record keeping transforms the HELOC strategy from theory into measurable results. By using spreadsheets, leveraging apps, conducting monthly reviews, and performing annual assessments, households create a disciplined system that documents progress, validates savings, and sustains motivation. This documented approach ensures the strategy remains transparent, adaptable, and effective over the long term.

***

Section 6: Implementing the Strategy

Troubleshooting Common Issues

HELOC balance not decreasing as expected One of the most common issues borrowers face is realizing that their HELOC balance is not shrinking as quickly as projected. This usually happens when surplus income is smaller than anticipated, expenses are higher, or interest accrual is underestimated. Documented financial guides emphasize the importance of reconciling monthly balances against your repayment plan. If balances are not decreasing, review whether deposits are being routed correctly, confirm that expenses are not exceeding surplus, and check for hidden fees or rising APRs. Adjusting chunk size or pausing new draws until repayment stabilizes can restore progress.

Discipline lapses The HELOC strategy requires strict discipline. Lapses occur when borrowers divert funds meant for repayment toward discretionary spending or fail to route income consistently into the HELOC. Even small lapses can extend repayment windows and increase interest costs. To counter this, set up automation—direct deposits, bill pay, and alerts—to reduce reliance on manual discipline. Documented case studies show that households who automate flows maintain stronger repayment cadence and avoid costly setbacks compared to those relying on memory or willpower alone.

Unexpected expenses Life events such as medical bills, car repairs, or home maintenance can disrupt repayment schedules. When unexpected expenses arise, they reduce surplus and extend HELOC days-held, increasing interest costs. Financial educators recommend maintaining a separate emergency fund outside the HELOC to absorb shocks without jeopardizing repayment. If expenses force you to use HELOC funds, log the transaction carefully and adjust repayment projections. Documenting these changes ensures transparency and helps you decide whether to pause chunking until surplus stabilizes.

Income disruptions Job loss, reduced hours, or delayed payments can quickly derail the strategy. Because surplus is the engine of repayment, income disruptions must be addressed immediately. Stress-testing your plan with scenarios like a missed paycheck or a 25% income reduction helps prepare for these risks. If disruptions occur, pause new HELOC draws, focus on stabilizing income, and use reserves to maintain minimum payments. Documented financial planning resources emphasize that flexibility and stop rules are essential to prevent the HELOC from becoming long-term debt.

Motivation challenges The HELOC strategy is a marathon, not a sprint. Over months and years, motivation can wane, especially when progress feels slow. To stay motivated, document milestones such as mortgage balance reductions, interest avoided, or years shaved off the timeline. Visual aids like charts or progress trackers reinforce the impact of discipline. Celebrating small wins—clearing a HELOC draw or reaching a $50,000 reduction—provides psychological reinforcement. Documented behavioral finance studies show that visible progress is one of the strongest motivators for sustaining long-term financial strategies.

Breakdown for Readers — Troubleshooting Checklist

HELOC balance: Reconcile monthly; confirm deposits, expenses, and APR; adjust chunk size if needed.

Discipline: Automate deposits and bill pay; set alerts to prevent lapses.

Unexpected expenses: Maintain emergency fund outside HELOC; log disruptions and adjust repayment projections.

Income disruptions: Pause new draws; stress-test scenarios; use reserves to maintain stability.

Motivation: Track milestones; use charts and progress reports; celebrate small wins to sustain discipline.

Conclusion: Troubleshooting common issues ensures the HELOC strategy remains resilient. By documenting balances, automating discipline, preparing for expenses and income shocks, and reinforcing motivation, households can navigate challenges without losing momentum. The key is transparency and adaptability—turning setbacks into lessons that strengthen the path toward mortgage freedom.

PART III:

ADVANCED STRATEGIES AND CONSIDERATIONS

This section moves beyond the fundamentals of setting up and launching your HELOC strategy. Here, we explore advanced techniques, risk management tools, and optimization methods that allow you to refine the process, adapt to changing conditions, and maximize long-term savings. While the earlier chapters focused on building discipline and establishing rhythm, Part III equips you with the foresight and flexibility needed to sustain success over years of implementation.

Why advanced strategies matter Financial environments are dynamic—interest rates shift, income streams fluctuate, and personal goals evolve. Advanced strategies help you anticipate these changes, stress-test your plan, and pivot when necessary. Documented financial case studies show that households who incorporate advanced considerations—such as sensitivity analysis, cash-flow optimization, and risk guardrails—achieve more consistent results and avoid common pitfalls.

Key themes in Part III

Sensitivity Analysis: Modeling "what-if" scenarios for interest rate hikes, income reductions, or expense increases.

Break-Even and Stress Testing: Identifying the exact point where the strategy pays off and ensuring it holds under adverse conditions.

Cash-Flow Optimization: Timing expenses, deposits, and windfalls to maximize efficiency.

Negotiation and Red Flags: Securing favorable HELOC terms while avoiding clauses or fees that erode savings.

Record Keeping and Troubleshooting: Building systems to track progress, document results, and correct course when issues arise.

Long-Term Strategy Integration: Aligning HELOC acceleration with broader financial goals such as retirement planning, investment growth, and legacy building.

Breakdown for Readers — Advanced Strategy Roadmap

Stress-test scenarios: Run models for rising rates, income shocks, and expense creep.

Break-even analysis: Document when avoided mortgage interest exceeds HELOC costs.

Cash-flow optimization: Align deposits, expenses, and windfalls to minimize float time.

Negotiation tactics: Secure lower rates, fee waivers, and favorable draw/ repayment terms.

Red flag awareness: Avoid balloon clauses, excessive fees, high rate caps, and prepayment penalties.

Tracking systems: Use spreadsheets, apps, and quarterly/annual reviews to document progress.

Troubleshooting: Prepare for discipline lapses, unexpected expenses, and motivation challenges.

Integration: Connect HELOC payoff with long-term financial planning goals.

Conclusion: Part III is about mastery. By layering advanced strategies onto the foundation built in earlier chapters, you transform the HELOC from a tactical tool into a comprehensive financial instrument. With documented systems, stress-tested models, and disciplined execution, you ensure that the strategy not only accelerates mortgage payoff but also strengthens your overall financial resilience.

CHAPTER 8:

Advanced Optimization Techniques

The Stacking Method

Using multiple HELOCs strategically The stacking method involves leveraging more than one HELOC to accelerate mortgage payoff. Instead of relying on a single line of credit, borrowers strategically open multiple HELOCs across different lenders to increase available borrowing power and flexibility. For example, one HELOC may be used for larger mortgage chunks while another serves as a short-term cash-flow buffer. Documented financial strategies highlight that stacking allows borrowers to diversify lender risk, negotiate better terms, and maintain liquidity while still aggressively reducing mortgage principal.

Timing considerations Timing is critical when stacking HELOCs. Each draw must be carefully scheduled to avoid overlapping repayment windows that strain surplus cash flow. A disciplined borrower might use HELOC A for the first chunk, repay it within 12–18 months, and then activate HELOC B for the next cycle. This staggered approach ensures that balances remain manageable and interest costs do not compound across multiple lines. Financial educators emphasize that timing should align with income stability and expense cycles, ensuring repayment capacity is never compromised.

Risk management Stacking increases both opportunity and risk. Multiple HELOCs mean multiple variable interest rates, fee structures, and repayment obligations. If interest rates rise or surplus shrinks, carrying balances across several lines can quickly erode savings. Risk management requires strict guardrails: maintain an emergency fund outside the HELOCs, stress-test repayment under higher APRs, and avoid simultaneous large draws. Documented case studies show that households who set stop rules—such as pausing new draws if surplus drops below a threshold—successfully mitigate stacking risks while still reaping accelerated payoff benefits.

When this makes sense The stacking method makes sense for borrowers with strong surplus cash flow, excellent credit, and stable income. It is particularly effective for households with high mortgage balances who want to maximize acceleration without waiting for a single HELOC to recycle. It also benefits borrowers who can negotiate favorable terms across multiple lenders, spreading risk and reducing reliance on one institution. However, stacking is not recommended for those with volatile income or minimal surplus, as the complexity and risk outweigh potential savings.

Breakdown for Readers — Stacking Method Checklist

Strategic use: Open multiple HELOCs to diversify lender risk and increase borrowing power.

Timing: Stagger draws; repay one HELOC before activating another to avoid overlapping balances.

Risk management: Stress-test APR increases; maintain emergency reserves; set stop rules for surplus drops.

Applicability: Use stacking if you have strong surplus, stable income, and high mortgage balances.

Avoid: Do not stack if income is volatile, surplus is minimal, or discipline is inconsistent.

Conclusion: The stacking method is an advanced optimization technique that magnifies the power of HELOC acceleration. By using multiple HELOCs strategically, timing draws carefully, managing risks, and applying the method only when conditions are favorable, borrowers can achieve faster mortgage payoff while maintaining financial resilience. Documented strategies show that stacking is most effective when paired with discipline, surplus stability, and clear guardrails.

***

Section 1: Implementing the Strategy

Incorporating Investment Returns

Should you invest while paying down mortgage? A common question for households using HELOC acceleration is whether to divert surplus into investments instead of mortgage payoff. The answer depends on your financial goals and market conditions. Paying down mortgage debt provides a guaranteed return equal to the interest rate avoided—for example, eliminating a 6% mortgage balance is equivalent to earning a risk-free 6% return. Investments, however, may yield higher returns but carry volatility. Documented financial planning resources emphasize that debt reduction offers certainty, while investing introduces risk but potential upside. The decision hinges on whether you value guaranteed savings or are willing to accept market fluctuations for possible growth.

The math on opportunity cost Opportunity cost is the trade-off between investing surplus funds and applying them to debt. If your mortgage rate is 6% and your HELOC APR is 8%, paying down debt saves you those rates in guaranteed returns. By contrast, the S&P 500 has historically averaged 7–10% annually, but with significant volatility. If investments underperform your mortgage rate, you lose money compared to debt reduction. Conversely, if investments outperform, you gain—but only if you can tolerate the risk. Documented case studies show that households who ignore opportunity cost often misallocate surplus, either missing guaranteed savings or exposing themselves to unnecessary risk.

Risk tolerance considerations Risk tolerance is central to deciding between investing and debt payoff. Conservative households may prefer the certainty of mortgage reduction, while aggressive investors may allocate surplus to equities, real estate, or retirement accounts. Age, income stability, and financial goals all influence tolerance. For example, younger borrowers with decades before retirement may accept volatility, while those nearing retirement often prioritize debt freedom. Financial advisors stress that risk tolerance should be documented and revisited annually, ensuring that strategy aligns with evolving circumstances.

Balanced approach strategies A balanced approach combines debt reduction with investment. For example, households may allocate 70% of surplus to HELOC repayment and 30% to retirement accounts. This ensures guaranteed savings while still capturing potential market growth. Another strategy is sequencing: aggressively pay down debt for several years, then redirect surplus into investments once mortgage balances are reduced. Documented financial planning guides highlight that balanced approaches reduce regret—providing both certainty and growth potential. The key is to document allocations, monitor results, and adjust as conditions change.

Breakdown for Readers — Investment vs. Mortgage Checklist

Debt payoff return: Paying down mortgage = guaranteed return equal to interest rate avoided.

Opportunity cost: Compare mortgage/HELOC rates vs. historical investment returns (7–10% average for equities).

Risk tolerance: Assess age, income stability, and goals; conservative = debt payoff, aggressive = investing.

Balanced strategy: Split surplus (e.g., 70/30 debt vs. investment) or sequence debt payoff before investing.

Documentation: Track allocations annually; stress-test scenarios to confirm strategy remains viable.

Conclusion: Incorporating investment returns into a HELOC strategy requires balancing certainty against opportunity. By weighing debt payoff against market potential, calculating opportunity cost, assessing risk tolerance, and adopting balanced approaches, households can align their strategy with both financial freedom and long-term wealth building. Documented evidence shows that the most resilient plans are those that combine guaranteed savings with disciplined investment.

***

Section 2: Tax Optimization

HELOC interest is only deductible under post-2017 tax law if the funds are used to "buy, build, or substantially improve" the home securing the loan, and total mortgage-related debt remains within IRS limits. Proper documentation and guidance from a tax advisor are essential.

HELOC interest deductibility rules (post-2017 tax law) The **Tax Cuts and Jobs Act of 2017 (TCJA)** significantly changed the rules for deducting HELOC interest. Prior to 2017, interest on up to $100,000 of home equity debt was deductible regardless of how the funds were used. Post-2017, the IRS restricts deductibility to funds used to **buy, build, or substantially improve** the home securing the loan. Additionally, the combined mortgage and HELOC debt eligible for deduction is capped at **$750,000 for joint filers** (or $375,000 for married filing separately).

When HELOC interest is deductible Interest is deductible only if the HELOC funds directly improve the property securing the loan. Examples include:

Renovating a kitchen or bathroom

Adding a new room or finishing a basement

Installing energy-efficient windows, HVAC systems, or solar panels

Major structural repairs such as roof replacement

Non-qualifying uses include debt consolidation, tuition, vacations, or personal expenses. Even if financially prudent, these uses do not meet IRS deductibility rules.

Documentation requirements To claim the deduction, you must **itemize deductions** on your tax return. Documentation should include:

Loan agreements showing the HELOC terms

Receipts and invoices proving funds were used for qualifying home improvements

Mortgage and HELOC statements showing balances and interest paid

Records of appraisals or permits for substantial improvements

Without clear documentation, the IRS may disallow the deduction. Maintaining organized records ensures compliance and simplifies tax filing.

Working with your tax advisor Because HELOC deductibility depends on both usage and debt limits, working with a tax advisor is crucial. Advisors can:

Confirm whether your HELOC use qualifies under IRS rules

Calculate deductible portions if your combined mortgage debt exceeds $750,000

Guide you on whether itemizing deductions provides more benefit than the standard deduction

Help allocate HELOC funds correctly if used for mixed purposes (e.g., part home improvement, part personal expense)

A tax advisor ensures you maximize benefits while avoiding costly errors or audits.

Breakdown for Readers — HELOC Tax Optimization Checklist

Rule: Deductible only if funds "buy, build, or substantially improve" the home securing the loan.

Limit: Combined mortgage + HELOC debt capped at $750,000 (joint filers).

Qualifying uses: Renovations, structural repairs, energy upgrades.

Non-qualifying uses: Debt consolidation, tuition, personal expenses.

Documentation: Keep receipts, loan statements, and improvement records.

Tax advisor: Consult for mixed-use funds, itemization decisions, and debt limit calculations.

Conclusion: Tax optimization with a HELOC requires strict adherence to post-2017 IRS rules. By ensuring funds are used for qualifying home improvements, maintaining thorough documentation, and consulting a tax advisor, households can capture legitimate deductions while avoiding compliance risks.

***

Section 3: Advanced Optimization Techniques

Refinancing During the Process

When refinancing makes sense Refinancing can be a powerful tool when interest rates drop, your credit profile improves, or your financial goals shift. For example, if your mortgage rate is significantly higher than current market averages, refinancing into a lower rate can reduce monthly payments and total interest costs. Refinancing also makes sense if you want to shorten your loan term (e.g., moving from a 30-year to a 15-year mortgage) or consolidate debt into a single, more manageable payment. Documented financial guides emphasize that refinancing is most effective when the savings outweigh closing costs and when you plan to stay in the home long enough to realize those savings.

How to incorporate refinancing into strategy When using a HELOC acceleration strategy, refinancing should be integrated carefully. If you refinance your primary mortgage, you reset the amortization schedule, which can affect how HELOC chunks reduce principal. The key is to align refinancing with your payoff plan: refinance into a lower rate or shorter term, then continue applying HELOC chunks to principal. This combination magnifies savings by reducing both the interest rate and the loan balance faster. Some borrowers also refinance to open a new HELOC with better terms, ensuring the line remains a flexible tool for acceleration.

Costs vs. benefits analysis Refinancing involves costs such as appraisal fees, origination charges, and closing costs, which typically range from 2–5% of the loan amount. The benefits include lower monthly payments, reduced interest over time, or faster payoff with a shorter term. A break-even analysis helps determine whether refinancing is worthwhile: divide total closing costs by monthly savings to calculate how many months it takes to recoup expenses. For example, if refinancing saves $250 per month but costs $5,000 upfront, the break-even point is 20 months. Documented financial planning resources stress that refinancing only makes sense if you expect to remain in the home beyond the break-even period.

HELOC considerations post-refinance Refinancing can affect your HELOC in several ways. Some lenders require closing the existing HELOC when refinancing the first mortgage, while others allow it to remain open. If your HELOC is closed, you may need to reapply for a new line of credit, potentially with different terms. Post-refinance, confirm whether your HELOC's loan-to-value ratio still qualifies under the new mortgage balance and appraisal. Additionally, ensure that refinancing does not introduce unfavorable clauses such as balloon payments or prepayment penalties that could undermine your acceleration strategy. Documented lender policies highlight the importance of reviewing HELOC terms after refinancing to maintain flexibility and avoid surprises.

Breakdown for Readers — Refinancing Checklist

When it makes sense: Lower rates, improved credit, shorter loan term, or debt consolidation.

Integration: Refinance into better terms, then continue HELOC chunking for maximum payoff acceleration.

Costs vs. benefits: Calculate break-even point; ensure savings exceed closing costs and time horizon.

HELOC impact: Confirm whether HELOC remains open; reapply if necessary; review new loan-to-value and terms.

Action step: Consult lender policies and run side-by-side comparisons before committing.

Conclusion: Refinancing during the HELOC process can amplify results when timed correctly. By lowering rates, shortening terms, and aligning with your acceleration strategy, refinancing transforms debt reduction into a more efficient system. The key is to weigh costs against benefits, confirm HELOC implications, and document the break-even analysis to ensure refinancing strengthens rather than complicates your path to mortgage freedom.

***

Section 4: Advanced Optimization Techniques

The Final Payoff Strategy

Last chunk considerations The final payoff moment requires careful planning. Your last HELOC draw should be sized to eliminate the remaining mortgage balance without overextending repayment capacity. Documented financial guides emphasize that the last chunk is often smaller than earlier ones, since the mortgage balance has already been reduced significantly. Before drawing, confirm that your surplus can comfortably repay the HELOC within 12–18 months, ensuring you finish strong without lingering debt.

Paying off mortgage vs. keeping HELOC open Once the mortgage is fully paid, you face a choice: close the HELOC or keep it open. Paying off the mortgage provides psychological and financial freedom, eliminating monthly obligations and securing full ownership of your home. However, keeping the HELOC open can serve as a flexible emergency line of credit, especially if terms are favorable. Financial experts recommend weighing your risk tolerance—those who value liquidity may keep the HELOC, while those who prioritize debt-free living may close it. Documented lender policies note that unused HELOCs may carry annual fees, so factor ongoing costs into your decision.

Closing costs and timing Closing out a mortgage or HELOC may involve fees, such as recording charges, cancellation fees, or early termination penalties. Timing matters: some lenders waive fees if the HELOC remains open for a minimum period (often 2–3 years). Before initiating final payoff, request a payoff statement from your lender to confirm the exact balance and any closing costs. A break-even analysis ensures that the timing of your final chunk maximizes savings while minimizing unnecessary fees.

Celebrating your success The final payoff is more than a financial milestone—it's a life achievement. Documented behavioral finance studies show that celebrating progress reinforces discipline and creates lasting motivation. Whether it's a family gathering, a symbolic "mortgage burning" ceremony, or simply updating your financial vision board, acknowledging success is essential. Celebrating not only honors the discipline required but also marks the transition from debt reduction to wealth building.

Breakdown for Readers — Final Payoff Checklist

Last chunk: Size draw to eliminate remaining mortgage balance; confirm surplus can repay HELOC quickly.

Mortgage vs. HELOC: Decide whether to close HELOC or keep it open for liquidity; weigh fees vs. flexibility.

Closing costs: Request payoff statement; confirm fees or penalties; time payoff to minimize costs.

Celebrate: Mark the milestone with a personal or family ritual; reinforce motivation for future financial goals.

Next step: Transition surplus from debt reduction into investments, retirement accounts, or legacy planning.

Conclusion: The final payoff strategy is the culmination of disciplined HELOC acceleration. By carefully sizing the last chunk, weighing the decision to keep or close the HELOC, managing closing costs, and celebrating success, households secure both financial freedom and emotional fulfillment. Documented strategies show that the payoff moment is not just the end of debt—it's the beginning of wealth building and legacy creation.

CHAPTER 9:

Risk Management and What Can Go Wrong

Interest Rate Risk

How rising rates affect your strategy HELOCs are typically variable-rate loans tied to the prime rate plus a margin. When interest rates rise, the cost of carrying a HELOC balance increases, which can erode or even eliminate the savings from mortgage acceleration. For example, if your HELOC APR climbs from 7% to 10%, the interest you pay on the line may exceed the mortgage interest you are avoiding. Documented financial guides emphasize the importance of stress-testing your plan by modeling higher rates and confirming that surplus income can still cover repayment. Rising rates don't necessarily end the strategy, but they demand vigilance and flexibility.

HELOC rate caps explained Most HELOCs include lifetime rate caps that limit how high the interest rate can rise. Caps are often set at prime + 12%, meaning rates could reach double digits in extreme environments. While caps provide a ceiling, they may still expose borrowers to significant payment shocks. Understanding your HELOC's margin and cap is essential: a lower margin and reasonable cap provide more protection. Documented lender disclosures show that borrowers who ignore caps risk underestimating worst-case scenarios, leaving them vulnerable if rates spike.

Fixed-rate HELOC conversion options Some lenders allow borrowers to convert portions of their variable-rate HELOC balance into fixed-rate loans. This option locks in predictable payments and shields you from rising rates. Fixed-rate conversions are particularly useful when carrying large balances or during periods of rate volatility. However, they may come with fees or slightly higher rates than the variable option. Documented case studies highlight that households who selectively convert balances maintain flexibility while reducing exposure to rate risk.

Hedging strategies Hedging against interest rate risk involves proactive planning. Strategies include:

Maintaining an emergency fund outside the HELOC to absorb shocks.

Using surplus income to accelerate repayment during low-rate periods.

Diversifying debt tools, such as combining HELOCs with fixed-rate products.

Monitoring Federal Reserve policy and market trends to anticipate changes.

Documented financial planning resources stress that hedging is less about complex instruments and more about disciplined cash-flow management and preparedness.

When to pause or abort There are times when continuing the HELOC strategy no longer makes sense. If rates rise so high that HELOC interest consistently exceeds mortgage interest avoided, or if surplus income shrinks due to job loss or expense creep, pausing or aborting the strategy is prudent. In such cases, focus on stabilizing finances, maintaining minimum payments, and reassessing conditions before resuming. Documented best practices emphasize that stop rules—clear thresholds for pausing—protect households from turning a strategy into a liability.

Breakdown for Readers — Interest Rate Risk Checklist

Rising rates: Stress-test repayment under higher APRs; confirm surplus can still cover costs.

Rate caps: Understand lifetime caps; evaluate whether ceilings are reasonable or expose you to shocks.

Fixed-rate conversion: Consider locking balances when rates rise; weigh fees vs. stability.

Hedging: Build emergency reserves; accelerate repayment during low-rate periods; diversify debt tools.

Pause/abort rules: Stop if HELOC interest exceeds mortgage savings or surplus shrinks significantly.

Conclusion: Interest rate risk is the most significant threat to HELOC acceleration. By understanding how rising rates affect your plan, reviewing caps, considering fixed-rate conversions, applying hedging strategies, and setting clear stop rules, you protect yourself from turning a powerful tool into a financial burden. Documented evidence shows that households who anticipate and manage rate risk sustain long-term success, while those who ignore it often face setbacks.

***

Section 1: Risk Management and What Can Go Wrong

Job Loss or Income Reduction

Emergency fund importance (keep 3–6 months separate) A HELOC strategy relies on surplus income to repay draws quickly. If income is disrupted, the plan can stall or even backfire. That's why maintaining a separate emergency fund—ideally 3–6 months of living expenses—is critical. This fund should be kept outside the HELOC to ensure liquidity during hardship. Documented financial planning resources emphasize that households with robust emergency reserves are far less likely to default or face foreclosure during income shocks. The emergency fund acts as a buffer, allowing you to continue minimum payments while stabilizing your situation.

How to handle income disruption When income is reduced or lost, the first step is to pause new HELOC draws. Focus on covering essential expenses and maintaining minimum payments to protect your credit. Reassess your budget immediately, cutting discretionary spending and prioritizing necessities. If possible, redirect any severance, unemployment benefits, or secondary income streams into the HELOC to keep balances manageable. Documented case studies show that households who act quickly during disruptions minimize long-term damage, while those who delay often face compounding debt.

HELOC suspension by lender Lenders have the right to freeze or reduce HELOC limits during financial instability, especially if property values decline or income verification changes. This can leave borrowers without access to funds just when they need them most. To mitigate this risk, avoid relying on the HELOC as your sole emergency source. Keep cash reserves accessible and monitor lender communications closely. The Consumer Financial Protection Bureau notes that HELOC suspensions are more common during economic downturns, making proactive planning essential.

Backup plans and exit strategies A strong risk management plan includes backup options if the HELOC strategy becomes unsustainable.

These may include refinancing into a fixed-rate loan, consolidating debt into a lower-interest product, or temporarily shifting surplus into savings until stability returns. Exit strategies should be documented in advance, with clear stop rules such as: "Pause chunking if surplus drops below $500/month" or "Abort strategy if HELOC APR exceeds mortgage rate." Financial educators emphasize that having predefined exit strategies prevents emotional decision-making and protects long-term financial health.

Breakdown for Readers — Job Loss/Income Reduction Checklist

Emergency fund: Maintain 3–6 months of living expenses outside the HELOC.

Income disruption response: Pause new draws; cut discretionary spending; redirect severance or benefits to minimum payments.

HELOC suspension: Be aware lenders can freeze/reduce limits; avoid relying solely on HELOC for emergencies.

Backup plans: Consider refinancing, debt consolidation, or pausing strategy until surplus stabilizes.

Exit rules: Document clear thresholds for pausing or aborting to prevent compounding debt.

Conclusion: Job loss or income reduction is one of the greatest risks to a HELOC acceleration plan. By maintaining a separate emergency fund, acting quickly during disruptions, preparing for potential HELOC suspensions, and documenting backup strategies, households can weather financial storms without derailing their long-term goals. The key is preparation—anticipating challenges before they arise ensures resilience when life takes unexpected turns.

***

Section 2: Risk Management and What Can Go Wrong

Spending Discipline Failures

Warning signs you're off track The HELOC acceleration strategy depends on strict spending discipline. Warning signs that you're drifting off track include consistently carrying higher HELOC balances than projected, missing surplus targets, or using HELOC funds for discretionary purchases rather than mortgage chunks. Another red flag is lifestyle creep—gradually increasing expenses without adjusting repayment schedules. Documented financial planning resources emphasize that early detection of these signs prevents small lapses from compounding into long-term debt problems.

Recovery protocols If discipline lapses occur, recovery requires immediate corrective action. First, pause new HELOC draws until balances stabilize. Next, re-evaluate your budget to identify discretionary spending that can be cut. Redirect all available surplus back into the HELOC to reduce balances quickly. Documented case studies show that households who implement recovery protocols within one or two months can restore progress without major setbacks, while those who delay often face extended repayment windows and higher interest costs.

Accountability systems Accountability is essential to maintaining discipline. Systems may include monthly reviews with a spouse or partner, using budgeting apps that track HELOC balances, or setting alerts for spending thresholds. Some households create visual dashboards showing mortgage reduction progress, reinforcing the impact of discipline. Financial educators stress that accountability systems transform the strategy from a private effort into a shared commitment, increasing the likelihood of long-term success.

When to admit the strategy isn't for you Not every household is suited for HELOC acceleration. If discipline lapses are frequent, surplus income is consistently insufficient, or HELOC balances remain high despite repeated efforts, it may be time to admit the strategy isn't working. In such cases, traditional mortgage payoff methods or refinancing into a shorter term may be more effective. Documented financial guides emphasize that recognizing misalignment early prevents compounding debt and protects long-term financial health. The strategy is powerful, but only when executed with discipline and consistency.

Breakdown for Readers — Spending Discipline Checklist

Warning signs: Rising HELOC balances, missed surplus targets, discretionary HELOC use, lifestyle creep.

Recovery protocols: Pause new draws; cut discretionary spending; redirect surplus into HELOC quickly.

Accountability systems: Use apps, alerts, dashboards, or partner reviews to reinforce discipline.

Exit decision: Admit strategy isn't working if lapses are frequent or surplus is insufficient; pivot to alternatives.

Conclusion: Spending discipline failures are one of the most common reasons HELOC strategies falter. By recognizing warning signs early, applying recovery protocols, building accountability systems, and knowing when to pivot, households can protect themselves from turning a powerful tool into a liability. Documented evidence shows that discipline is not optional—it is the foundation of success in mortgage acceleration.

***

Section 3: Risk Management and What Can Go Wrong

Market Value Decline

How falling home values affect HELOCs Home equity lines of credit (HELOCs) are directly tied to the value of your property. When home values decline, your available equity shrinks, reducing the lender's collateral. This can affect your borrowing power and, in some cases, leave you "underwater" if your mortgage and HELOC balances exceed the home's market value. Documented financial guidance from the Consumer Financial Protection Bureau notes that declining property values are one of the most common triggers for lenders to reassess or restrict HELOC terms.

Lender freeze or reduction of credit line Lenders have the right to freeze or reduce HELOC limits if property values drop significantly or if they believe repayment risk has increased. For example, during the 2008 housing crisis, many banks froze HELOCs nationwide to protect themselves from losses. A freeze means you cannot draw additional funds, while a reduction lowers your available credit limit. Even if you are current on payments, lenders may act preemptively to minimize exposure. Documented case studies show that borrowers caught off guard by freezes often struggled with cash-flow planning, highlighting the importance of anticipating this risk.

Strategies to protect yourself To protect against market value decline, maintain a conservative loan-to-value (LTV) ratio by avoiding maxing out your HELOC. Keep an emergency fund outside the HELOC so you are not dependent on credit access during downturns. Regularly monitor your home's value through appraisals or online tools, and stress-test your plan by modeling scenarios where equity drops by 10–20%. If your area shows signs of declining values, consider accelerating repayment to reduce outstanding balances. Documented financial planning resources emphasize that proactive repayment and liquidity reserves are the best defenses against lender restrictions.

Geographic considerations Real estate markets vary widely by geography. Homes in areas with volatile markets—such as regions dependent on a single industry or prone to natural disasters—are more susceptible to value declines. Conversely, properties in stable, diversified economies tend to hold value better. Geographic considerations also include local housing supply, employment trends, and demographic shifts. For example, urban centers with strong job growth may be more resilient than rural areas facing population decline. Documented housing market analyses show that borrowers who factor in geographic risk when planning HELOC strategies are better prepared for downturns.

Breakdown for Readers — Market Value Decline Checklist

Impact: Falling home values reduce equity and borrowing power; may leave you underwater.

Lender actions: HELOC freezes or reductions can occur even if you are current on payments.

Protection strategies: Maintain conservative LTV, keep emergency funds outside HELOC, monitor property values, stress-test scenarios.

Geographic risk: Assess local market stability, employment trends, and demographic shifts; plan accordingly.

Action step: Document stop rules—pause new draws if equity declines significantly or lender signals risk.

Conclusion: Market value decline is a critical risk in HELOC strategies. By understanding how falling values affect equity, anticipating lender freezes, implementing protective strategies, and factoring in geographic considerations, households can safeguard their financial plans. Documented evidence shows that proactive monitoring and conservative borrowing are the keys to resilience when property markets shift.

***

Section 4: Risk Management and What Can Go Wrong

Lender Actions

HELOC suspension or closure Lenders reserve the right to suspend or close a HELOC under certain conditions, such as a significant decline in property value, changes in your financial situation, or broader economic instability. During the 2008 housing crisis, many borrowers experienced sudden freezes on their HELOCs, leaving them without access to funds even though they were current on payments. The Consumer Financial Protection Bureau (CFPB) notes that lenders may legally reduce or suspend credit lines if they believe repayment risk has increased. This underscores the importance of maintaining liquidity outside the HELOC so you are not solely dependent on it during downturns.

Rate increases beyond caps While most HELOCs are variable-rate loans tied to the prime rate, they typically include lifetime rate caps. However, borrowers often misunderstand these caps. A cap does not prevent rates from rising sharply—it only sets a maximum ceiling, which can still be very high (e.g., prime + 12%). If rates rise quickly, monthly interest costs can spike long before the cap is reached. Documented lender disclosures emphasize that borrowers should stress-test repayment scenarios at higher rates to ensure the strategy remains viable. Ignoring this risk can lead to balances that cost more than the mortgage interest avoided.

Change in terms Lenders may also change HELOC terms mid-stream, including adjustments to draw periods, repayment schedules, or fee structures. For example, some HELOCs transition from interest-only payments during the draw period to fully amortizing payments once the draw period ends. If borrowers are unprepared, this shift can create sudden payment shocks. Additionally, lenders may introduce new fees or alter margin requirements. Documented case studies show that households who fail to review updated disclosures often face unexpected costs that erode savings.

Your rights and recourse Borrowers have rights under federal law when lenders take adverse actions. The CFPB requires lenders to provide written notice explaining the reason for a HELOC suspension, reduction, or closure. If you believe the action was unjustified, you can request reinstatement by providing updated financial documentation or property appraisals. Borrowers also have the right to shop for new HELOCs or refinance with another lender if terms become unfavorable. Documented consumer protection resources emphasize that proactive communication with lenders and maintaining thorough records are the best ways to exercise your rights and seek recourse.

Breakdown for Readers — Lender Actions Checklist

Suspension/closure: Lenders may freeze or close HELOCs due to property value decline or financial risk.

Rate increases: Caps limit maximum rates but do not prevent sharp increases; stress-test repayment scenarios.

Change in terms: Watch for draw period expirations, amortization shifts, or new fees.

Rights/recourse: Lenders must provide written notice; you can request reinstatement or seek new financing.

Action step: Maintain liquidity outside HELOC and review disclosures regularly to avoid surprises.

Conclusion: Lender actions are outside your control but can dramatically impact your HELOC strategy. By understanding the risks of suspension, rate increases, and term changes—and by knowing your rights—you can prepare for disruptions and protect your financial plan. Documented evidence shows that households who anticipate lender actions and maintain backup liquidity are far more resilient when markets shift.

***

Section 5: Risk Management and What Can Go Wrong

Divorce, Death, and Life Changes

How life events affect the strategy Major life events such as divorce, death, or significant lifestyle changes can disrupt even the most disciplined HELOC acceleration plan. Divorce may split household income and assets, reducing surplus available for repayment. Death of a spouse or co-borrower can trigger estate complications, leaving heirs with debt obligations or property disputes. Other life changes—such as relocation, retirement, or caring for dependents—may alter financial priorities and cash-flow stability. Documented financial planning resources emphasize that these events often require immediate reassessment of debt strategies to prevent compounding risk.

Legal considerations Legal implications are central when life events occur. In divorce, property division and debt responsibility must be clarified through settlement agreements. Courts may assign HELOC or mortgage obligations to one party, but lenders are not bound by divorce decrees—they still hold both borrowers liable unless the loan is refinanced or closed. In cases of death, probate law governs how property and debts are transferred. Heirs may inherit both the home and its associated HELOC obligations. Documented estate planning guides stress the importance of wills, trusts, and clear titling to minimize disputes and ensure smooth transitions.

Unwinding the strategy if necessary Sometimes life events make continuing the HELOC strategy impractical. In such cases, unwinding the plan may involve refinancing into a fixed-rate mortgage, consolidating debt, or selling the property to eliminate obligations. The key is to act quickly and document the unwinding process to protect credit and preserve equity. Financial advisors recommend setting "stop rules" in advance—for example, pausing chunking if household income drops below a threshold or if ownership changes. Documented case studies show that households who proactively unwind avoid long-term damage, while those who delay often face escalating costs.

Insurance considerations Insurance plays a critical role in protecting against life-event risks. Life insurance can provide funds to pay off a mortgage or HELOC in the event of death, ensuring heirs are not burdened with debt. Disability insurance can replace income if illness or injury prevents work, sustaining repayment capacity. Homeowner's insurance protects property value, which underpins HELOC collateral. Documented financial planning resources emphasize that integrating insurance into debt strategies creates resilience, ensuring that unexpected events do not derail long-term financial goals.

Breakdown for Readers — Life Event Risk Checklist

Impact: Divorce, death, or lifestyle changes reduce surplus and disrupt repayment.

Legal: Divorce decrees don't release liability; probate governs debt transfer; use wills/trusts for clarity.

Unwinding: Refinance, consolidate, or sell property if strategy becomes impractical; set stop rules in advance.

Insurance: Use life, disability, and homeowner's insurance to protect against income loss and debt burdens.

Action step: Document contingency plans for major life events to safeguard credit and equity.

Conclusion: Divorce, death, and life changes are unpredictable but inevitable risks. By anticipating their impact, understanding legal obligations, preparing unwinding protocols, and integrating insurance safeguards, households can protect themselves from financial disruption. Documented evidence shows that resilience in the face of life events comes from preparation—ensuring that even when circumstances change, the path to financial freedom remains secure.

***

Section 6: Risk Management and What Can Go Wrong

The Worst-Case Scenario Planning

Foreclosure risk (minimal if managed properly) Foreclosure is the most severe consequence of mismanaging a HELOC strategy, but the risk is minimal if borrowers maintain discipline. Foreclosure occurs when borrowers fail to make required payments, allowing lenders to seize the property. According to the Consumer Financial Protection Bureau (CFPB), foreclosure is rare for households that maintain surplus cash flow, keep emergency reserves, and avoid overleveraging their HELOC. The key is to treat the HELOC as a tool for acceleration, not as a source of lifestyle spending. With proper monitoring and stop rules, foreclosure risk remains low.

Bankruptcy implications Bankruptcy is another worst-case scenario, typically triggered by overwhelming debt or income collapse. If a borrower files for bankruptcy, HELOC balances are treated as secured debt, meaning lenders have claims against the property. Chapter 7 bankruptcy may result in liquidation, while Chapter 13 allows repayment plans that restructure debt. Documented legal resources emphasize that bankruptcy severely impacts credit scores and future borrowing ability. Planning ahead—by maintaining conservative loan-to-value ratios and avoiding unnecessary draws—reduces the likelihood of bankruptcy becoming necessary.

Multiple simultaneous setbacks The most dangerous scenario is when several setbacks occur at once—for example, rising interest rates combined with job loss and declining home values. These simultaneous shocks can overwhelm even disciplined households. Documented case studies from the 2008 housing crisis show that borrowers facing multiple setbacks often struggled to recover without selling property or restructuring debt. Worst-case planning requires stress-testing your strategy under combined scenarios, ensuring you have backup liquidity and exit strategies ready.

Building resilience into your plan Resilience is built by anticipating risks and preparing safeguards. This includes maintaining a 3–6 month emergency fund outside the HELOC, setting stop rules for pausing draws, diversifying income streams, and monitoring property values. Insurance products—such as life, disability, and homeowner's insurance—add further resilience by protecting against income loss and property damage. Documented financial planning resources emphasize that resilience is not about eliminating risk but about ensuring setbacks do not derail long-term goals.

Breakdown for Readers — Worst-Case Scenario Checklist

Foreclosure risk: Minimal if surplus is maintained; avoid overleveraging HELOC.

Bankruptcy: HELOC treated as secured debt; severe impact on credit and borrowing ability.

Simultaneous setbacks: Rising rates + job loss + value decline = compounded risk; stress-test scenarios.

Resilience: Emergency fund, stop rules, diversified income, insurance safeguards, property monitoring.

Action step: Document contingency plans and rehearse exit strategies before crises occur.

Conclusion: Worst-case scenario planning is about preparing for the unlikely but possible. By understanding foreclosure and bankruptcy risks, anticipating multiple setbacks, and building resilience into your plan, households can safeguard their financial freedom. Documented evidence shows that those who plan for the worst are best positioned to achieve the best outcomes.

CHAPTER 10:

Legal and Regulatory Considerations

Legal Structure of HELOCs

Secured debt implications A Home Equity Line of Credit (HELOC) is a form of **secured debt**, meaning it is backed by your home as collateral. Unlike unsecured loans, lenders have a legal claim against the property if repayment obligations are not met. This structure lowers risk for lenders, which is why HELOCs often carry lower interest rates than credit cards or personal loans. However, it also raises the stakes for borrowers: defaulting on a HELOC can lead to foreclosure, even if the balance is relatively small compared to the home's value. Documented financial guidance from the Consumer Financial Protection Bureau (CFPB) emphasizes that borrowers must treat HELOCs with the same seriousness as their primary mortgage.

Junior lien position explained Most HELOCs are recorded as a **junior lien**, meaning they sit behind the first mortgage in repayment priority. In the event of foreclosure, the first mortgage lender is paid first, and the HELOC lender receives whatever remains. This junior position increases risk for lenders, which is why HELOCs often have stricter terms, variable interest rates, and caps. For borrowers, the junior lien status means that while the HELOC is flexible, it is still legally enforceable and can complicate refinancing or selling the property. Documented real estate law resources note that junior liens can also affect negotiations with lenders during hardship, since HELOC lenders may be more aggressive in protecting their position.

Your obligations as borrower Borrowers are legally obligated to make timely payments, maintain property insurance, and uphold the terms of the HELOC agreement. This includes adhering to draw limits, repayment schedules, and any covenants outlined in the loan documents. Failure to comply can trigger penalties, rate increases, or even acceleration clauses requiring immediate repayment of the full balance. Documented lender disclosures stress that borrowers must read agreements carefully, as HELOC contracts often include clauses that allow lenders to freeze or reduce credit lines under certain conditions, such as declining property values or income changes.

Lender's rights and remedies Lenders have broad rights under HELOC agreements. These include the ability to:

Freeze or reduce the credit line if property values decline or borrower risk increases.

Accelerate repayment if terms are violated.

Place foreclosure proceedings if payments are missed.

Report delinquencies to credit bureaus, impacting borrower credit scores.

Borrowers also have rights, including receiving written notice of adverse actions and the ability to dispute or request reinstatement. Documented consumer protection laws, such as those enforced by the CFPB, require lenders to provide transparency and fair treatment, but the remedies available to lenders remain powerful. Understanding these rights and remedies ensures borrowers can anticipate lender actions and protect themselves legally.

Breakdown for Readers — Legal Structure Checklist

Secured debt: HELOCs are backed by your home; default can lead to foreclosure.

Junior lien: HELOCs sit behind the first mortgage; lenders face higher risk, borrowers face stricter terms.

Borrower obligations: Timely payments, insurance, compliance with draw/repayment rules, and adherence to covenants.

Lender rights: Freeze/reduce credit lines, accelerate repayment, foreclose, and report delinquencies.

Action step: Review HELOC agreements carefully and consult legal/tax advisors before signing.

Conclusion: The legal structure of HELOCs defines both the borrower's obligations and the lender's remedies. By understanding secured debt implications, junior lien status, contractual obligations, and lender rights, households can navigate HELOC strategies with clarity and confidence. Documented evidence shows that informed borrowers are better equipped to avoid pitfalls and protect their financial freedom.

***

Section 1: Legal and Regulatory Considerations

Federal Regulations

Truth in Lending Act (TILA) requirements The **Truth in Lending Act (TILA)** requires lenders to clearly disclose the terms and costs of credit products, including HELOCs. This means borrowers must receive transparent information about interest rates, fees, repayment schedules, and potential changes in terms. TILA also provides a **three-day right of rescission** for HELOCs secured by a primary residence, allowing borrowers to cancel the agreement without penalty. Documented consumer protection resources emphasize that TILA ensures borrowers can make informed decisions by comparing credit offers on an equal basis.

Real Estate Settlement Procedures Act (RESPA) The **Real Estate Settlement Procedures Act (RESPA)** protects borrowers during the mortgage and HELOC settlement process. RESPA requires lenders to provide clear disclosures about closing costs, prohibits kickbacks between service providers, and ensures borrowers receive a **Loan Estimate** and **Closing Disclosure**. For HELOCs, RESPA ensures transparency in settlement services and prevents abusive practices. Documented legal guidance highlights that RESPA empowers borrowers to understand the full cost of their loan and avoid hidden fees.

Fair Credit Reporting Act (FCRA) The **Fair Credit Reporting Act (FCRA)** governs how lenders and credit bureaus handle borrower information. For HELOCs, this means your payment history, balances, and credit inquiries are reported to credit agencies. FCRA gives borrowers the right to access their credit reports, dispute inaccuracies, and place fraud alerts or credit freezes if needed. Documented consumer rights resources emphasize that FCRA protections are critical for maintaining accurate credit profiles, which directly affect HELOC eligibility and terms.

Consumer protections you have Together, TILA, RESPA, and FCRA provide a framework of consumer protections. Borrowers have the right to:

Receive clear disclosures about loan terms and costs.

Cancel certain HELOC agreements within three days (TILA rescission).

Understand and challenge settlement costs (RESPA).

Access and correct credit report information (FCRA).

Be protected against unfair, deceptive, or abusive practices by lenders.

Documented evidence shows that these protections are designed to level the playing field between borrowers and lenders, ensuring transparency, fairness, and accountability in the HELOC process.

Breakdown for Readers — Federal Regulation Checklist

TILA: Transparent loan disclosures; three-day rescission right for HELOCs on primary residences.

RESPA: Clear settlement disclosures; prohibition of kickbacks; Loan Estimate and Closing Disclosure required.

FCRA: Rights to access, dispute, and correct credit reports; fraud alerts and freezes available.

Consumer protections: Transparency, fairness, and recourse against abusive practices.

Conclusion: Federal regulations safeguard borrowers by requiring transparency, protecting against hidden costs, and ensuring credit accuracy. By understanding TILA, RESPA, and FCRA, households can confidently navigate HELOC strategies, knowing their rights are documented and enforceable.

***

Section 2: Legal and Regulatory Considerations

State-Specific Variations

Community property states considerations In community property states—such as California, Texas, Arizona, Nevada, and others—debts incurred during marriage are generally considered joint obligations, even if only one spouse signs the loan agreement. This means a HELOC opened by one spouse may legally bind both, creating shared liability. Documented state law resources emphasize that borrowers in these jurisdictions must account for spousal consent and liability when structuring HELOC strategies. Failure to do so can complicate divorce settlements or estate planning, as both parties remain responsible for repayment unless the loan is refinanced or closed.

Homestead protection laws Homestead exemptions vary widely by state and protect a portion of a primary residence's value from unsecured creditors. For example, Florida and Texas offer **unlimited homestead protection**, shielding the entire value of a primary residence from most creditor claims. Other states cap exemptions, often between $30,000–$75,000. While these protections safeguard equity from unsecured creditors, they do not apply to mortgage or HELOC lenders, who hold secured claims. Documented comparisons show that understanding your state's homestead laws is vital for risk management, as protections can dramatically affect outcomes in bankruptcy or creditor disputes.

Usury laws and rate caps Usury laws set maximum interest rates lenders can charge, and these limits differ by state. Some states impose strict caps on consumer loans, while others allow higher rates for certain loan types. Although federally chartered banks often operate under federal preemption, state usury laws still apply to local lenders. Borrowers should review whether their HELOC includes a lifetime rate cap and how state usury laws interact with lender terms. Documented financial law guides note that ignoring usury protections can expose borrowers to unexpectedly high interest costs, especially in states with weaker caps.

Foreclosure procedures by state Foreclosure rules vary significantly across the U.S. In judicial foreclosure states (e.g., Florida, New York), lenders must go through the court system, which can take months or years and often provides borrowers more opportunities to cure defaults. In non-judicial foreclosure states (e.g., Texas, Georgia), lenders can repossess property more quickly through trustee sales, often within weeks. Documented foreclosure law resources emphasize that borrowers must understand their state's process, as it affects timelines, costs, and opportunities for negotiation. Judicial states tend to favor borrower protections, while non-judicial states favor lender efficiency.

Breakdown for Readers — State-Specific Risk Checklist

Community property: Debts may bind both spouses; consider liability in marriage, divorce, or estate planning.

Homestead laws: Unlimited protection in states like Florida/Texas; capped exemptions elsewhere; secured lenders not exempt.

Usury laws: State caps vary; federal preemption applies to national banks; review lifetime HELOC rate caps.

Foreclosure: Judicial states = longer timelines, more protections; non-judicial states = faster repossession.

Action step: Research your state's statutes before implementing HELOC strategies to avoid legal surprises.

Conclusion: State-specific variations can dramatically alter the risks and outcomes of HELOC strategies. By understanding community property rules, homestead protections, usury limits, and foreclosure procedures, borrowers can tailor their approach to their legal environment. Documented evidence shows that proactive awareness of state laws builds resilience and prevents costly surprises.

***

Section 3: Legal and Regulatory Considerations

Tax Implications

Mortgage interest deduction limits The mortgage interest deduction allows taxpayers to reduce taxable income by the amount of interest paid on qualifying home loans. However, the **Tax Cuts and Jobs Act (TCJA) of 2017** lowered the cap: interest is deductible only on up to **$750,000 of mortgage debt** for joint filers (or $375,000 for married filing separately). Prior to 2017, the limit was $1 million. This change means households with larger mortgages may not be able to deduct all interest, making careful documentation essential.

HELOC interest deductibility (qualified residence interest) HELOC interest is deductible only if the funds are used to **"buy, build, or substantially improve"** the home securing the loan. This is known as **qualified residence interest**. Using HELOC funds for personal expenses—such as tuition, vacations, or debt consolidation—does not qualify. The IRS clarified in Notice 2018-32 that the deduction applies only when the HELOC directly improves the property. Borrowers must track how funds are used to ensure compliance.

2017 Tax Cuts and Jobs Act impact The TCJA reshaped the landscape for mortgage and HELOC deductions. In addition to lowering the debt cap, it eliminated the blanket deduction for home equity debt up to $100,000. Now, only qualified residence interest is deductible. The TCJA also nearly doubled the standard deduction, meaning fewer taxpayers benefit from itemizing mortgage interest. Documented tax analyses show that many households no longer itemize, reducing the practical value of mortgage and HELOC deductions.

Record keeping for tax purposes Accurate record keeping is critical for substantiating deductions. Borrowers should maintain:

Loan agreements and closing documents

Receipts and invoices for home improvements funded by HELOCs

Annual mortgage and HELOC statements showing interest paid

Property appraisals or permits for substantial improvements

Without documentation, the IRS may disallow deductions. Organized records ensure compliance and simplify tax filing.

IRS Form 1098 considerations Lenders issue **IRS Form 1098** annually, reporting the amount of mortgage interest paid. This form is essential for claiming deductions. However, Form 1098 may not distinguish between deductible and non-deductible HELOC interest. Borrowers must reconcile the form with their own records to ensure only qualified residence interest is claimed. Tax advisors recommend attaching supporting documentation to returns if HELOC funds were used for improvements, reducing audit risk.

Breakdown for Readers — Tax Implications Checklist

Mortgage interest deduction: Limited to $750,000 of debt (post-2017 TCJA).

HELOC interest: Deductible only if funds "buy, build, or substantially improve" the home.

TCJA impact: Eliminated blanket home equity deduction; fewer taxpayers itemize due to higher standard deduction.

Record keeping: Maintain loan docs, receipts, statements, and permits to substantiate deductions.

Form 1098: Review carefully; reconcile with records to ensure only qualified interest is claimed.

Conclusion: Tax implications are a critical part of HELOC strategy. By understanding deduction limits, applying qualified residence rules, documenting expenses, and reconciling Form 1098, households can maximize legitimate tax benefits while avoiding compliance risks. Documented evidence shows that proactive record keeping and consultation with tax advisors are the keys to leveraging HELOCs responsibly under current law.

***

Section 4: Legal and Regulatory Considerations

Estate Planning Considerations

How HELOCs affect your estate A Home Equity Line of Credit (HELOC) is a secured debt tied to your property, meaning it does not disappear upon death. The outstanding balance becomes part of your estate's liabilities, and heirs may inherit both the home and the obligation to repay the HELOC. If the estate lacks sufficient assets, the lender can enforce repayment through foreclosure. Documented estate planning resources emphasize that borrowers should account for HELOC balances when calculating net estate value, ensuring heirs are not surprised by hidden obligations.

Beneficiary implications Beneficiaries who inherit a home with a HELOC must decide whether to repay, refinance, or sell the property. Unlike life insurance proceeds, which pass directly to named beneficiaries, real estate transfers are subject to liens and debts. If multiple heirs are involved, disagreements may arise over whether to keep or liquidate the property. Documented probate law guides highlight that clear communication and estate planning documents reduce conflict and ensure heirs understand their responsibilities.

Life insurance considerations Life insurance can serve as a critical safeguard in estate planning when HELOCs are involved. A properly structured policy can provide heirs with funds to pay off outstanding balances, preventing forced sales or foreclosure. Mortgage protection insurance or term life policies are often recommended to cover the remaining debt. Documented financial planning resources stress that integrating life insurance into estate plans ensures heirs inherit property free of burdensome debt, preserving family wealth.

Will and trust provisions Wills and trusts are essential tools for managing HELOC obligations after death. A will can specify how debts should be repaid and which heirs inherit the property. Trusts, particularly revocable living trusts, can streamline the transfer of property and provide instructions for handling HELOC balances. Documented estate planning guides emphasize that trusts can avoid probate, reduce disputes, and ensure continuity in repayment. Including HELOC obligations explicitly in estate documents prevents confusion and protects heirs from unexpected liabilities.

Breakdown for Readers — Estate Planning Checklist

HELOC impact: Outstanding balances remain secured against the property; heirs inherit both home and debt.

Beneficiaries: Must decide to repay, refinance, or sell; clear estate documents reduce disputes.

Life insurance: Provides funds to cover HELOC balances; prevents foreclosure or forced sales.

Wills/trusts: Specify repayment instructions; trusts streamline transfers and avoid probate.

Action step: Integrate HELOC obligations into estate planning documents and align with insurance coverage.

Conclusion: HELOCs introduce unique estate planning challenges. By understanding how secured debt affects inheritance, preparing beneficiaries, integrating life insurance, and drafting clear wills or trusts, households can ensure their legacy is preserved. Documented evidence shows that proactive estate planning transforms HELOCs from potential burdens into manageable obligations, protecting heirs and securing family wealth.

***

Section 5: Legal and Regulatory Considerations

When to Consult Professionals

Real estate attorney consultation points A real estate attorney can provide critical guidance when dealing with HELOCs and mortgage acceleration strategies. Attorneys help review loan agreements, explain lien positions, and ensure compliance with state-specific property laws. They are especially valuable in complex situations such as divorce, estate planning, or disputes with lenders. Documented legal resources emphasize that attorneys can also negotiate with lenders if terms change unexpectedly or if foreclosure proceedings are threatened. Consulting an attorney ensures borrowers fully understand their obligations and rights under the law.

Tax advisor engagement Tax advisors play a key role in maximizing the financial benefits of HELOC strategies. They can clarify deductibility rules under the **Tax Cuts and Jobs Act (TCJA)**, calculate whether itemizing deductions is more beneficial than taking the standard deduction, and ensure compliance with IRS requirements for qualified residence interest. Advisors also help reconcile IRS Form 1098 with actual HELOC usage, ensuring only legitimate deductions are claimed. Documented tax guidance stresses that professional advice prevents costly errors and reduces audit risk.

Financial planner integration A financial planner helps integrate HELOC strategies into broader wealth-building goals. Planners evaluate whether mortgage acceleration aligns with retirement savings, investment strategies, and risk tolerance. They can also stress-test scenarios such as job loss, rising interest rates, or market value decline to ensure resilience. Documented financial planning resources highlight that planners provide accountability, helping households stay disciplined and avoid spending failures that undermine the strategy.

When professional fees are worth it Professional fees may seem like an added burden, but they are often worth the investment. Attorneys prevent costly legal mistakes, tax advisors maximize deductions and compliance, and financial planners ensure strategies align with long-term goals. Documented case studies show that households who consult professionals avoid pitfalls that can cost far more than advisory fees. Fees are especially justified when facing complex legal issues, large loan balances, or uncertain income streams.

Breakdown for Readers — Professional Consultation Checklist

Attorney: Review loan agreements, explain liens, handle disputes, advise on divorce/estate issues.

Tax advisor: Clarify deductibility rules, reconcile Form 1098, ensure IRS compliance, maximize tax benefits.

Financial planner: Align HELOC strategy with retirement, investments, and risk management; provide accountability.

Fees worth it: Prevent legal/tax mistakes, maximize savings, ensure resilience; justified in complex or high-risk cases.

Conclusion: Consulting professionals transforms HELOC strategies from risky undertakings into well-managed financial tools. Attorneys, tax advisors, and financial planners each provide specialized expertise that protects households from costly errors and ensures strategies align with long-term goals. Documented evidence shows that professional guidance is not an expense—it is an investment in financial security.

***

Section 6: Legal and Regulatory Considerations

Legal Structure of HELOCs

Secured debt implications A Home Equity Line of Credit (HELOC) is a **secured debt**, meaning it is backed by your home as collateral. Unlike unsecured loans such as credit cards, lenders have a legal claim against the property if repayment obligations are not met. This structure lowers risk for lenders, which is why HELOCs often carry lower interest rates. However, it raises the stakes for borrowers: defaulting on a HELOC can lead to foreclosure, even if the balance is relatively small compared to the home's value. The Consumer Financial Protection Bureau (CFPB) emphasizes that borrowers must treat HELOCs with the same seriousness as their primary mortgage because the home itself is at risk.

Junior lien position explained Most HELOCs are recorded as a **junior *lien***, meaning they sit behind the first mortgage in repayment priority. In foreclosure, the first mortgage lender is paid first, and the HELOC lender receives whatever remains. This junior position increases risk for lenders, which is why HELOCs often come with variable interest rates and stricter terms. For borrowers, the junior lien status means that while the HELOC provides flexibility, it can complicate refinancing or selling the property. Real estate law resources note that junior liens can also affect negotiations with lenders during hardship, since HELOC lenders may be more aggressive in protecting their position. You must guarantee the payment on this plan with a strict payment resources, if renting the property do so with a high expectations on the renters, through the screening process.

Side Note: **Junior Lien Position — Plain Language Rewrite**

Most HELOCs (home equity lines of credit) are recorded as a junior lien. That means the HELOC is behind the first mortgage in priority. If the property is foreclosed and sold, the first mortgage lender is paid first. The HELOC lender only gets paid from whatever funds remain after the first mortgage is satisfied. Because of that lower priority, HELOCs are riskier for lenders; lenders typically protect themselves with variable rates, stricter terms, or higher costs.

For borrowers, having a HELOC as a junior lien gives flexible access to equity but can make refinancing or selling the property more complicated. In hardship situations, HELOC lenders may be more aggressive about protecting their position, which can affect negotiations and options available to the owner.

Suggested Plain-English Addendum about Payment Guarantee and Rental Plan

To support a repayment plan that relies on rental income, include clear, enforceable requirements and backup protections. Below are the practical elements you should require and sample contract language you can adapt.

Key protections and expectations to include:

A minimum monthly payment guarantee (how it's funded if rent lapses)

Required reserve fund or security deposit amount (number of months' payments)

Tenant standards and landlord responsibilities (screening, lease term, allowed rent)

Proof and timing of rent collection (rent roll, bank statements)

Remedies and actions if payments miss (draw from reserves, demand cure, termination)

Additional protections: rental income insurance, co-signed guarantee, escrow for proceeds, automatic ACH withdrawal

Sample plain-language clauses you can adapt

Guaranteed Payment Reserve

Client will maintain a Payment Reserve equal to [X] months of required payments. The Payment Reserve will be deposited into an escrow account at signing and may be drawn by Company to cover missed payments until the Client cures the default.

Rental Income Expectations and Tenant Standards

If the property is rented to support payments, tenants must meet these minimums: (a) credit score ≥ *[]; **(b) monthly rent** ≥ [%] of required payment; (c) lease term ≥ [_]* months; (d) landlord provides proof of tenant screening (application, credit report, ID) prior to move-in.

Proof of Rent and Payment Flow

Client must provide a signed lease and evidence of rent collection (rent roll, tenant-paid receipts, or bank deposits) within [__] days of occupancy.

Payments to Company are to be made by ACH from rental receipts or by automated withdrawal from Client's designated account.

Alternatives and Backstops

If rent does not cover the required payment for more than [__] consecutive months, Company may (a) apply the Payment Reserve; (b) require a cosigner or additional security; (c) place recovered proceeds into escrow; or (d) pursue remedies under this Agreement.

Insurance and Property Management

Client agrees to maintain landlord insurance covering loss of rental income and to use a licensed property manager if requested by Company. Property manager contact and agreement must be provided within [__] days of execution.

Remedies for Breach

Failure to maintain reserves, meet tenant standards, or provide timely proof of rent constitutes a breach. On breach, Company may suspend services, demand immediate cure, draw on reserves, or terminate the plan and pursue recovery of fees and damages.

Example Short Paragraph for Marketing / Client Instructions

If you plan to rent the property to guarantee payment, make sure you: (1) set aside a reserve equal to [X] months of payments; (2) screen tenants carefully (credit, income, ID); (3) require a lease at or above the minimum rent threshold; (4) supply proof of rent collection quickly; and (5) keep active landlord insurance that covers lost rental income. These steps protect your recovery plan and let us act quickly if rent falls short.

Your obligations as borrower Borrowers are legally obligated to make timely payments, maintain property insurance, and comply with the terms of the HELOC agreement. This includes adhering to draw limits, repayment schedules, and covenants outlined in the loan documents. Failure to comply can trigger penalties, rate increases, or acceleration clauses requiring immediate repayment of the full balance. Lender disclosures stress that borrowers must read agreements carefully, as HELOC contracts often include clauses allowing lenders to freeze or reduce credit lines if property values decline or income changes.

Lender's rights and remedies Lenders have broad rights under HELOC agreements, including:

Freezing or reducing the credit line if property values decline or borrower risk increases.

Accelerating repayment if terms are violated.

Initiating foreclosure proceedings if payments are missed.

Reporting delinquencies to credit bureaus, impacting borrower credit scores.

Borrowers also have rights, such as receiving written notice of adverse actions and the ability to dispute or request reinstatement. Consumer protection laws, enforced by the CFPB, require lenders to provide transparency and fair treatment, but the remedies available to lenders remain powerful.

Breakdown for Readers — Legal Structure Checklist

Secured debt: HELOCs are backed by your home; default can lead to foreclosure.

Junior lien: HELOCs sit behind the first mortgage; lenders face higher risk, borrowers face stricter terms.

Borrower obligations: Timely payments, insurance, compliance with draw/repayment rules, and adherence to covenants.

Lender rights: Freeze/reduce credit lines, accelerate repayment, foreclose, and report delinquencies.

Action step: Review HELOC agreements carefully and consult legal/tax advisors before signing.

Conclusion: The legal structure of HELOCs defines both borrower obligations and lender remedies. By understanding secured debt implications, junior lien status, contractual obligations, and lender rights, households can navigate HELOC strategies with clarity and confidence. Documented evidence shows that informed borrowers are better equipped to avoid pitfalls and protect their financial freedom.

***

Section 7: Federal Regulations (HELOC Focus)

Fair Credit Reporting Act (FCRA) — what it is and why it matters for HELOCs

The FCRA governs how credit reporting agencies and entities that provide consumer credit information must collect, use, correct, and share credit data. For businesses that originate, service, or underwrite HELOCs—or that use credit reports for loan approvals, tenant screening, or loss-mitigation decisions—this means you must have a lawful, documented purpose to pull consumer reports, obtain required authorizations, and follow strict dispute and accuracy procedures when a consumer challenges information on their file.

Practical compliance steps tied to consumer-reporting rules for HELOC work

Require a signed, explicit authorization before pulling a borrower's credit report.

Log the permissible purpose and store the authorization with the file.

Keep copies of any reports you rely on and note the date and reason for the pull.

Follow furnisher obligations: investigate disputes promptly, correct or update information when required, and retain evidence of dispute responses.

Limit credit-report access internally to staff with a business need and train them on FCRA responsibilities.

Real Estate Settlement Procedures Act (RESPA) — scope and HELOC implications

RESPA and Regulation X regulate settlement practices, escrow accounts, and certain fee/referral arrangements in real-estate financing. For HELOC servicing or any activity that touches borrower escrow accounts, payoff statements, or post-closing disbursements, RESPA's rules on proper escrow handling, required disclosures, and prohibitions on kickbacks and referral fees are directly relevant.

How RESPA should shape HELOC operational practices

Provide clear, timely disclosures when you open or service escrow accounts tied to HELOCs.

Maintain accurate settlement and escrow records and produce required statements on request.

Avoid referral/fee-splitting arrangements with real-estate vendors that could be construed as kickbacks.

Train staff on Regulation X disclosure timing and how to document escrow inflows/outflows.

Truth in Lending Act (TILA) / Regulation Z — disclosures and consumer protections for HELOCs

TILA/Regulation Z requires transparent disclosures for consumer credit secured by a dwelling, including APR, payment terms, and certain consumer protections (for example, right of rescission for some home-secured transactions). Because many HELOCs are home-secured revolving lines, TILA rules affect how you advertise rates, present terms, and notify borrowers about changes to variable rates or billing.

Practical steps to satisfy TILA/Regulation Z when handling HELOCs

Ensure all HELOC disclosures (initial, periodic, and rate-change notices) meet Regulation Z content and timing requirements.

Clearly disclose variable-rate mechanics, index and margin, and examples of payment changes when required.

If offering or referring borrowers to credit or refinance products, ensure any advertised terms are accurate and include requisite APR or repayment examples.

Business controls to reduce regulatory risk (FCRA, RESPA, TILA) — HELOC checklist

Maintain a compliance matrix mapping HELOC tasks to statutes (e.g., credit pulls → FCRA; escrow/payoff handling → RESPA; disclosures/marketing → TILA).

Use standardized intake templates that capture required authorizations and disclosure acknowledgments.

Implement role-based access to credit and borrower data; log each access and pull.

Keep template disclosures reviewed by counsel and update them when federal guidance or rules change.

Train staff on red flags for prohibited referral fees and the timing/ contents of required disclosures.

Retain documentary evidence (signed authorizations, copies of notices, dispute responses) in each borrower file.

Consumer protections to highlight to borrowers of HELOCs

You have the right to accurate credit reporting and to dispute errors with both the lender and credit bureaus.

You will receive required loan disclosures that explain APR, payment terms, and how variable rates work.

If your HELOC involves escrowed monies or settlement handling, you will receive clear statements and disclosures about those funds.

Our firm will limit use of your personal data to purposes necessary for the HELOC and will document authorizations, disclosures, and any dispute resolutions.

Client-facing summary (one paragraph)

When you apply for or use a HELOC, federal rules protect how your credit is checked, how loan terms and rate changes are disclosed, and how escrow or settlement funds are handled. We obtain written permission before pulling reports, give you clear TILA disclosures about rates and payments, and follow RESPA rules when managing escrow or payoff activity. If you see an error on your credit report or a disclosure you don't understand, we'll explain your rights and the steps we'll take to correct it.

***

Community Property States

In community property states, most assets and debts acquired during marriage are treated as jointly owned. That means a HELOC taken out during marriage may be considered community debt, and both spouses' consent or signatures are often required for lien placement, modification, payoff, or release. Lenders and title agents typically demand proof of spousal joinder or a court order to clear or subordinate a HELOC when a property is sold, refinanced, or goes through a foreclosure process. For borrowers, this increases documentation needs and can slow transactions that involve HELOC lien work.

Homestead Protection Laws

Homestead rules can limit how a lender enforces a HELOC against a primary residence and may affect the portion of home equity available to secure or satisfy a HELOC. In states with strong homestead protections, a borrower's exempt equity may reduce the recoverable balance and change creditor remedies. Practically, this means:

Title and payoff calculations must account for state homestead exemptions.

Lenders and servicers may face procedural steps before attaching or foreclosing on a homestead property.

Borrowers may have additional defenses or statutory notice rights that delay enforcement.

Usury Laws and Rate Caps

State usury laws and statutory rate caps affect HELOC pricing and permissible post-default interest adjustments. Because many HELOCs carry variable rates, the applicable state ceiling, indexing method, and anti-usury exemptions (for national banks or certain secured loans) determine whether a lender may raise rates, add default interest, or charge certain fees. For operations and servicing:

Verify state rate caps and exemptions before applying any increased or default interest.

Ensure advertised or contracted rate terms comply with both state law and any federal preemption rules.

When structuring payment plans or modifications, disclose how rate caps affect monthly payments and outstanding balances.

Foreclosure Procedures and HELOCs

HELOC enforcement follows the state's foreclosure framework, and the HELOC's lien priority (usually junior to the first mortgage) shapes remedies and recovery prospects. Key implications:

In judicial states, HELOC lenders typically must file suit to foreclose, adding time, expense, and public record activity.

In non-judicial states, HELOCs governed by power-of-sale clauses may proceed to auction more quickly.

Redemption periods, notice requirements, and sale procedures determine how much (if any) a junior HELOC holder might recover after a sale.

Priority rules mean first mortgage payoff takes precedence; HELOC holders receive proceeds only after senior liens are satisfied. Operationally, servicers should track local timelines tightly, serve required notices precisely, and assess whether pursuing foreclosure or working a modification is more cost-effective given the HELOC's subordinate position.

Practical Business Controls

To manage state variation risk for HELOCs, implement these controls:

Maintain a state-by-state matrix showing marital consent rules, homestead exemptions, usury caps, and foreclosure type.

Build intake prompts that surface borrower marital status, homestead claims, and existing first-mortgage priority.

Consult local counsel before filing or enforcing in unfamiliar jurisdictions.

Standardize disclosures and fee language to reflect state rate constraints and borrower protections.

Client Guidance Summary

When advising borrowers about HELOCs, emphasize:

If married, check whether spousal joinder is needed.

Confirm homestead protections may shield some equity and change enforcement options.

Understand state rate caps before agreeing to variable or default interest terms.

Foreclosure timing and recovery likelihood depend on whether your state uses judicial or non-judicial procedures and the HELOC's junior lien status.

***

Section 8: Tax Implications for HELOCs

Mortgage interest deduction limits

Interest on home-secured debt is deductible only up to statutory limits that combine all qualified residence debt. For loans originated after December 15, 2017, the limit for deductible home mortgage interest is generally $750,000 of total qualified residence indebtedness ($375,000 if married filing separately); higher legacy limits may apply for older debt.

HELOC interest deductibility (qualified residence interest)

Interest on a HELOC is tax-deductible only when the loan proceeds are used to "buy, build, or substantially improve" the home that secures the loan. If HELOC proceeds are spent on non-housing purposes (for example, debt consolidation or personal expenses), that interest is not deductible under current IRS guidance.

2017 Tax Cuts and Jobs Act impact

The 2017 Tax Cuts and Jobs Act narrowed deductibility for home-equity borrowing by tying the deduction to qualified residence improvements and folding home equity debt into the overall mortgage cap described above. This changed prior rules that allowed broader deductibility of home-equity interest regardless of use.

Record keeping for tax purposes

Borrowers should document exactly how HELOC funds are used and keep contemporaneous records (invoices, contractor agreements, cancelled checks, bank statements) that trace funds to qualifying home improvements. Retain documentation supporting interest calculations and proofs of payment for at least the period recommended by tax counsel or the IRS, since the deduction depends on demonstrable use of funds for the residence.

IRS Form 1098 considerations

Lenders report mortgage interest paid by borrowers on IRS Form 1098. If your HELOC interest is paid to a single lender or servicer, expect Form 1098 showing interest paid during the tax year; retain that form for your records and for preparing deductibility calculations. If interest is not reported on Form 1098 or you have multiple lenders, maintain your own detailed interest payment records and consult your tax advisor for reporting and substantiation requirements.

Practical action items for borrowers and servicers

Before closing or disbursing HELOC proceeds, document the borrower's stated use of funds and provide clear borrower guidance about tax treatment if funds are used for nonqualified purposes.

Maintain loan files with clear, dated evidence tying disbursements to qualifying home improvements (invoices, contracts, escrow receipts) to support deduction claims.

Ensure lenders issue Form 1098 when required and advise borrowers to keep that form with their tax documents; if reporting is complex, flag accounts for borrower tax counseling or referral to a CPA.

***

When to Consult Professionals — HELOC Focus

Real Estate Attorney Consultation Points

Title, lien priority, and deed issues: Confirm HELOC lien placement, check for past subordination or release language, and resolve title defects before sale, refinance, or probate.

Foreclosure and enforcement strategy: Evaluate state-specific foreclosure pathways (judicial vs non-judicial), redemption rights, and likely recovery outcomes; advise on whether to negotiate, defend, or settle.

Community property and spouse joinder: Advise on spousal consent requirements, quitclaim needs, and joint-owner documentation in community property states.

Homestead and exemption planning: Review homestead protections that may affect lien enforcement and creditor claims.

Drafting and review of POA/escrow/settlement documents: Prepare limited powers, escrow instructions, and any third-party agreements so actions comply with lender and local rules.

Sample questions to bring: "How does local foreclosure law affect a junior HELOC holder?"; "What documents prove a valid spousal joinder here?"; "Can we subordinate or restructure this HELOC without triggering default?"

Tax Advisor Engagement

Deductibility and documentation: Confirm whether interest is deductible (qualified residence interest) given intended use of proceeds; outline required substantiation for home-improvement uses.

Form 1098 and reporting: Clarify how HELOC interest will be reported, how to reconcile multiple lenders, and implications for year-end tax filing.

Estate and gift tax interactions: Advise on life-insurance sizing and liquidity planning to cover HELOC obligations on death.

Timing and planning for large draws: Assess tax effects of using HELOC funds for investments, business, or large property projects.

Sample questions to bring: "If I use HELOC proceeds for X, is the interest deductible?"; "What records should I retain to substantiate deductions?"; "How will a HELOC affect my estate liquidity and tax exposure?"

Financial Planner Integration

Cash-flow modeling and contingency plans: Fit HELOC payments into short- and long-term budgets, stress-test scenarios where rates rise or rental income drops.

Refinance vs. repay decisioning: Model when refinancing, paying down principal, or converting to a fixed product makes sense given rate forecasts and household goals.

Insurance and liquidity solutions: Recommend life or disability coverage sized to cover HELOC balances in an estate plan; evaluate emergency reserve targets.

Investment trade-offs: Compare using HELOC for investments versus preserving home equity; quantify risk/reward and margin call scenarios.

Sample questions to bring: "At current rates, what payment and cash-flow risk does this HELOC introduce?"; "How much reserve should we maintain to cover worst-case payment scenarios?"

When Professional Fees Are Worth It

Complex title, marital, or probate issues: Hire a real estate attorney when ownership or spousal consent is unclear, when probate or trust funding interacts with the HELOC, or when foreclosure risk is present.

Material tax exposure or unclear deductibility: Retain a tax advisor when projected HELOC use is large, when funds are used partly for nonqualified purposes, or when multiple lenders complicate Form 1098 reporting.

Significant financial decisions or leverage: Engage a financial planner when HELOC use could materially change retirement plans, debt ratios, or investment strategies.

High-stakes negotiations or litigation: Pay for counsel if negotiating payoff terms, sue/defend in foreclosure, or when a lender pursues aggressive remedies.

Rule of thumb: If the decision affects six-figure amounts, the family home, or estate transferability, professional fees are usually justified.

Practical Checklist Before You Meet a Professional

Bring: loan agreement, HELOC note and rider, deed, title report, recent payoff statement, escrow records, insurance policy, recent bank statements showing draws, Form 1098 (if available).

Prepare: clear timeline of draws and disbursements; explanation of intended use of funds; list of other liens and mortgage balances; marital status and trust/will copies if applicable.

Goals: state desired outcomes (e.g., refinance, protect estate, dispute chargeoffs, secure deduction), preferred risk tolerance, and liquidity constraints.

Quick Triage Guide (Do this first)

If you plan major home improvements and want tax benefits → consult tax advisor before drawing funds.

If title, spouse consent, or foreclosure is possible → consult real estate attorney immediately.

If HELOC use changes cash flow or retirement strategy → schedule financial planner review.

If you face an urgent lender notice, sale, or legal filing → prioritize attorney engagement over planning conversations.

PART IV:

MAKING IT WORK FOR YOU

1. Overview and core objective

Use the HELOC to accelerate mortgage payoff, support strategic cash flow needs, or fund value-adding home projects while protecting your home from acceleration risk and preserving liquidity. This strategy balances disciplined repayment, lender-communication protocols, and contingency protections so the HELOC is a tool — not a hazard.

2. Key risks to manage (short list)

Acceleration clause triggers (missed payments, bankruptcy, unauthorized title transfers, large value declines) — can force full repayment demand.

Variable interest and rising rates that increase payment burden.

Using HELOC proceeds for nonqualified purposes (tax and planning consequences).

Overleveraging home equity and losing emergency liquidity.

3. Clear decision criteria before you start

Do you have stable cash flow and a 3–6 month emergency reserve?

Is the HELOC rate competitive and subject to clear index/margin disclosure?

Will draws be used for home improvements or high-return debt paydown (where interest deductibility or ROI is clear)?

Can you meet monthly debt service even if rates rise materially?

4. Safe operational playbook (step-by-step)

Know your contract: catalog acceleration triggers, required notices, and lender cure periods; highlight anything that could void or accelerate the HELOC.

Build a Payment Reserve: maintain a dedicated reserve equal to 3 months of HELOC payments (or higher if using rental-backstop) accessible by ACH or escrow.

Use "chunk" principal payments tactically: make large, scheduled principal reductions when cash flow permits to reduce interest exposure and replenish reserve before the next draw.

Automate cash flow into the HELOC: route income (payroll deposits, rental receipts) to the HELOC account to minimize average daily balance and interest accrual when using velocity banking techniques.

Limit purpose of draws: prefer home improvements or high-interest debt paydown to preserve tax deductibility and ROI.

Communicate with lender proactively if payment stress appears: negotiate temporary forbearance or modified terms before missing payments.

Monitor property value and insurance: maintain property condition, adequate hazard and landlord insurance, and a quarterly valuation alert to flag rapid declines that could concern the lender.

5. Tactical strategies (options you can deploy)

Velocity / cash-flow banking: draw a controlled chunk to pay down mortgage principal, then channel monthly income into the HELOC to pay it down quickly; repeat as cash flow allows to shorten mortgage life and reduce interest expense.

Hybrid repayment: combine scheduled HELOC minimums with occasional lump principal payments from windfalls or rental cash flow to lower outstanding balance.

Rental income backstop: if you rent the property to cover payments, require tenant screening and a payment reserve (see Escrow Instructions template previously drafted).

Rate-cap planning: if your HELOC has a teaser or initial low period, plan to accelerate paydown during that window and avoid large draws near known cap resets.

6. Warning signs and stop actions (when to pause the strategy)

Two consecutive months of missed or late payments — stop draws and draw on reserves.

Notice of intent to accelerate or foreclosure filing — retain counsel and halt non-essential draws immediately.

Rapid home-value decline (loss > X% in 12 months) — reassess leverage and consider refinancing to fixed terms.

Variable rate spikes that send required payment above an acceptable stress threshold (predefined in your plan).

7. Sample 12-month HELOC acceleration plan (illustrative)

Month 0: Establish Payment Reserve = 3× monthly HELOC payment; confirm escrow and ACH setup.

Month 1: Draw $X to make a principal reduction on the mortgage; record transaction and adjust target reserve.

Months 2–6: Direct monthly income deposits to HELOC; make one additional lump payment in month 4 from bonus/savings.

Month 7: Reassess interest rate and property value; if rates remain favorable, repeat draw + chunk payment sequence; if rates rose, halt and pay down.

Month 12: Reconcile year results, update reserve target, and document all transactions for tax and audit purposes.

8. Governance, tracking, and reporting (minimum controls)

Weekly cash-flow dashboard showing HELOC balance, average daily balance, reserve balance, and next reset date.

Signed authorizations for any automated income routing and owner attestations if rental income is used.

Quarterly review with tax advisor about deductibility and with counsel if any title/transfer action occurred.

Maintain clear file evidence: loan docs, payoff receipts, valuation snapshots, insurance certificates, and reserve escrow records.

9. When to bring in pros (quick guide)

Counsel: immediately if you receive acceleration/foreclosure notices or if title transfers are contemplated.

Financial planner: before major draws that alter retirement or debt plans.

Tax advisor: before using HELOC funds for investments or mixed-purpose spending (deductibility questions).

10. Quick checklist (one-page)

[ ] Read and flag acceleration clause and cure periods in HELOC note.

[ ] Establish Payment Reserve (3× monthly payment) in escrow/accessible account.

[ ] Set up automated income routing and ACH payments.

[ ] Schedule chunk principal payments and document each draw/payment.

[ ] Maintain insurance, monitor home value, and run quarterly reviews.

[ ] Stop draws if 2 months of missed payments or acceleration notice received; contact counsel.

[ ] Reconcile annually and consult tax advisor about interest deductibility.

CHAPTER 11:

The Psychological Game — Mindset Shifts Required

Transforming your approach to a HELOC begins with shifting identity from someone weighed down by debt to someone who actively manages debt as a strategic financial instrument. Instead of seeing the balance as a moral failure or a permanent burden, reframe it as a lever you can use — when used deliberately, it accelerates goals, funds value-adding projects, or smooths short-term cash flow. That mental shift changes decisions: you stop making reactive, panic-driven moves and start designing plays (reserve rules, cooling-off periods, chunk payments) that keep control with you rather than with the lender.

Mastering delayed gratification is the muscle that makes acceleration work in practice. Short-term impulses—an attractive purchase, an unplanned vacation, or an emotional draw on the line—can erode the long-term gains you're building. Practice concrete tactics: impose a 24–72 hour cooling off before any discretionary draw, automate transfers that force saving before spending, and celebrate non-spending wins. Over time those small acts of restraint compound into a pattern where choosing future freedom becomes easier than instant pleasure because the evidence of progress is visible and motivating.

Prioritizing a long-term vision over short-term pleasure keeps daily tradeoffs aligned with what matters most. Create a vivid Freedom Vision—a clear description of life mortgage-free, the practical benefits it brings, and the timeline you aim for—and revisit it often. When decisions come up, run them through a quick test: "Does this move advance my Freedom Vision or delay it?" If it delays, treat it as a conscious trade-off, not a default. This practice converts vague hope into disciplined action and helps you tolerate temporary discomfort for a measurable future payoff.

Finally, reframe your relationship with money from scarcity or guilt to information and agency. Money is data about choices: it tells you what you value and where to apply attention. When you view balances, reserves, and payments as neutral feedback rather than moral verdicts, you reduce shame, make clearer plans, and respond creatively to setbacks. Build practical rituals—weekly balance checks, a monthly "wins" log, and a simple dashboard—that turn emotional noise into actionable signals. That new stance—curious, pragmatic, and purposeful—lets you use the HELOC as a calibrated tool, not a looming threat.

Mindset Shifts Required

A HELOC acceleration strategy succeeds as much in the mind as it does in the ledger. This chapter focuses on the mental moves, habits, and guardrails that turn intentional plans into sustained action without sacrificing emotional wellbeing or financial prudence.

Mindset Shifts (core)

From debtor to strategic debt manager — view the HELOC as a flexible financial tool you control, not a sentence you endure.

Delayed gratification mastery — trade short-term consumption for documented long-term freedom; treat each sacrifice as a planned investment.

Long-term vision over short-term pleasure — keep a clear mortality- and legacy-anchored "why": family security, retirement freedom, or business choices.

Reframing relationship with money — money becomes information and energy: a signal of choices, not a moral scoreboard.

Emotional Triggers and Reframes

Fear of interest spikes → reframe as an early warning system that forces prudent reserve behavior.

Impulse spending after a draw → reframe draws as conditional lines of credit; require an "intent to repay" checklist before each use.

Comparison to peers with different strategies → reframe: your timeline is your values, not their optics.

Set short, calming interventions: 24-hour rule before any nonessential draw; three-breath pause before discretionary purchases.

Daily and Weekly Habits (practical)

Daily balance check (60 seconds): HELOC balance, reserve balance, upcoming rate resets.

Weekly cash-flow review (15 minutes): income in/out, chunk planned this month, reserve delta.

Monthly ritual: reconcile HELOC activity, record "wins" (principal reduced), and note one corrective action.

Quarterly reflection: rate environment check, valuation snapshot, and psychological temperature (stress level 1–10).

Decision Rules and Guardrails (hard limits)

Reserve rule: never draw if reserve < 3× monthly HELOC payment.

Draw purpose rule: only for approved categories (home improvement that increases value; high-interest debt payoff; documented investment with ROI threshold).

Stop rule: pause all new draws after 2 missed payments or any acceleration notice.

Review rule: any draw > $X requires a 3-day cooling period and written plan for repayment.

Accountability Tools and Social Support

Visible tracker: a single-page dashboard posted where you pay bills (balance, reserve, next reset).

Accountability partner: weekly 10-minute check with a spouse, advisor, or finance buddy.

Auto-controls: automated transfers to reserve, auto-payments to HELOC principal, alerts at thresholds.

Reward system: small, nonfinancial rewards tied to milestones (e.g., after three chunk payments, schedule a free family outing).

Quick Checklist (one page)

[ ] Write your primary "why" for accelerating the mortgage.

[ ] Set reserve target (3× monthly payment) and fund it.

[ ] Define allowable draw purposes and document ROI/need.

[ ] Put decision rules in writing and post the dashboard.

[ ] Automate transfers and payment flows where possible.

[ ] Choose an accountability partner and set weekly check-ins.

[ ] Schedule monthly reconciliation and quarterly professional check (tax/counsel/planner).

Small psychological shifts compound. The point isn't to be rigidly austere; it's to replace reactive money behavior with predictable, values-aligned actions that make the HELOC an engine for control rather than anxiety.

***

Section 1: The Psychological Game — Building Discipline and Habits

Behavioral economics principles that help you win

Loss aversion: Frame missed payments or slower progress as a loss (visualize the extra interest) to motivate avoidance behavior.

Present bias workaround: Use commitment devices (automated transfers, signed pledges) to lock future behavior now.

Default effects: Make the desired behavior the default — auto-pay, auto-transfer to reserve, scheduled chunk payments.

Small-wins reinforcement: Break big goals into tiny, repeatable actions so progress compounds and momentum builds.

Habit stacking techniques (practical recipes)

Anchor habit: attach a new HELOC habit to an existing daily routine.

Example: After morning coffee, open HELOC dashboard for 60 seconds (balance + reserve).

Example: After paying rent, immediately transfer X% to HELOC reserve account.

Micro-commitments: require a tiny, nonthreatening action before bigger ones (write the draw purpose on a sticky note, wait 24 hours).

Implementation intention: use "If/Then" rules to remove friction.

Example: If I receive unexpected income, then I will apply 50% to HELOC principal within 3 business days.

Habit bundling: combine a habit you love with one you need.

Example: Listen to a favorite podcast while reconciling monthly HELOC transactions.

Accountability partners and structures

Choose the right partner: spouse, trusted advisor, financial coach, or peer with similar goals.

Make it specific: weekly 10–15 minute check-ins, a shared dashboard screenshot, and one agreed metric (e.g., reserve balance or principal-paid this month).

Simple script for check-ins: 1) What I did this week, 2) What I'll do next week, 3) One obstacle and how I'll handle it.

Public commitment tools: text groups, Trello board, or calendar invites to reinforce social cost of slipping.

Professional accountability: schedule quarterly reviews with a planner or CPA tied to milestones.

Tracking for motivation — minimal, high-impact metrics

Daily (60 seconds)

HELOC balance; Reserve balance; Days until next rate reset.

Weekly (10–15 minutes)

Income received; Planned chunk payments; Any draws this week; Action items completed.

Monthly (30–45 minutes)

Principal paid this month; Interest paid this month; Reserve status vs. target; One corrective action if behind.

Quarterly (30–60 minutes)

Net change in outstanding balance; Rate environment check; Property valuation snapshot; Tax/timing check with advisor.

Metric template (one line each)

Date | HELOC balance | Reserve balance | Principal paid | Interest paid | Draws this period | Notes/action

Motivation techniques and rewards

Celebrate micro-wins: small nonfinancial rewards after chunk payments (favorite meal, family outing).

Visual progress: one-page dashboard on the fridge or phone widget showing days saved or interest avoided.

Loss framing for discipline: show month-by-month projected interest if you skip a chunk vs. if you pay it.

Gamify: streak counters for daily checks and leaderboard with accountability partner.

Quick implementation plan (30/60/90 day)

Days 1–30: Set up auto-transfers, fund reserve to 1× target, pick accountability partner, start daily 60-second checks.

Days 31–60: Increase reserve to full target (3×), schedule first chunk payment, introduce weekly check-ins.

Days 61–90: Automate one chunk per quarter, run monthly reconciliation ritual, hold first professional review.

Decision rules to prevent derailment

Stop draws if reserve < 3× payment.

Require 24–72 hour cooling period for discretionary draws > $X.

Pause strategy and consult advisor after 2 missed payments or any acceleration notice.

Checklist (one page)

[ ] Pick anchor habit and stack new actions.

[ ] Set up automated transfers and auto-payments.

[ ] Fund initial reserve and set target.

[ ] Choose accountability partner and schedule check-ins.

[ ] Create daily/weekly/monthly tracking template.

[ ] Define reward and loss frames for motivation.

[ ] Publish decision rules and stop triggers.

***

Staying Motivated Through the Journey

Staying motivated across a long financial plan begins with a clear mental picture of the outcome. Start each week with a short visualization exercise: sit quietly for five minutes and imagine the mortgage paid off, the daily ease that follows, and the concrete benefits—lower monthly bills, more discretionary time, and greater financial flexibility. Visualization helps align daily choices with long-term goals and makes future rewards feel more real, which reduces the temptation to trade progress for short-term pleasures.

Celebrate milestones intentionally but without spending. Create low- or no-cost rituals that honor forward motion—write a gratitude note, take a free family hike, enjoy a home movie night, or record a short journal entry describing what you accomplished. These small ceremonies reinforce the habit loop and provide emotional rewards without eroding the financial gains you're working to build.

Turn goals into measurable momentum with a progress-tracking dashboard. Use a one-page snapshot that displays current HELOC balance, reserve level, principal paid this month, upcoming rate reset dates, and a rolling projection of interest avoided. Update it weekly so abstract aspirations become concrete metrics you can act on. Seeing steady, quantifiable progress reduces anxiety and increases confidence to continue the plan.

Build or join a community for accountability and encouragement. An accountability partner, a small peer group, or a virtual mastermind can meet weekly to report a single metric and one actionable plan for the coming week. Share templates, celebrate wins, and offer non-judgmental feedback when setbacks occur. Community transforms solitary discipline into shared momentum and makes it easier to recover from missteps.

Weave these practices into a simple routine: daily visualization (5 minutes), weekly dashboard update (15 minutes), a monthly milestone ritual, and a regular community check-in. This blend of internal focus, measurable tracking, purposeful celebration, and social support keeps motivation steady, reinforces disciplined behavior, and protects progress over the long haul.

***

Section 2: The Psychological Game — Handling Spouse and Partner Alignment

Before you move forward with a HELOC acceleration plan, secure genuine buy-in from your spouse or partner. A clear, calm conversation up front prevents costly misunderstandings later. Explain the strategy's purpose, the specific steps you'll take, and the safety nets you'll put in place — reserves, cooling-off rules for discretionary draws, and a plan for worst-case scenarios. Present the numbers: current balances, projected monthly impacts under different rate scenarios, and the target timeline. When both partners see the facts and the contingency plans, commitment is more likely to be real rather than reluctant.

Ongoing communication keeps alignment intact as reality unfolds. Set a regular, brief cadence for money conversations — a weekly 10-minute check and a monthly review where you look at the dashboard together. Keep updates factual and focused: what changed in the balance, what draws were made or planned, how the reserve looks, and any rate or valuation alerts. Use a shared one-page dashboard or app so both partners have the same view of progress; that removes ambiguity and reduces the "he said / she said" friction that often derails plans.

Disagreements will happen; prepare a respectful framework for resolving them. Agree in advance on decision rules for common conflict points — for example, require a cooling-off period before any discretionary draw over a set threshold, or a two-week notice before refinancing actions. When an argument emerges, pause the emotional escalation by reverting to the agreed facts and rules: refer to the dashboard numbers, the reserve rule, and the stop triggers. If you still can't reach consensus on a major move, use a neutral third party — a financial coach, trusted advisor, or mediator — to facilitate a solution that preserves the relationship and the plan.

Make celebration part of the alignment strategy so both partners feel rewarded by progress. Design shared, no-spend rituals that mark milestones: a handwritten note of gratitude, a home-cooked celebratory meal, a photo of the dashboard progress on the fridge, or a short family outing that costs little. Recognizing achievements together reinforces teamwork and keeps morale high without undoing financial gains. Over time, these shared moments transform the plan from an individual chore into a joint accomplishment.

Finally, treat alignment as ongoing work, not a one-time checkbox. Revisit goals annually (or with any major life change), update the plan when incomes or priorities shift, and keep the conversation compassionate — acknowledge fears, validate the other person's concerns, and share credit when progress happens. A robust alignment practice reduces surprise, strengthens trust, and makes it far more likely that the HELOC strategy turns into a shared path to long-term financial freedom.

***

Section 3: The Psychological Game — The Freedom Vision

Imagine life without a mortgage and let that picture guide daily choices. Start by describing specific activities you'll do when the house is paid off: hours reclaimed each month, travel you'll prioritize, time you'll spend with family, or new work you'll pursue without mortgage pressure. Making this concrete—where you'll go, who you'll be with, and how a thinner monthly budget will feel—turns an abstract goal into vivid motivation you can return to during tight months.

Mortgage freedom opens doors for retirement acceleration. Without a monthly mortgage drain you can redirect cash flow into retirement accounts, taxable investments, or guaranteed-income products that shorten the timeline to financial independence. Model scenarios: the effect of redirecting one mortgage payment a month into retirement accounts, the trade-off between extra mortgage prepayments versus increased retirement savings, and the breakeven horizon for different allocations. Use simple projections to choose whether extra principal payments or boosted retirement contributions best serve your long-term plan.

A mortgage-free home is also a foundational asset for generational wealth building. Paid-off property reduces estate liabilities, simplifies transfers to heirs, and can be leveraged strategically—through home equity for legacy financing, rental income, or down-payment assistance for younger family members. Plan how you want equity to function across generations: funding education, seeding businesses, or providing a safety net. Document intentions in estate and trust documents so the asset becomes a reliable tool for intergenerational goals rather than an unplanned liability.

Clarify your "why" with a short, focused exercise. Write a single paragraph answering: Why do I want mortgage freedom? Then expand into three concrete benefits you most value (for example: time with family, earlier retirement, less stress). Next, identify one emotional obstacle (fear, temptation, impatience) and one practical barrier (cash flow, variable rates, unexpected expenses). Finally, tie each barrier to a specific countermeasure you will use (reserve fund, cooling-off rule, accountability partner). Keep this "why" statement visible and revisit it monthly to renew purpose and align actions with the vision.

Bring these elements together into a simple Freedom Vision document: a short narrative of post-mortgage life, a numeric plan for retirement acceleration, a one-page generational equity strategy, and your written "why" with countermeasures. Review it quarterly and use it as the anchor for decisions about draws, lump payments, and trade-offs—so every financial move either advances your Freedom Vision or is consciously deferred for a stronger future.

CHAPTER 12:

Common Questions and Concerns

"Isn't this just robbing Peter to pay Paul?"

Many people hear "use a HELOC to pay down a mortgage" and instinctively think it's a wash — moving debt around without real progress. The difference lies in timing, interest mechanics, and disciplined cash flow management. A HELOC acceleration strategy intentionally uses a low-cost, flexible revolving line to reduce higher-cost, amortizing debt faster, then channels incoming cash flow to pay the HELOC down quickly. The aim is not to shuffle balances indefinitely but to alter the sequence of interest accrual and principal reduction so that more dollars hit principal sooner. That change in cash-flow pattern, when combined with guardrails (reserves, cooling-off rules, chunk payments), delivers genuine reduction in total interest paid and shortens the mortgage timeline. It isn't "robbing Peter to pay Paul" when the plan reduces total interest and increases net equity rather than merely moving unpaid balances back and forth.

A clear way to see the difference is to separate the mechanical transfer from disciplined intent. Randomly transferring balances without a repayment plan is exactly the risky behavior critics fear. The acceleration strategy, by contrast, pairs each draw with an explicit repayment sequence: a funded reserve, an automated income routing to the HELOC, and scheduled chunk principal payments on the mortgage. Those controls prevent the cyclical use of credit and ensure the HELOC functions as a temporary lever — a purposeful step toward net interest savings and an earlier mortgage payoff.

The mathematics that prove the concept hinges on reducing the amortizing loan's principal early. Mortgage interest accrues on the outstanding principal; paying additional principal early lowers future interest because subsequent interest is calculated on a smaller base. Compared to making only scheduled mortgage payments, a plan that moves an extra principal chunk onto the mortgage immediately reduces the amortization path and total interest. In simple terms: if you pay an extra principal amount P toward a mortgage balance, the future interest saved approximates the sum of scheduled interest that would have accrued on that portion over the remaining term.

A concise illustrative example helps:

Mortgage balance: $200,000 at 4.5% fixed, 30 years.

HELOC available at 6.0% variable (short window or promotional period might be lower).

Strategy: draw $20,000 from the HELOC to make a one-time principal reduction on the mortgage, then direct monthly cash flow to rapidly pay down the HELOC.

Basic formulas to compare outcomes:

Mortgage interest for a given period is roughly interest = outstanding_balance × rate_period. Use $\text{interest} = B \cdot r$ for a simple monthly estimate where r is the monthly rate.

The present value of interest saved by prepaying principal depends on remaining term; early principal reduction reduces future interest payments proportional to how long that principal would have stayed on the mortgage.

Numerical intuition: paying $20,000 off a 4.5% mortgage immediately saves approximately $20{,}000 \times 0.045 = \$900$ in interest in the first year alone, and continues to reduce interest each subsequent year as amortization on the remaining balance shrinks. Even if the HELOC carries a higher rate temporarily, the net effect can be positive if the HELOC is paid down fast enough so that the higher interest window is short and the larger, ongoing mortgage interest savings compound over many years.

Interest calculation differences matter greatly to the outcome. Key distinctions:

Mortgage (amortizing fixed loan): interest is computed against a steadily declining principal; each payment contains interest then principal. Early principal payments reduce the schedule and compound savings over the remaining term.

HELOC (revolving line): interest is typically variable and charged on the average daily balance; payments may be interest-only or include principal. Because HELOC interest accrues on the day-by-day balance, rapid repayment (via automated deposits and chunk payments) minimizes the days large balances persist and thus reduces total interest on the HELOC.

Compounding and timing: mortgages have fixed amortization schedules that lock in long-term interest exposure, while HELOC exposure is highly time-sensitive — a large HELOC balance held for a single month costs far more than one kept for a single week. Shortening the duration of HELOC-funded exposure is therefore critical.

A simple comparison table of mechanics (conceptual):

Mortgage: long-term rate stability; principal declines slowly unless you prepay; interest costs spread over many years.

HELOC: short-term flexibility; variable pricing and daily interest; optimal when used briefly and paid down quickly.

Practical sensitivity points and risk considerations: if HELOC rates spike, costs can temporarily exceed savings; if the borrower lacks discipline and does not channel income to the HELOC, the plan fails and becomes circular debt. Therefore, the plan's success depends on three pillars: (1) a disciplined repayment cadence that keeps HELOC duration short, (2) reasonable rate spreads and/or promotional windows that make temporary borrowing efficient, and (3) strong governance (reserves, stop triggers, and accountability).

In short, the strategy is not intrinsically "robbing Peter to pay Paul" when executed with discipline because it changes the time value of money: it shifts when principal is reduced on the amortizing loan so that cumulative interest paid over the life of the mortgage declines. The math favors the approach when the incremental interest cost for the HELOC is low relative to the mortgage rate savings achieved by early principal reduction and when repayment of the HELOC is rapid. Always model scenarios before drawing: test best-case, base-case, and worst-case rate paths, and confirm that the net present value of the strategy under realistic timelines is positive before proceeding.

***

Section 1: Common Questions and Concerns — What if Interest Rates Skyrocket?

Interest-rate spikes are the single biggest macro risk to any HELOC acceleration plan, so start by putting the risk in perspective with historical context. Rates move in cycles and have gone through long periods of both low and high levels; short-term shocks can be sharp, but long-term averages smooth out. Understanding past moves helps you model plausible scenarios (mild, moderate, severe) instead of imagining only the worst case. Use historical ranges to set stress-test bands for your plan: what happens if rates rise 200, 400, or 800 basis points and remain elevated for 6, 12, or 36 months? Modeling those bands turns anxiety into actionable contingencies.

Risk mitigation is about reducing exposure and shortening the window of vulnerability. First, limit the time a large HELOC balance remains outstanding: make HELOC draws as brief as possible and prioritize rapid paydown with automated cash flow. Maintain a robust reserve (three months of HELOC payments or more) so short spikes don't force missed payments. Consider hybrid protections: use interest-rate caps or lender conversion options to lock a portion of outstanding balances into fixed payments, or stagger draws so you never carry your full target exposure at one rate point. Finally, build behavioral controls—cooling-off periods for discretionary draws, mandatory check-ins with your accountability partner, and pre-set stop rules if rates or payment stress hit your thresholds.

Break-even calculations let you test whether an acceleration move still makes sense under higher rates. The core calculation compares the interest saved on the long-term mortgage by prepaying principal to the incremental interest cost of carrying the HELOC funds during the paydown period. Compute: incremental_HELOC_cost = HELOC_rate_excess × average_HELOC_balance × duration_in_years; mortgage_interest_savings ≈ mortgage_rate × prepayment_amount × effective_remaining_years (adjusted for amortization). Run best-case, base-case, and worst-case scenarios and include the probability-weighted outcomes you find most realistic. If the HELOC incremental cost in the worst-case still leaves a positive net present value when compared to mortgage savings, the strategy remains robust; if not, pause or scale back.

Exit strategies are the final line of defense and should be defined before you draw. Common and practical exits include: (1) Rapid repayment — accelerate payments, use reserves and windfalls to retire the HELOC quickly; (2) Convert to a fixed-rate installment loan — lock outstanding balance into predictable payments if rates are rising; (3) Refinance — roll the HELOC into a longer fixed product if market conditions and closing costs make sense; (4) Close the line and rely on savings — if you can't manage volatility, close the HELOC to eliminate future variable risk. Each exit has costs and timing implications, so predefine triggers that prompt each option (for example, HELOC rate > X% for Y days, or reserve depleted to <Z% of target).

Operationalize protection with concrete rules: require a pre-draw checklist that verifies reserve level and cooling-off status; run a weekly stress dashboard showing current HELOC rate, days until next reset, reserve coverage, and break-even sensitivity; and set automatic alerts for your exit triggers. Finally, simulate an adverse scenario once a year with your planner or advisor so the team understands mechanics and emotional responses are less likely to drive rash choices. Done well, rate risk becomes a managed variable rather than a show-stopper for an otherwise effective acceleration strategy.

***

Section 2: Common Questions and Concerns — Why Don't Banks Advertise This?

Banks and mortgage lenders operate in an ecosystem where their primary revenue comes from long-term interest streams and related servicing fees. Encouraging borrowers to accelerate principal paydown reduces the life of those interest streams and therefore diminishes the predictable income the bank expects from a mortgage portfolio. A strategy that intentionally shortens loan duration or shifts interest exposure to short, self-managed bursts runs counter to the commercial incentives that shape typical lender product design and marketing.

There is a clear conflict of interest baked into that incentive structure. Lenders make more money when loans remain outstanding longer, and many institutional processes—secondary market packaging, servicing operations, and investor yield models—are optimized for predictable, long amortization schedules. While banks will offer tools that improve customer retention or cross-sell products, they rarely promote tactics that materially accelerate payoff of the core product that funds their margins.

Beyond direct profit motives, practical and regulatory factors mute bank promotion of acceleration techniques. Banks must design products and communications for broad compliance, credit risk management, and consumer protection; recommending strategies that rely on disciplined borrower behavior, rapid payoff of variable lines, or aggressive cash-flow manipulation could be viewed as risky or outside standard servicing guidance. Promoting HELOC-driven acceleration could increase operational complexity and potential liability for lenders if borrowers misapply the technique and then default.

Industry structure also matters. Mortgage origination, loan servicing, and HELOC lines often sit with different entities or are bundled into distinct investors' portfolios. That separation creates friction for any unified messaging that would cross-promote one product as a tool to defeat the revenue profile of another. In addition, the secondary mortgage market and investor covenants can constrain how aggressively a lender markets alternatives that might lead to prepayment concentrations they did not underwrite.

Finally, consumer heterogeneity means the strategy isn't universally appropriate. Banks prefer one-size-fits-most messages that avoid suggesting nuanced financial engineering; advertising a tactic that requires disciplined cash flow, risk controls, and contingency planning could bring a surge of ill-prepared consumers and reputational risk. For those reasons, you're more likely to find independent educators, planners, and fintech coaches explaining acceleration mechanics than mortgage banks advertising them.

Understanding why banks don't promote this approach helps you evaluate it more clearly: the lack of marketing is not proof the idea is invalid, but it does signal the need for careful modeling, personal discipline, and professional advice before implementation.

***

Section 3: Common Questions and Concerns — Can I Still Build an Emergency Fund?

Using a HELOC as part of your cash-management toolkit can feel like a shortcut to liquidity, but it's important to separate the conceptual convenience of a line of credit from the financial safety that a dedicated emergency fund provides. A HELOC offers on-demand access to cash, which makes it tempting to treat as your safety net. That access is valuable, yet unlike a funded emergency account it is contingent on lender terms, market rates, and credit availability — any of which can change quickly. Relying solely on a HELOC for emergencies exposes you to funding risk and interest cost at the precise moment you can least afford either.

A robust approach keeps the HELOC and emergency fund as complementary tools rather than substitutes. A cash emergency fund — typically held in a liquid, low-volatility account — provides immediate, no-interest access for short-term shocks (car repairs, short job gaps, urgent medical expenses). A HELOC can serve as a secondary backstop: a contingent line to lean on when the cash fund is depleted or when you need larger, short-term liquidity (urgent home repairs, temporary business shortfalls). Prioritize building a primary cash reserve first, then treat the HELOC as an extra layer of protection rather than the first line of defense.

Balance considerations matter: how much cash to hold versus how much to rely on a HELOC depends on your income stability, household expenses, and risk tolerance. For most households, a three-to-six-month cash reserve remains a sensible baseline; more conservative plans raise that to six-plus months if income is uncertain or expenses are volatile. If you maintain a smaller cash reserve while carrying a HELOC, increase the HELOC-specific reserve rule (for example, enough to cover three months of HELOC payments) and document explicit triggers for when to draw from cash versus the line. This hybrid sizing reduces rollover risk and gives you clear rules during stress.

There are situations where using both makes strong sense. Households with stable income but seasonal cash needs can keep a modest cash buffer for day-to-day shocks while relying on a HELOC for larger, predictable seasonal shortfalls. Investors or landlords often pair a liquid emergency fund with a HELOC because property repairs can require larger, unpredictable sums that are impractical to hold in cash. In all cases, define decision rules up front: when to tap cash, when to use the HELOC, repayment priorities after a draw, and how to replenish the cash reserve. Those rules prevent reactive borrowing and protect the household from compounding interest costs.

Operational safeguards help the hybrid model work. Maintain a written emergency flowchart (cash first for X events; HELOC for Y events), automate transfers that rebuild cash reserves after any draw, and keep the HELOC unused and monitored (annual review, line-availability check). Run stress tests annually imagining scenarios such as job loss or interest spikes and confirm your combined plan still covers living costs for your target horizon. When done deliberately, a funded emergency account plus a HELOC backstop gives you both immediate security and strategic liquidity without sacrificing discipline or exposing you to unnecessary funding risk.

***

Section 4: Common Questions and Concerns — What About Investing Instead?

Choosing between using extra cash to accelerate mortgage payoff or directing it into investments is a common and important trade-off. The core distinction lies in guaranteed versus uncertain returns: paying down mortgage principal gives a predictable, risk-free return equal to the mortgage's interest rate because you permanently reduce future interest costs. Investing exposes you to market risk and volatility with the possibility of higher long-term returns, but those returns are not guaranteed and can be negative in the short term. Framing the choice this way helps you weigh certainty against potential upside and anchors decisions in measurable comparisons rather than emotion.

Guaranteed return versus market risk is fundamentally a question of math and probability. A dollar used to reduce mortgage principal at a 4% rate effectively "earns" you a 4% after-tax return (adjusted for deductibility rules). That return is certain and immediate because it lowers future interest. By contrast, historical stock market returns have averaged higher than typical mortgage rates over long horizons, but they come with variance—years of losses can wipe out nominal gains and make timing important. Compare expected investment returns net of fees and taxes to your effective mortgage rate; if your mortgage rate is low and your expected after-tax investment return is meaningfully higher, investing may be attractive, but only with the temperament to tolerate volatility.

Psychological factors often tip the scale as much as arithmetic does. Many people prefer the emotional security of owning their home outright and the stress reduction that comes with lower monthly obligations. Others thrive on market exposure and are comfortable with short-term swings for long-term gain. Behavioral biases matter: investors prone to panic selling could lose gains in market downturns, making a mortgage-payoff path emotionally safer and more likely to succeed. Be honest about how you respond to risk and which outcome—guaranteed debt reduction or potential higher returns—keeps you calmer and more consistent over time.

Balanced approach options let you capture both benefits without committing fully to one path. Dollar-cost averaging into investments while making modest extra mortgage payments spreads risk and keeps momentum on both fronts. Another hybrid is the 60/40 rule: allocate a percentage of extra cash to mortgage prepayment and the remainder to retirement or taxable investments, then rebalance annually. You can also prioritize a short emergency fund, pay down high-interest consumer debt first, and then split marginal savings between investments and HELOC/mortgage acceleration based on regular reviews of rates and goals.

Your personal risk tolerance and time horizon should drive the decision. If you have a long investment horizon, diversified retirement accounts, and an emergency fund in place, leaning toward investments may maximize long-term wealth. If you value liquidity, predictability, and lowering monthly obligations—especially approaching retirement or with unstable income—accelerating mortgage payoff or maintaining a HELOC reserve may be wiser. Model scenarios: run a five- and ten-year projection comparing net worth under different allocation splits, and test outcomes under adverse market and rate environments to see which path you can live with psychologically.

Finally, make the decision reversible and reviewable. Start with a defined experiment—redirect a fixed portion of monthly surplus to investments for six months while maintaining planned chunk payments on the mortgage—and measure how you feel and what the numbers show. Revisit the plan annually or when life changes occur (job shift, major expense, rate move). Whatever path you choose, document the rules that guide reallocation so choices remain intentional, defensible, and aligned with both your financial goals and how you actually behave when markets and rates move.

***

Section 5: Common Questions and Concerns — Is This Legal?

Yes — using a HELOC as part of an intentional acceleration strategy is legal when executed transparently and within the terms of your loan documents. Homeowners have the contractual right to borrow against an approved line of credit, make principal prepayments on their mortgage, and allocate their own cash and credit as they see fit. The strategy relies on lawful actions: drawing on an agreed HELOC, applying funds to mortgage principal, and managing repayments according to the contracts you signed with your lender. Where laws or lender rules place limits (for example, prepayment penalties in rare loans or specific servicer requirements), those are contractual constraints to respect, not legal barriers to the overall approach.

There are no loopholes or hidden tricks required to make this work — the effectiveness comes from disciplined cash flow and timing, not deception. Successful implementation depends on following disclosure and authorization rules, honoring loan covenants, and avoiding any misrepresentation to lenders or title companies. Do not manipulate documents, misstate use of funds, or attempt to conceal encumbrances; doing so risks default, legal exposure, and loss of lender protections. The ethical, sustainable path is fully aboveboard: model outcomes, document decisions, keep clear records of draws and uses, and execute according to the HELOC and mortgage terms.

Everything is above board when you prioritize transparency and sound record-keeping. Keep copies of loan agreements, draw notices, application forms, and confirmations of principal reductions. If you use HELOC funds for home improvements and expect tax deductibility, retain invoices and proofs of payment; if transfers involve joint owners or trusts, document required consents. When you follow the paperwork and maintain clear financial records, you create an audit trail that protects you and demonstrates legitimate intent to actuaries, lenders, or tax authorities if questions arise.

Maintaining constructive bank relationships preserves access and reduces operational friction. Notify your servicer if required by your agreement for certain transactions, and respond promptly to any lender inquiries. Avoid behaviors that would signal credit risk — large, unexplained draws without repayment plans, bounced payments, or sudden title transfers — because those actions invite scrutiny and can trigger remedies like acceleration. If a HELOC is part of a broader refinance or estate plan, coordinate with counsel and the lender so all parties understand the sequence and no contractual covenant is unintentionally breached.

In practice, sensible safeguards keep the strategy legal and durable: review loan documents for prepayment or draw restrictions; model stress scenarios and stop triggers; document the purpose and timing of each draw; consult a real estate attorney or tax advisor for complex situations; and keep communications with lenders professional and proactive. When you follow the contracts, preserve full disclosure, and manage risk responsibly, the HELOC acceleration approach is a lawful, practical method to shorten mortgage life and build equity.

***

Common Questions and Concerns — 25+ Frequently Asked Questions and Answers

Technical

What exactly is a HELOC and how does it differ from a home mortgage? A HELOC is a revolving line of credit secured by your home that you can draw from as needed, while a mortgage is typically a fixed or amortizing loan with set monthly payments; the HELOC's flexibility and variable interest make it useful for short-term liquidity and targeted principal-paydown strategies.

How is HELOC interest calculated? Interest on a HELOC is usually calculated on the average daily balance using a variable index plus margin, so the amount you owe changes with daily usage and rate resets rather than the fixed amortization schedule of a standard mortgage.

When do HELOC rates reset and what should I watch for? Rate resets depend on your contract (monthly, quarterly, etc.); monitor the next reset date, the index published, margin changes, and any floor or cap provisions because those determine payment volatility and risk exposure.

Are there prepayment penalties on HELOCs or mortgages I should know about? Most HELOCs and modern mortgages don't have prepayment penalties, but some older or specialized loans may; always check the loan documents for prepayment clauses before initiating an acceleration plan.

Can I use HELOC funds to pay off my mortgage principal directly? Yes — you may draw on an approved HELOC and instruct the funds to be applied as a principal reduction on your mortgage, provided you follow lender procedures and any contractual requirements for payoff application.

How does amortization change if I make chunk principal payments? Making large principal reductions shortens the amortization path: future interest accruals decrease and the loan either pays off earlier or requires smaller future payments depending on whether the lender reamortizes or leaves payments unchanged.

Will using a HELOC trigger automatic reviews or covenants from my mortgage servicer? Generally not if you act within contract terms, but large title changes, transfers, or other covenant breaches can prompt servicer review; document transactions and consult servicers if your loan has special conditions.

Financial

How do I compare the math between HELOC interest costs and mortgage interest savings? Compare the HELOC incremental cost (rate × average balance × duration) to the mortgage interest reduced by the prepayment (mortgage rate × prepayment amount × effective remaining years); run multiple scenarios to test sensitivity to rate moves.

What size reserve should I keep before using a HELOC for acceleration? A prudent minimum is three months of HELOC payments; more conservative households keep six months. The reserve protects against rate spikes, income shocks, and prevents missed payments that could trigger acceleration.

Does HELOC interest remain tax-deductible? Interest deductibility depends on how funds are used and current tax rules; typically only funds used to buy, build, or substantially improve the secured home qualify, so document uses carefully and consult your tax advisor.

How frequently should I run break-even and stress models? Run break-even and stress tests before major draws and at least quarterly thereafter, or whenever rates move materially, so you understand if the strategy remains financially advantageous under new conditions.

What happens to my net worth if rates spike temporarily? Short-term rate spikes increase interest expense and reduce monthly cash flow, but if the HELOC exposure is short and principal was applied to the mortgage, the long-term net worth may still improve; guardrails determine whether short-term pain becomes permanent loss.

Should I prioritize mortgage prepayment or retirement investing? It depends on effective after-tax mortgage rate, expected investment returns, horizon, and psychological preference; run comparative scenarios and consider a hybrid approach that advances both goals modestly.

How should I treat windfalls or bonuses in the strategy? Use windfalls primarily for chunk principal payments and reserve replenishment; a pre-agreed split (for example, 70% principal / 30% discretionary) keeps momentum while allowing small rewards.

Practical

How do I document draws and principal applications for audits or tax purposes? Keep copies of draw confirmations, transfer receipts, mortgage payoff credits, invoices for home improvements, and dated screenshots of account activity to create a clear audit trail.

What simple automation saves the most effort? Automate income routing to the HELOC for core cash flow, set recurring transfers to your reserve account, and schedule calendar reminders for weekly dashboard updates to maintain discipline with minimal friction.

How do I handle unexpected expenses while engaged in the acceleration plan? Use your cash emergency fund first; if insufficient, draw from the HELOC with a written plan for rapid repayment and prioritize replenishing the cash reserve immediately after resolving the expense.

When should I stop drawing from the HELOC? Stop new draws when reserves fall below the threshold, after two missed payments, or upon receiving any lender acceleration notice; predefine these stop triggers and adhere to them strictly.

How do I communicate this strategy to service providers or co-owners? Share a concise one-page summary, the planned timeline, and contact information; if co-owners or trustees are involved, get written consent where required and document any joint decisions.

What tools make tracking easiest? A simple spreadsheet or one-page dashboard that tracks HELOC balance, reserve balance, principal paid, upcoming reset dates, and a rolling 12-month interest-avoided projection provides high signal with low maintenance.

Can I run this strategy on a rental property HELOC? Yes, but rental HELOCs carry different rules, tax considerations, and cash-flow dynamics; ensure tenant income stability, separate accounting, and consult your CPA about deductibility and depreciation interactions.

Personal

How do I get my partner on board? Start with transparent numbers, share the dashboard, agree on decision rules (cooling-off, reserve levels), and set short review cadences so both parties feel informed and heard rather than surprised.

What if I'm not disciplined enough to make rapid HELOC repayments? Don't start the acceleration strategy until you can automate transfers, establish reserves, or secure accountability support; otherwise the HELOC can become persistent high-cost debt rather than a temporary tool.

How do I stay motivated over the long timeline? Use visualization, track small wins on your dashboard, celebrate non-spend milestones, and engage an accountability partner to sustain behavior through plateaus and setbacks.

Is it ever appropriate to use the HELOC for non-home investments? It can be, but that increases complexity, tax uncertainty, and risk; only do so with a clear ROI plan, professional tax advice, and heightened guardrails to avoid jeopardizing your home.

How often should I review the plan with professionals? Meet with your tax advisor and financial planner at least annually and consult legal counsel any time title, trust, or estate interactions arise; more frequent reviews are wise when rates or life circumstances shift.

What emotional pitfalls should I watch for? Watch for overconfidence during early wins (leading to larger risky draws), shame during setbacks (which can cause hiding activity), and comparison-driven decisions; have pre-agreed stop rules and an accountability process to counteract emotions.

Can the strategy be scaled down for modest mortgages or modest incomes? Yes — scale the plan to fit your cash flow: smaller, less frequent chunk payments, lower reserve targets, and conservative draw caps let lower-income households still gain benefit without undue risk.

These concise FAQs cover technical mechanics, financial math, practical operations, and personal behavior. Use them as a quick reference when evaluating or running a HELOC acceleration plan, and adapt any answers to your circumstances with professional advice where needed.

CHAPTER 13:

Your Personalized Action Plan — Self-Assessment Checklist

Begin with a clear financial readiness score to understand whether your current balance sheet supports a HELOC acceleration plan. Tally liquid reserves, stable monthly cash flow, emergency fund size, and current debt obligations; convert these into a simple score (for example, 0–100) where higher values indicate stronger readiness. Use this score to set minimum gating conditions—such as a reserve equal to three months of HELOC payments and no recent missed obligations—so you only proceed when the numbers show a reasonable margin for error.

Assess discipline honestly with a short behavioral inventory. Track recent financial behaviors for 90 days: did you stick to budgets, avoid impulse draws, and apply windfalls to goals? Rate consistency, impulse control, and use of automation (auto-payments, transfers) to produce a discipline score. If automation and accountability are weak, strengthen those systems first—install guards like cooling-off periods, mandatory approvals, and an accountability partner—before committing to HELOC-driven moves.

Evaluate risk tolerance with scenarios, not adjectives. Create three stress tests (mild, moderate, severe) that model rate spikes, temporary income loss, and property value declines; then record how each outcome affects cash flow, reserve depletion, and the need to exit the strategy. Your tolerance is the set of outcomes you can withstand without sacrificing essential living standards or triggering irreversible actions like forced sales. Use this analysis to set hard numerical limits—maximum HELOC exposure, acceptable rate thresholds, and minimum reserve levels.

Analyze life situation factors that materially change the strategy's suitability. Consider near-term events (job changes, planned large purchases, family additions), medium-term plans (retirement horizon, business launches), and legal or estate complexities (co-ownership, trusts). If major life transitions are imminent, either postpone aggressive acceleration or scale the plan conservatively so it remains flexible. Document any conditional clauses (e.g., pause if job changes within 12 months) to keep the plan responsive to real life.

Assemble a go/no-go decision matrix that maps your readiness, discipline, risk tolerance, and life situation to a simple action outcome. For example: green = proceed with full plan if readiness ≥ 75, discipline ≥ 70, and risk cushion met; yellow = proceed with conservative pilot (smaller draws, higher reserve) if scores fall in midrange; red = pause and build reserves or automation if scores are low. Tie each color to exact operational rules—reserve size, draw caps, cooling periods, and professional consultation requirements—so the matrix is an executable control, not just a diagnostic.

Turn assessment into a short implementation checklist and timeline. If you land in green or yellow, list immediate steps: fund reserve to target, enable automated income routing, set up the weekly dashboard, choose an accountability partner, and schedule a modeling review with a planner or CPA. Assign dates and owners for each task so momentum begins. If you land in red, document the remediation plan (target reserve, automation steps, behavioral goals) and set a re-assessment date so the decision to pause becomes proactive rather than passive.

Finally, treat the action plan as living governance: review readiness scores and the decision matrix quarterly, rerun stress scenarios when rates or life events change, and keep clear records of all draws, repayments, and communications. A personalized assessment that is honest, numeric, and tied to concrete operational rules gives you the confidence to act when conditions are right and the clarity to stop or pivot when they are not.

***

Section 1: Your Personalized Action Plan — Your Numbers Worksheet

Start with your current mortgage details and make them explicit. Record the outstanding principal, interest rate, remaining term, monthly payment breakdown (principal vs interest), next reset or recast date if applicable, and any prepayment penalties or re-amortization policies. These facts set the baseline for every comparison and should be pulled from your most recent statement, so projections use current numbers rather than memory.

Next, run a focused income and expense analysis to establish true monthly cash flow available for acceleration. List all reliable income sources (after-tax amounts) and routine monthly obligations (mortgage, utilities, insurance, taxes, minimum debt payments, and living expenses). Subtract essentials from income to calculate discretionary cash flow available for reserve funding, chunk payments, and extra HELOC servicing. Do a 3-month average if income is variable and include a line for predictable seasonality or bonus timing.

Calculate available equity precisely before sizing any HELOC draw. Start with an up-to-date estimated market value (recent appraisal, comparable sales, or broker price opinion) then subtract total liens and an appropriate buffer for valuation volatility (for example 10–20% depending on market). The result is conservative usable equity; note lender LTV limits and any second-lien rules so your practical available credit reflects both value and underwriting constraints.

Determine a prudent HELOC size using the usable equity and your operational rules. Base the line amount on (1) the maximum LTV your lender allows, (2) your personal exposure limit (percentage of equity you're comfortable borrowing), and (3) reserve and repayment cadence — for example, set a target HELOC cushion equal to planned draws plus a three-month payment reserve. Express the working HELOC target as two numbers: the institutional cap (what lender may offer) and your personal cap (what you will actually use).

Project a realistic timeline that ties numbers to sequencing. Model scenarios showing how a single chunk payment of size X applied to the mortgage today reduces remaining term and interest, then show the expected HELOC repayment schedule given your weekly or monthly automated contributions. Produce three timeline variants (conservative, base, aggressive) using differing chunk sizes and repayment speeds so you can see days-to-zero for the HELOC and years shaved from the mortgage. Include key checkpoint dates: reserve funded, first chunk paid, three-month review, and annual reconciliation.

Finish by turning raw numbers into an actionable one-page worksheet: fields for mortgage snapshot, monthly cash-flow summary, usable equity and HELOC caps, reserve target, planned chunk amounts, and a three-scenario timeline with checkpoint dates. Keep this worksheet current, update it weekly during execution, and use it to power your dashboard, decision matrix, and go/no-go triggers so every draw and payment is justified by the numbers.

***

Section 2: Your Personalized Action Plan — 90-Day Implementation Plan

Week 1–2: Preparation and research Begin by gathering all essential documents and running the numbers that will drive decisions: your latest mortgage statement, recent property valuation or comps, pay stubs or income statements, and a three-month snapshot of bank activity. Use these to complete the Numbers Worksheet (mortgage balance, effective interest rate, monthly principal/interest split, discretionary cash flow). Simultaneously, set behavioral foundations: choose an accountability partner, enable basic automations (bill pay and a dedicated reserve account), and write a short Freedom Vision paragraph that clarifies why you'll endure temporary restraint. These preparatory steps create both the factual baseline and the personal commitment you'll need to act decisively.

Week 3–4: HELOC shopping and application Shop competitively and document offers so you can compare true costs and terms: index and margin, payment options (interest-only vs principal + interest), reset frequency, availability periods, fees, and any caps/floors. Request lender disclosures and ask about conversion options or fixed-rate locks for outstanding balances. While applications are in process, finalize your reserve target (minimum three months of HELOC payments recommended) and draft your pre-draw checklist: reserve funded, cooling-off rule in place, and automation triggers tested. Submit applications only when your paperwork is complete and your personal cap (how much you will actually use) is set.

Week 5–8: Approval and setup When approval arrives, verify every material term against the offer you compared. Establish account access, link ACH for income routing, and confirm how draws are executed (checks, transfers, or direct pay). Set up the one-page dashboard and schedule your weekly 10–15 minute review time on the calendar. Fund the reserve to the target level before making any non-emergency draws and test the automated flows so income deposits apply as intended. If any lender conditions require disclosure or action (e.g., notice for large draws or ownership verification), complete them now to prevent compliance issues later.

Week 9–12: Strategy launch and rhythm establishment Launch with a conservative pilot draw and a single chunk principal payment sized to your base-case scenario. Execute the pre-draw checklist and document the transaction thoroughly. For the first month, focus on discipline: hit automated repayment targets, perform daily 60-second balance checks, and hold weekly dashboard reviews with your accountability partner. At the end of week 12, run a formal 30-/60-/90-day reconciliation: measure actual cash flows vs. projections, review reserve sufficiency, confirm lender communications are clean, and re-run break-even/stress tests given current rates. Use this checkpoint to decide whether to scale to your planned cadence, maintain the conservative pilot, or pause for adjustments.

Operational rules to enforce across the 90 days

Reserve rule: never make discretionary draws until the reserve equals the agreed target.

Cooling rule: require 24–72 hours for discretionary draws above your threshold.

Stop triggers: halt new draws if reserves fall below target, if two payments are missed, or on any acceleration notice.

Documentation: record every draw, transfer, and principal application with timestamps and receipts.

Deliverables by day 90

One-page Numbers Worksheet updated with actuals.

Live dashboard and weekly review habit established.

Reserve funded and automated flows operational.

First chunk payment executed and reconciled.

A go/no-go decision recorded for scaling the strategy.

This 90-day plan emphasizes measured action, documentation, and behavioral scaffolding so you move from planning to tested execution with controls in place. After day 90, continue quarterly stress tests, annual professional reviews, and maintain the governance habits that keep the HELOC a tool for acceleration rather than a source of risk.

***

Section 3: Your Personalized Action Plan — Tracking Templates

A simple, reliable monthly HELOC balance tracker is the backbone of disciplined execution. Create a one-page template that records the opening balance, draws, repayments, interest charged, and the closing balance for each month. Include a column for average daily balance if your lender reports it, and a running total of principal applied to the mortgage from HELOC funds. Use this tracker to spot creeping usage, measure whether automated repayments are arriving on schedule, and verify that chunk payments actually reduced mortgage principal. Keep prior months visible so trendlines are obvious and reconciliation is quick.

A focused cash flow monitor turns abstract inflows and outflows into operational decisions. Build a month-by-month cash flow sheet that lists net income, fixed obligations, discretionary spending, emergency fund transfers, HELOC servicing (interest + principal), and planned chunk payments. Include a reconciliation row showing "available for HELOC strategy" after essentials and reserve funding. Update it weekly during execution to catch timing gaps (payroll lags, one-off bills) that could undermine planned repayments, and keep a short notes cell to record anomalies that require follow-up or reserve replenishment.

A progress visualization chart makes momentum visible and motivating. Transform core metrics from the trackers into visual elements: a stacked area showing mortgage balance vs HELOC balance over time, a bar chart of monthly principal paid, and a small line for reserve coverage as a percentage of target. Add a projected trajectory overlay for your base, conservative, and aggressive scenarios so you can see divergence from plan immediately. Visual cues are powerful: color-code stop triggers (red) and safety buffers (green) so a glance tells you whether actions are on track or require intervention.

An annual review template formalizes the lessons and course corrections you need to stay solvent and effective. The template should prompt a summary of year-end balances (mortgage, HELOC, reserves), a review of all draws and their purposes, an updated stress test for current rate scenarios, tax documentation status (invoices, improvements, deductibility notes), and a short behavioral review (wins, slips, changes in discipline). Conclude with a concise action list for the coming year: reserve target adjustments, timeline updates, professional consultations needed, and any changes to decision rules or escape triggers.

Bundle these four templates into a single tracking pack: a monthly sheet for operational detail, a weekly cash-flow snapshot, a visual dashboard for quick status checks, and an annual review for governance. Keep digital copies that auto-populate charts from your monthly inputs and maintain a secure, versioned folder for receipts and lender statements. When templates are simple, current, and routinely reviewed, they convert intention into reproducible practice and make the HELOC strategy measurable, manageable, and far less emotionally risky.

***

Section 4: Your Personalized Action Plan — Milestone Map

First chunk payoff celebration The first significant principal reduction is a critical psychological and operational milestone: it proves the mechanics work and confirms your discipline. Mark the moment with a simple, cost-free ritual—take a photo of the updated dashboard, write a short note describing what you did and why it mattered, or share the win with your accountability partner. Use the occasion to verify paperwork (confirm the mortgage received the principal credit), replenish any reserves used to execute the chunk, and log lessons learned so you don't repeat avoidable friction on later moves.

25% mortgage reduction Reaching a quarter reduction in principal shifts the math and morale. Revisit your timeline and recompute break-even and stress scenarios so the new balance informs next-stage decisions about chunk sizing and cadence. Treat this as a governance checkpoint: confirm reserve health, update your HELOC exposure cap if appropriate, and review rate risk with your dashboard. Celebrate with a no-spend ritual that reinforces partnership—an at-home themed dinner or a shared evening of reflection on progress—so psychological rewards stay aligned with financial discipline.

50% mortgage reduction Hitting the halfway mark is both symbolic and materially powerful: your monthly interest burden has meaningfully declined and the remaining term becomes more controllable. At this stage, assess whether to shift strategy toward faster retirement acceleration or maintain the existing cadence to maximize interest avoidance. Conduct a deeper professional check: meet with a financial planner or CPA to re-run long-term projections, revisit tax treatment of interest, and ensure estate documents still reflect your goals. A milestone note in your file—what worked, what surprised you, and how behaviors held up—creates institutional memory for the rest of the journey.

75% mortgage reduction At 75% paid down, the finish line is visible and choices change from aggressive accumulation to preservation. Tighten risk controls: consider reducing HELOC usage, increasing reserve targets, and testing exit options (lock portions into fixed payments or plan a refinance) so you protect gains from late volatility. Use this milestone to transition celebrations from small rewards to tangible planning for Freedom Vision outcomes—book a preparatory trip, begin mapping how freed cash will be reallocated, and schedule an annual review to align retirement and legacy plans with the nearly-completed mortgage.

Final payoff countdown The final months require precision and emotional management—one misstep can feel disproportionate after so much progress. Create a short countdown plan with weekly execution checks: confirm final payoff amount, schedule the final transfer(s), ensure all lender communications are clear, and plan the administrative steps to remove the mortgage lien (payoff letter, recorded release). Protect the moment by pausing discretionary spending two to four weeks before the final payments and communicate clearly with any co-owners so the finish isn't delayed by overlooked approvals.

Freedom day! When the mortgage is paid, document the legal release, archive all supporting records, and celebrate intentionally in a way that honors the journey without undoing financial gains. Host a modest at-home celebration or family ritual that marks the transition from obligation to optionality—then translate monthly mortgage cash flow into a new plan: bolster retirement, seed generational goals, grow an opportunity fund, or simply increase quality time. Capture a short "Freedom Manifesto" in writing: what you'll start doing differently now and the small governance habits you'll keep to ensure the payoff delivers lasting benefit.

***

Section 5: Your Personalized Action Plan — Your Personal Success Contract

Commitment statement I commit to treating the HELOC acceleration strategy as a disciplined project with clear rules, measurable milestones, and transparent record-keeping. I will prioritize preserving my home, protecting my household cash flow, and advancing my Freedom Vision. I make this commitment to myself and my household with the intent to act consistently, revisit decisions with data, and pause the plan if core safeguards are threatened.

Rules you'll follow I will maintain a minimum reserve equal to three months of HELOC payments before any discretionary draw, require a 24 to 72 hour cooling period for non-essential draws above my threshold, automate transfers that prioritize HELOC repayment and reserve replenishment, and run weekly dashboard reviews. I will update my Numbers Worksheet monthly, run break-even and stress tests quarterly, and consult a financial or tax professional before major structural moves.

Lines you won't cross I will not draw funds from the HELOC for speculative investments, non-essential luxury purchases, or to cover habitual living expenses. I will not allow the HELOC balance to exceed my personal cap relative to usable equity, and I will not skip reserve replenishment after a draw. I will avoid behaviors that materially increase default risk such as missing scheduled payments, hiding transactions from co-owners, or transferring title without lender notification where required.

Accountability structure I will name an accountability partner and schedule a weekly 10–15 minute check-in to review the dashboard, acknowledge wins, and surface risks. I will keep written records of each draw, repayment, and principal application and share quarterly reconciliations with my financial advisor or CPA. If I breach any stop trigger—reserve below target, two missed payments, or HELOC rate above my predefined threshold—I will pause new draws immediately and follow the pre-agreed remediation steps with my accountability partner.

Signature and date By signing below I affirm this contract as my operative governance for the HELOC acceleration plan. I will honor these commitments and review this contract at least annually or whenever life or market conditions change.

Signed: ______________________________ Date: ______________________________

PART V: BEYOND MORTGAGE FREEDOM

Part V reframes mortgage payoff as the beginning of a new financial chapter rather than the end of a project. Freedom from a mortgage frees cash flow, reduces fixed obligations, and creates both emotional bandwidth and practical capacity to pursue larger goals. This section explores how to convert the monthly dollars once dedicated to housing into durable wealth, meaningful choices, and resilient systems that protect your gains and multiply their impact.

Reallocating freed cash wisely turns relief into momentum. Decide intentionally what the monthly mortgage amount will become: turbocharged retirement contributions, a diversified investment portfolio, an opportunity fund for business or education, or a combination of these. Use a short reallocation plan that assigns percentages (for example, 50% retirement, 30% opportunity fund, 20% lifestyle upgrade) and revisit it annually. Treat the first year of reallocation as an experiment—track outcomes, measure emotional satisfaction, and adjust allocations so new spending aligns with long-term goals rather than impulse.

Generational planning elevates mortgage freedom into legacy building. Paid-off property is a keystone asset that can be leveraged prudently—through estate planning, trust structures, or strategic loans to family for education or housing starts—to transfer advantage across generations. Map the pathways now: decide whether equity will be preserved, partially monetized for legacy investments, or used to fund intergenerational entrepreneurship. Pair those choices with clear legal documents and conversations so wealth transfers amplify freedom rather than create friction.

Reinventing work and purpose becomes feasible when fixed costs fall. With lower monthly obligations you can say yes to higher-value but riskier options: a career pivot, starting a business, reduced hours for caregiving, or purposeful sabbaticals. Create a staged plan for any occupational change that uses a portion of freed cash as a runway—three to twelve months depending on the risk—and maintain a conservative reserve so opportunity decisions remain reversible and stress-free.

Protecting gains demands the same discipline that paid the mortgage. Scale up your governance tools: increase automation for savings and investments, raise reserve targets appropriate to your new lifestyle, and formalize annual reviews with advisors for tax, investment, and estate alignment. Rewire rituals: a quarterly "freedom review" replaces mortgage checks with forward-looking planning—are your reallocations producing the life you imagined, and what course corrections are needed?

Finally, celebrate intentionally but modestly. Recognize mortgage freedom as a cultural and psychological milestone—hold a documented ritual, capture lessons learned in a short manifesto, and commit one visible act that signals the shift (a charitable donation, a micro-retreat, or a family story night). That act marks not only the end of payments but the start of choices governed by purpose. Part V is an invitation to steward new capacity with humility and strategy so mortgage freedom becomes the first step toward sustained financial flourishing rather than a singular destination.

CHAPTER 14:

Life After the Mortgage — The Transition Period

Adjusting to no mortgage payment The first months after your mortgage disappears create a curious mix of relief and disorientation: a line item you budgeted for years is suddenly gone and you must decide, deliberately, what replaces it. Start by pausing for a short inventory—confirm the payoff is recorded, obtain the lien release, and archive payoff paperwork—then give yourself a single week of low-stakes celebration to mark the accomplishment. After the brief celebration, resume with structure: keep your previous monthly mortgage amount in a holding bucket for 30–90 days while you observe how its absence affects cash flow, emotions, and spending impulses. That holding period prevents immediate splurges, helps you notice behavioral tendencies, and creates space to make thoughtful reallocation choices.

Cash flow reallocation Turn the former mortgage payment into a strategic resource by preassigning percentages to clear priorities rather than leaving it unstructured. Common allocations include bolstering retirement accounts, enlarging your opportunity or business fund, increasing liquid reserves, and funding meaningful experiences. Create a simple allocation rule (for example, 50% retirement; 25% opportunity fund; 15% reserve; 10% lifestyle) and automate transfers so the money moves before temptation arises. Revisit the split after six months and again at one year to fine-tune based on actual satisfaction and changing goals; automation plus periodic review converts windfall cash flow into durable progress.

Avoiding lifestyle inflation Lifestyle inflation is the stealth risk that erodes long-term benefit from mortgage freedom. Protect against it by declaring a modest, intentional lifestyle upgrade allowance—small, planned improvements that reward progress without undoing financial gains. Pair that allowance with a written rule: any discretionary spend above the allowance must be pre-approved and linked to a documented reason (celebration, investment in wellbeing, family goal). Keep a visible monthly dashboard that contrasts "new discretionary spending" with progress metrics (retirement funded, reserve level, net worth change) so you can see the tradeoff in real time and choose intentionally rather than habitually.

New financial goals setting Use the momentum of mortgage payoff to set refreshed, concrete financial goals with timelines and ownership. Translate broad aims (retire earlier, build generational wealth, fund education, start a business) into specific, measurable actions: contribution amounts, target dates, legal documents to prepare, and the professionals you'll consult. Create a short One-Year Plan that lists three priority goals, funding rules for each, and the checkpoints you'll use to measure progress quarterly. Documenting these goals turns the psychological win of mortgage freedom into a governance framework for scalable growth rather than a fleeting relief.

Operational governance during transition Keep the governance disciplines that carried you to payoff and adapt them for your new phase. Maintain a monthly review ritual to track the reallocation plan, run an annual stress test on reserves and lifestyle, and continue sharing results with your accountability partner or advisor. Update estate documents and beneficiary designations if the freedom materially changes your legacy intentions. By converting relief into rules, automated flows, and measured goals, the transition period becomes a deliberate launchpad for the next phase of financial life rather than an undefined pause.

Emotional and relational adjustments Finally, acknowledge the emotional and relational shifts that accompany mortgage freedom: partners, family members, or your inner voice may react in unexpected ways to new choices. Schedule a calm conversation about how the freed cash will be used and create a small ritual to mark the transition that includes everyone affected. Recognize mixed feelings—gratitude, anxiety about new choices, or pressure to spend—and name them aloud so decisions remain collaborative and intentional. Life after the mortgage is as much a relational and psychological transition as it is financial; addressing those dimensions early preserves the long-term benefits you earned.

***

Section 1: Life After the Mortgage — Keeping or Closing Your HELOC

Pros and cons of keeping it open Keeping your HELOC open after the mortgage is paid gives you flexible, low-friction access to capital for opportunistic needs—large home repairs, short business cash-flow gaps, or strategic investments—without having to reapply for credit. It functions like an insurance layer: unused, it costs nothing beyond potential minimal fees; used judiciously, it preserves liquidity while you redeploy freed mortgage cash toward longer-term goals. The downsides are real: an open HELOC can tempt discretionary borrowing, exposes you to future variable-rate increases, and may complicate estate or sale transactions. If you keep it, enforce strict personal rules (draw caps, cooling-off periods, reserve targets) so the line remains contingency capital, not a replacement for disciplined saving.

HELOC as an emergency fund alternative A HELOC can serve as a contingent backstop to a cash emergency fund, offering access to larger sums when catastrophic or infrequent expenses occur. However, it should not replace a core cash buffer because credit availability and interest costs can change precisely when you need funds most. Treat the HELOC as secondary protection: maintain a primary liquid fund for immediate, no-interest access and use the HELOC only for larger or longer-duration liquidity needs that would otherwise force asset sales. Document clear triggers for tapping the HELOC (reserve depleted, expense exceeds X, urgent home repair over Y dollars) and pair every draw with an automatic repayment plan to avoid rolling high-cost, long-term debt.

Opportunity fund concept An open HELOC is a powerful complement to an opportunity fund—a deliberately maintained pool (part cash, part contingent credit) for time-sensitive investments like business acquisitions, real estate bargains, or one-time education opportunities. The blended model preserves immediate buying power (cash) while allowing optional leverage (HELOC) for larger or faster deals, provided rules govern use: set a maximum leverage percentage, require a minimum cash cushion post-transaction, and demand a documented ROI or exit strategy before drawing. Use scenario planning to ensure the combined opportunity fund covers worst-case repayments without jeopardizing essential reserves or long-term goals.

Credit score implications Keeping a HELOC open can affect your credit profile in multiple ways: it increases available revolving credit which can lower utilization ratios and potentially boost scores, but high outstanding balances or frequent large draws can raise utilization and perceived risk. Inquiries and new accounts can produce short-term dips, while a long-standing, well-managed HELOC contributes positively to credit age and mix. If you decide to close the line, understand the tradeoffs: you eliminate future rate and behavioral risk but may reduce available credit and impact scoring dynamics. Monitor credit reports after any decision, and if you keep the HELOC, maintain low active utilization, timely payments, and periodic reviews to balance liquidity benefits against score effects.

Decision framework and rules of thumb Decide based on psychology, liquidity needs, and governance capacity. Keep the HELOC if you: 1) value optionality for large, infrequent needs; 2) have disciplined repayment processes; and 3) can tolerate variable-rate exposure. Close it if you: 1) are prone to impulsive draws; 2) prefer absolute debt elimination and simplicity; or 3) expect to sell or transfer the property soon and want a clean title. If keeping it, adopt strict rules: personal cap at a conservative percentage of usable equity, maintain a minimum cash reserve equal to three to six months of living or HELOC payments, require a 72-hour cooling period for discretionary draws, and run an annual stress test on rate spikes. That framework preserves the HELOC's strategic value while protecting the freedom you just earned.

***

Section 2: Life After the Mortgage — Wealth Acceleration Strategies

Retirement account maximization With your mortgage gone, redirecting the freed cash into tax-advantaged retirement accounts is one of the highest-leverage moves you can make. Max out employer-matched contributions first to capture free money, then prioritize IRAs or Roth IRAs based on your current tax bracket and future expectations. If you have access to a 401(k) or similar plan, consider increasing pre-tax contributions to lower taxable income or boosting Roth contributions for tax-free growth—whichever aligns with your long-term tax plan. Treat the first 12 months after payoff as an experiment window: automate the increased contributions, track the impact on your projected retirement timeline, and adjust allocation once you've validated cash-flow comfort.

Investment portfolio building Build a diversified, goal-aligned investment portfolio to translate monthly mortgage savings into long-term wealth. Start with a core allocation—broad domestic and international equity index funds, high-quality bonds, and a modest allocation to alternatives if appropriate—then layer tax-efficient strategies across taxable and retirement accounts. Reinvest dividends and use dollar-cost averaging to avoid timing risk as you scale contributions. Periodically rebalance to maintain target risk and to harvest gains or tax losses as strategy permits. As your asset base grows, introduce more granular planning: target glidepaths for horizon goals, tactical tilts for valuation or yield opportunities, and a written rebalancing rule to remove emotion from portfolio drift.

Real estate investment options Freeing monthly mortgage cash creates a runway to diversify into other real estate opportunities without jeopardizing liquidity. Consider turnkey rental purchases in well-researched markets, BRRRR (buy-rehab-rent-refinance-repeat) strategies if you want active value creation, or passive exposure through REITs and real estate mutual funds for lower operational burden. Evaluate each option with clear underwriting: expected cash-on-cash returns, cap-rate sensitivity, vacancy and maintenance stress tests, and exit scenarios. Use conservative leverage, especially early on, and require a minimum equity cushion and contingency fund for property-specific shocks so real estate investments enhance, rather than imperil, your newly gained stability.

Business investment opportunities Mortgage freedom can fund entrepreneurial moves that previously felt too risky. Whether you seed your side hustle, buy an existing small business, or scale a proven concept, treat business investment like any capital allocation: demand a business plan, cash runway, break-even timeline, and clear metrics for success. Protect downside by keeping a dedicated opportunity fund (cash + contingency credit), setting strict capital deployment thresholds, and staging investments based on milestone achievements. If you lack operational appetite, consider minority investments, revenue-share deals, or trusteeship in a business where you provide capital and governance but not day-to-day management.

Integrating strategies and governance Combine these pathways with a simple governance frame: set target allocation percentages for retirement, taxable investments, real estate, and business opportunities; automate transfers to each bucket; and review allocations quarterly. Maintain or increase emergency reserves as your asset mix becomes less liquid, and run at least one annual stress test to ensure growth plans survive job loss, market drawdowns, or property vacancies. Document decision rules for deploying larger sums—minimum due diligence, required advisor sign-off, and stop-loss thresholds—so the transition from mortgage payer to wealth builder happens with discipline and preserves the financial freedom you worked to achieve.

***

Section 3: Life After the Mortgage — Paying It Forward

Teaching others the strategy Turn your practical experience into clear lessons so others can benefit without repeating your mistakes. Break the strategy into teachable modules: the numbers worksheet, the 90-day pilot, risk controls, and behavioral guardrails. Offer short workshops or write a concise guide that uses your own before-and-after data to illustrate tradeoffs, how to run stress tests, and the exact governance rules that made the plan safe for you. Emphasize transparency: teach people to document draws, verify principal postings, and consult tax or legal advisers for special situations so they adopt the method responsibly rather than as a risky hack.

Mentoring opportunities Deepen impact by mentoring individuals or small groups through their first implementation steps. A mentor's value is behavioral and procedural—help mentees build their Numbers Worksheet, test automations, and run realistic scenarios for their specific income volatility and life stage. Set a simple mentorship cadence: an initial intake review, a co-built 90-day plan, weekly short check-ins during launch, and quarterly reconciliation for the first year. Use your experience to spot common pitfalls early—insufficient reserves, emotional overspending after windfalls, or ignoring lender disclosures—and provide corrective nudges that keep learners on the safe path.

Charitable giving from newfound cash flow Direct a portion of the freed mortgage cash into charitable giving as a disciplined habit that compounds social value and personal fulfillment. Create a giving plan that ties amounts to milestones (first chunk, 25% paid, Freedom Day) or a fixed percentage of the monthly mortgage savings. Consider impactful structures beyond one-off gifts: a donor-advised fund for tax-efficient, strategic giving; small, recurring grants to local organizations that align with your values; or funding micro-scholarships for opportunities you care about. Document the giving rationale publicly or within your family to model stewardship and create a legacy of generosity tied to financial independence.

Legacy planning Translate mortgage freedom into intentional legacy design so your gains benefit heirs and causes without creating confusion or conflict. Review and update estate documents—wills, trusts, beneficiary designations, and powers of attorney—so they reflect new asset allocations and philanthropic goals. Decide whether paid-off property will be preserved, partially monetized, or used as a legacy lever (loans to family for education or housing). Pair legal documents with family conversations that explain values, intentions, and any conditions on inherited assets; clarity reduces later disputes and ensures your freedom fuels the outcomes you intend.

Amplifying impact through cohorts and resources Multiply your influence by forming small cohorts or producing modular resources: short video tutorials, one-page worksheets, and checklist templates that lower the barrier for others to implement responsibly. Host periodic cohort check-ins where participants share wins and troubleshooting lessons under your facilitation. Partner with local nonprofits or financial education programs to bring the method to underserved communities—adapted with conservative guardrails—so paying it forward becomes structural, not anecdotal. By packaging your learning into repeatable, safe formats, you expand both financial literacy and the real-world impact of mortgage freedom.

Sustaining the giving and mentorship habit Make paying it forward sustainable by embedding it into your new budget and routine: allocate a fixed monthly time block for mentoring and a fixed percentage of freed cash for giving. Treat mentorship outcomes as measurable goals—number of mentees who complete a 90-day pilot, documented improvements in mentee reserves—and apply the same accountability you used on your own plan. This disciplined approach preserves your financial momentum while ensuring that the freedom you worked for creates perpetual value in other people's lives.

***

Section 4: Life After the Mortgage — The Next Financial Goal

Rental property acquisition Purchasing a rental property is a natural next step for many who free up mortgage cash: it recycles housing equity into an income-producing asset that can accelerate net worth growth and create passive cash flow. Begin with clear underwriting: target markets with positive cash-on-cash returns, conservative rent and vacancy assumptions, and realistic maintenance reserves. Use your freed mortgage payment as seed equity or to shore up down-payment and contingency funds, then size leverage prudently so a single vacancy or repair doesn't derail your household cash flow. Treat the first property as a disciplined experiment—document actual operating results against your pro forma, refine systems for tenant selection and property management, and only scale once you've proven the model and governance.

Children's education funding Redirecting mortgage savings into dedicated education accounts secures future choices for your children while offering tax or financial-aid planning benefits depending on the vehicle you choose. Decide the funding vehicle that best matches your goals—529 plans for college with tax-advantaged growth, custodial accounts for broader use, or a dedicated brokerage for maximum flexibility—and automate monthly contributions that grow with your confidence and cash flow. Build an education roadmap with target amounts by age, and pair that with contingency rules: maintain emergency reserves separately, prioritize education contributions only after retirement and debt safety thresholds are met, and revisit assumptions when major life changes occur.

Early retirement planning Mortgage freedom compounds the most powerful lever for early retirement: lowered fixed expenses. Convert the former mortgage payment into accelerated retirement savings and a flexible withdrawal runway. Max out employer matches, prioritize tax-advantaged accounts, and build a taxable investment ladder sized to cover the pre-retirement gap or sequence-of-returns risk. Model retirement timing under multiple scenarios—conservative, base, and optimistic—and stress-test them for market drawdowns and unexpected expenses. If early retirement is the goal, build a multi-bucket plan (cash runway, taxable, tax-deferred) and set concrete milestones—net worth targets, passive income thresholds, and required safe withdrawal rates—so you can convert aspiration into a staged, measurable exit plan.

Whatever freedom means to you Freedom after mortgage payoff is deeply personal—some choose entrepreneurship, others travel, extended caregiving, or artistic pursuits—so translate abstract desire into specific, fundable projects. Write a short "Freedom Statement" that names the top three things you'll do with the liberated cash and assign funding rules and timelines for each. Break large dreams into phased experiments with small, measurable bets: pilot a short sabbatical before quitting a job, run a 6-month business cohort before scaling, or set aside an annual experience fund to test lifestyle changes. Anchor each choice with the same governance that guided payoff: automation, reserves, stop triggers, and a quarterly review so freedom becomes sustainable rather than fleeting.

Integrating goals into a unified plan Choose one or two priority goals rather than fragmenting the entire freed cashflow across many initiatives; clarity increases impact. Create a simple allocation rule—percentages or fixed amounts—for each priority and automate transfers into the respective buckets. Reassess annually with your Numbers Worksheet and stress tests to ensure liquidity and resilience are maintained as you pursue growth or lifestyle changes. By turning the abstract promise of freedom into defined goals, funding rules, and measurable checkpoints, you ensure the next financial chapter delivers sustained value aligned with the life you want to lead.

CHAPTER 15:

Alternative Applications — Using This Strategy for Other Debts

Student loan acceleration Applying a HELOC-style cash-flow acceleration approach to student loans can make sense when the student debt carries a higher interest rate than the secured line and when loan terms allow prepayment without penalty. Convert the logic: use the HELOC as temporary liquidity to make larger principal reductions on the student loan, then prioritize rapid HELOC repayment so you avoid carrying unsecured interest. This works best when your HELOC rate is low relative to the student loan rate, you have stable income to service short-term draws, and the student loans are not tied to special forgiveness programs where changing payment patterns could reduce future benefits. Always run the numbers and examine loan forgiveness or income-driven repayment consequences before redirecting funds.

Auto loan payoff Auto loans are often shorter term with relatively modest balances, so using a HELOC to accelerate an auto loan can be efficient if it reduces total interest paid and simplifies cash flow. The key conditions are a HELOC rate that, net of fees and risk, produces a lower total interest burden for the period involved and a plan to retire the HELOC quickly to avoid rolling the debt into long-term variable interest. Since vehicles depreciate, avoid using secured home credit to fund investments in rapidly depreciating assets unless the behavioral and contingency rules (reserves, draw caps, cooling periods) are strictly enforced.

Credit card debt elimination Using a HELOC to extinguish high-interest credit card balances is a common and often sound arbitrage when executed responsibly: you replace very high unsecured interest with typically much lower secured interest and then attack the HELOC principal aggressively. This can materially reduce monthly interest drain and accelerate net worth restoration. However, the strategy fails if it simply converts revolving credit into a long-term secured obligation without behavior change—if card usage continues, or HELOC repayments are only minimal, you've traded one problem for another. Set strict rules: use the HELOC only as a bridge to pay cards in full, freeze or cut cards as needed, and automate aggressive HELOC amortization until the balance is cleared.

When it works versus when it doesn't The approach works when three conditions align: (1) the HELOC's effective cost is lower than the debt being retired after accounting for fees and tax considerations; (2) you have disciplined repayment plans and reserves that prevent the HELOC from becoming persistent debt; and (3) the debt being addressed does not carry unique protections or future benefits that prepayment would sacrifice (for example, certain student loan forgiveness eligibility). It doesn't work when the HELOC rate is volatile and likely to surpass the debt's cost during the repayment window, when behavioral discipline is weak, or when using home-secured credit would dangerously increase foreclosure risk relative to the benefit. Always model worst-case rate and income scenarios, define stop triggers, and ensure the swap reduces overall risk rather than merely shifting the liability from one pocket to another.

Operational safeguards and behavioral rules For any non-mortgage use, apply the same governance standards you used for mortgage acceleration: maintain a separate core cash reserve, establish cooling-off rules for discretionary draws, document each transaction, and automate repayments to the HELOC with a prioritized schedule. Require a written ROI or payoff rationale for each conversion (amount saved in interest, timeline to repay, contingency plans). Engage professional advice for tax or legal implications—especially for student loans or business debts—and treat HELOC conversions as tactical, short-duration moves rather than structural fixes.

Final decision checklist Before using home equity to retire other debts, answer these questions clearly: Will this reduce total interest and fees under conservative rate scenarios? Can I repay the HELOC on the planned timeline without dipping into essentials? Will I maintain or grow my emergency reserve through the process? If you can answer yes to all three, the approach is a viable, high-impact tool; if not, favor simpler strategies—debt snowball, targeted consolidation loans with fixed rates, or professional debt counseling—until readiness and rules are in place.

***

Section 1: Alternative Applications — Business Applications

Business loan payoff Using a HELOC-style acceleration approach to retire business loans can be effective when the cost of short-term home-secured liquidity is meaningfully lower than the outstanding business debt and when personal collateral exposure is acceptable to you. Treat any draw as a tactical, short-duration bridge: deploy HELOC funds to eliminate high-rate or short-term commercial notes, then prioritize rapid repayment from business cash flow or a planned refinancing. Before executing, run a lender and legal review to ensure no covenants or cross-collateralization issues arise, and document the business rationale—interest savings, improved cash-flow coverage, or simplification of creditor relationships—so the move is strategic rather than reactive.

Cash flow management For many small businesses, timing mismatches between receivables and payables create persistent cash stress; a personal HELOC can smooth those cycles if used cautiously. Use the line to cover temporary payroll, supplier, or inventory gaps with an explicit repayment plan tied to incoming receivables or a near-term financing event. Protect both household and business by maintaining strict caps on how much of personal equity you'll expose and by keeping separate accounting records that track business draws, repayments, and the precise business purpose for each transfer. Avoid routine reliance on personal credit for recurring operational shortfalls; if the business shows chronic shortfalls, prioritize structural fixes—pricing, collections, or a dedicated business line—over repeated HELOC draws.

Business line of credit strategies A business line of credit and a HELOC serve similar liquidity purposes but differ in collateral, cost, and governance. When possible, prioritize establishing or growing a business line of credit: it keeps personal assets insulated, builds your business credit profile, and often better matches enterprise risk. Use a HELOC as emergency or opportunity overlay—available for rapid deployment when business LOC approval would take too long or when you must act quickly on an acquisition or supplier discount. If you maintain both, adopt layered rules: primary use business LOC for recurring working capital, reserve HELOC for strategic, one-off investments or temporary bridge financing that you will retire immediately upon receivable realization or refinancing.

Entrepreneur considerations Entrepreneurs must weigh the upside of accelerated business growth against the personal risk of using home equity. Explicitly define your tolerance for personal collateralization and document exit strategies for each HELOC-funded business move: timeline to repay, revenue milestones, contingency liquidity sources, and minimum retained household reserves. Consider governance additions such as investor approval, board consent, or escrowed milestone releases before drawing significant personal equity for business use. If bringing partners or investors on board, disclose personal HELOC usage and include it in capitalization tables so everyone understands true leverage and downside exposure. Finally, test each decision with a conservative stress scenario—loss of a major client, delayed product launch, or 30–60 day receivable lag—and confirm your household finances remain secure under those shocks.

Operational safeguards and best practices Apply the same strict operational controls used for mortgage acceleration: maintain a dedicated business-HELOC ledger, require a 72-hour cooling period for discretionary draws above a small threshold, automate repayment flows tied to business inflows, and run monthly reconciliations with your accountant. Limit cumulative HELOC exposure relative to usable equity and never borrow amounts that would force a sale of the primary residence if the business fails to perform. Document every draw's business purpose and outcome to build accountability and to support tax and legal clarity.

When the strategy makes sense and when to avoid it This approach makes sense for time-sensitive growth opportunities with clear near-term cash returns (inventory discounts, short vendor terms that unlock margin, asset purchases with quick payback) or to replace high-cost short-term business debt. Avoid using personal HELOC funds for chronic operating losses, speculative ventures without validated demand, or capital needs better suited to equity or dedicated business lending. If you are uncomfortable with personal collateral risk, or if business cash flow is unstable without a clear near-term inflection, prioritize business credit channels, investors, or restructuring rather than loading personal home equity into the enterprise.

Summary operational checklist

Confirm legal and covenant implications with lenders and counsel.

Quantify interest arbitrage and worst-case scenarios.

Maintain separate accounting and detailed transaction logs.

Set strict draw caps, cooling periods, and automated repayment triggers.

Require milestone-based releases for large draws and annual professional reviews.

When entrepreneurs thread discipline, transparency, and conservative stress testing into HELOC-backed business moves, the tool can accelerate growth without sacrificing household safety. When those disciplines aren't present, the personal downside outweighs potential upside—choose structural business financing instead.

***

Section 2: Alternative Applications — Real Estate Investor Version

Multiple property management Scaling from one rental to a multi-property portfolio requires disciplined systems; a HELOC can be a liquidity bridge, but portfolio scale succeeds or fails on operations. Use a single, simple property management playbook that standardizes tenant screening, lease terms, maintenance workflows, and reserve requirements so you can add assets without reinventing processes each time. Track each property with discrete ledgers that capture cash-on-cash return, vacancy risk, cap-rate, and blended repair reserves; treat the HELOC as a short-term tool to solve known timing gaps (a security deposit shortfall, an urgent roof repair) rather than as permanent working capital. As you multiply properties, increase centralized reserves proportionally and tighten draw approvals—require documented ROI and a contingency repayment source before any HELOC deployment for property needs.

HELOC for down payments Using the HELOC to fund down payments can accelerate acquisitions when opportunities move faster than your cash accumulation, but it changes both underwriting and risk dynamics. Structure HELOC-funded down payments only when you have a clear exit or repayment plan—sale within a defined window, immediate refinancing to a rental mortgage, or committed incoming capital—so the HELOC exposure is temporary and planned. Underwrite the deal conservatively with stress tests for vacancy, capex, and interest-rate shifts; ensure the property's projected cash flow covers HELOC servicing plus mortgage and operating costs under downside scenarios. Keep documentation showing the source and intended repayment of HELOC funds to simplify refinancing and to preserve tax and underwriting clarity.

Portfolio acceleration A HELOC can be an effective accelerator for rolling acquisitions, renovations, and forced-appreciation strategies when governed by strict allocation rules. Define a portfolio acceleration fund composed of cash plus an agreed HELOC contingency; cap HELOC utilization to a conservative percentage of usable equity and require pre-approved project budgets, contractor bids, and timelines before release.

Prioritize projects with short payback (rental re-rent at higher rate, efficiency upgrades that reduce costs, or cosmetic rehabs that unlock higher rents) and tie repayment schedules to realized increases in net operating income. Use automated dashboards to monitor portfolio leverage ratios, DSCR (debt service coverage ratio) trends, and reserve depletion so you see early signs of stress and can throttle activity before it becomes systemic.

Advanced investor strategies Experienced investors can layer HELOCs into more sophisticated techniques—bridge financing for 1031 exchange timelines, seasoning properties for better refinance terms, or cross-collateralized rehab programs that rotate capital through a series of buys and sells—but those strategies demand higher governance and contingency planning. Add professional touchpoints: formal underwriting checklists, third-party appraisal or market reports, legal review for cross-collateralization, and quarterly portfolio stress tests that model tenant loss, interest spikes, and regional market declines. Always separate household exposure from portfolio risk with explicit caps on personal HELOC usage and require milestone-based draws (percent released on completion) for larger projects. When executed with clear rules, HELOCs become flexible capital accelerants for investors; when used without structure they convert leverage into fragile tail risk—treat them as tactical, tightly managed instruments within a broader, stress-tested investment thesis.

***

Section 3: Alternative Applications — The Financial Independence Connection

FIRE movement alignment The HELOC acceleration framework aligns with core FIRE principles by converting disciplined cash-flow management into faster debt elimination and amplified investment capacity. Where traditional FIRE strategies emphasize lowering expenses and increasing savings rate, a controlled HELOC strategy is a tactical lever: it shortens the time spent paying high interest on a mortgage, frees up recurring cash, and creates optionality to redeploy those funds into tax-advantaged accounts or productive investments. Alignment requires translating HELOC maneuvers into the language of FIRE—savings rate improvement, safe withdrawal thresholds, and time to target net worth—so every draw and repayment is evaluated against the movement's long-term tradeoffs rather than short-term convenience.

Path to early retirement Using HELOC tactics to accelerate mortgage payoff can materially move your retirement timeline by reducing fixed living costs and increasing investable cash sooner. The pathway is practical: apply controlled HELOC chunks to reduce mortgage principal, repurpose the recurring mortgage payment into retirement contributions and taxable investments, and keep a conservative reserve to protect the runway. Model multiple retirement scenarios that incorporate the strategy's net interest savings, tax implications, and the modest risk of variable HELOC rates. Early retirement becomes a staged decision supported by measurable milestones—net worth targets, passive income thresholds, and a tested cash runway—so you can choose the exact moment to lean out of work with confidence.

Passive income acceleration Post-mortgage cash plus any retained HELOC optionality can be directed to build passive income faster: buy dividend-paying equities, accumulate cash-flowing rental properties, or fund business structures that generate recurring revenue. The key is a disciplined capital allocation rule that prioritizes durable, scalable income sources over speculative bets. Use the freed payment as seed capital for acquisition funds, down-payment reserves, or fractional real estate investments; concurrently maintain a conservative contingency reserve to avoid forced liquidations. Track incremental passive income per dollar deployed and require a minimum cash-on-cash return or yield before committing HELOC leverage to income properties.

Freedom number calculation Translate aspiration into a concrete "freedom number"—the amount of passive income or investable assets needed to sustain your desired lifestyle—then use HELOC strategy outcomes to accelerate reaching that number. Calculate required annual expenses, apply a safe withdrawal rate (or a passive income target), and convert that target into a portfolio size or recurring income goal. Model how mortgage acceleration shortens the timeline by reducing baseline expenses and freeing monthly cash flow for investment. Recompute the freedom number annually to reflect lifestyle shifts, tax changes, or new income streams so the HELOC's role remains tactical and measured within a clear path to financial independence.

By intentionally linking HELOC tactics to FIRE metrics—savings rate, passive income targets, and a defined freedom number—you convert an operational mortgage strategy into a deliberate accelerator toward early retirement. Maintain conservative stress tests, strong reserves, and governance rules so leverage serves the objective of durable freedom rather than introducing brittle risk into your plan.

CONCLUSION:

Your Journey Starts Now

Recap of Key Principles Begin by grounding yourself in the essential lessons you've practiced throughout this book. Your Numbers Worksheet, the 90-day pilot, and the governance rules are not optional checklists but the scaffolding that makes everything else possible. Revisit the core metrics regularly—mortgage balance, usable equity, reserve level, and HELOC repayment cadence—and let those numbers guide tactical choices. Keep documentation current and visible so decisions are driven by facts rather than emotion.

Income velocity is everything Accelerating how quickly money moves from income to principal and back into productive use multiplies every dollar you have. Focus on increasing the speed and intentionality of cash flows: automate transfers, prioritize windfalls for high-impact actions, and shorten the time between HELOC draw and repayment whenever possible. Faster cycles reduce interest drag, create clearer feedback loops, and convert small behavioral wins into outsized terminal gains.

Discipline beats complexity The smartest results rarely come from clever hacks but from simple rules applied consistently. Choose a small set of unambiguous rules—reserve minimums, cooling periods, draw caps, and stop triggers—and enforce them without exception. Simplicity makes adherence realistic; predictability reduces stress; and repeated disciplined actions compound into durable outcomes far beyond any single tactical advantage.

Strategy requires commitment This approach is a committed project rather than a one-off maneuver. It demands weekly reviews, honest reconciliations, and the humility to pause when stop triggers occur. Anchor your commitment with a Personal Success Contract, a named accountability partner, and a cadence of short checkpoints so the plan survives real life—job changes, family needs, or market shifts. Commitment is not rigidity; it is the consistent willingness to return to your rules and metrics when choices get noisy.

Freedom is worth it The financial gains are practical but the deepest value is the expanded margin of choice that mortgage freedom creates.

When obligations shrink, possibilities broaden: invest, give, mentor, pivot work, or simply breathe. Treat the payoff as the start of a new stewardship phase—protect your gains, plan your next goals, and use the discipline you built to sustain them. Your journey starts now; the daily acts of governance, curiosity, and restraint will convert the strategy into lasting freedom.

***

The Decision Point

Why waiting costs you money Every month you delay disciplined action is a month interest compounds on a larger principal and an opportunity to redeploy cash that goes unrealized. Small procrastinations multiply: delayed chunk payments mean more interest paid, postponed reallocations slow wealth accumulation, and undiscovered inefficiencies persist. Market and rate uncertainty cut both ways, but in most realistic scenarios earlier, disciplined payoff and redeployment produce materially better outcomes than perfect timing. Treat inaction as an expense line—quantify the cost of waiting in your Numbers Worksheet and let that visible cost tilt decisions toward timely execution.

Fear versus calculated risk Fear is a natural signal; it becomes useful when converted into a structured risk-assessment rather than a decision veto. Replace vague worry with clear scenarios: best, base, and worst cases for interest, income, and reserves. For each scenario, record the exact step you will take and the stop triggers that force a pause. Calculated risk looks like a conservative draw limit, an automatic repayment plan, and contingency sources for stress events. When fear meets process, it becomes a guardrail that preserves upside without immobilizing you.

Your future self will thank you Decisions made today compound into options for tomorrow: more investable cash, shorter work horizons, and greater capacity to give or pivot. Imagine a future budget where the mortgage line is repurposed entirely for opportunity—retirement, education, or a business runway—and then work the math backward to today's actions. The gratitude you earn from your future self is concrete: interest saved, time reclaimed, and a simpler set of choices later. Frame each small action as a gift to that future self and let that orientation steady your daily discipline.

Taking the first step Begin with a low-friction pilot: update your Numbers Worksheet, run a 90-day plan with one conservative chunk, and set two non-negotiable rules (reserve minimum and cooling period). Automate one transfer to the repayment plan, name an accountability partner, and schedule your first weekly checkpoint. The first step should be designed to teach—small enough to be reversible, large enough to prove the mechanics. Momentum builds from repeatable micro-wins; the most important move is the one you can and will repeat.

Final encouragement Decision-making is a muscle, not an event. Commit to process over perfection, measure every action, and let disciplined iteration convert anxiety into competence. The tools and rules in this book are a framework—your consistent application is the variable that changes outcomes. Start now with one clear, conservative action and watch how cumulative discipline reshapes your financial future. Your journey begins at the decision point; choose motion over delay and let progress compound.

Final Encouragement

You can do this You have more control than you think; the HELOC acceleration method is a set of repeatable actions, not a secret reserved for experts. Start with small, measurable steps—update your Numbers Worksheet, set a conservative reserve, and run a 90-day pilot—so each win builds confidence. Focus on process over perfect outcomes: consistency compounds, and the discipline you practice now becomes the habit that carries you through setbacks and breakthroughs alike.

Thousands have succeeded This approach is not theoretical; countless homeowners have shortened mortgage timelines by combining intentional cash flow, clear rules, and steady execution. Their common pattern is simple: they began with conservative tests, tightened governance after early lessons, and scaled only when systems proved reliable. Let those examples be evidence that the path is practical and repeatable—use others' stories as templates for governance rather than blueprints for risk-taking.

Support is available You do not need to navigate the plan alone—advisors, mentors, accountability partners, and community cohorts can shorten your learning curve and catch blind spots. Seek professional input for tax, legal, and complex refinancing decisions, and recruit a trusted partner for weekly check-ins to preserve behavioral discipline. Leverage templates, trackers, and the small governance rituals in this book so external support amplifies, rather than replaces, your ownership of the process.

Your mortgage-free future awaits: The payoff is more than a removed line item; it's a structural shift in your options and your time. Keep the end in view—freedom to invest, give, pivot work, or spend time differently—and let that vision anchor the daily choices that feel small now but compound into lasting change. Begin with one conservative, reversible action today and let momentum do the rest: your future self will thank you.

Author's Personal Note

Why I wrote this book: I wrote this book to translate a complex financial technique into a practical, repeatable playbook that real people can use. Too often powerful strategies stay locked behind jargon, professional gatekeeping, or one-off anecdotes; my goal was to create a clear, disciplined pathway you can test, govern, and adapt to your life. This book is purposefully tactical—templates, rules, and checkpoints—because freedom is engineered, not hoped for.

My own journey: I learned the lessons in these pages the hard way: through missed assumptions, recalibrations, and incremental wins that added up. Early experiments taught me the value of conservative pilots, documented decisions, and accountability structures that keep emotion from eroding discipline. Those early, modest successes built confidence to scale safely; the governance I describe is the same governance that protected my household through surprises and preserved optionality when markets shifted.

What mortgage freedom meant to me: Mortgage freedom changed daily reality: it moved a recurring obligation out of the center of decisions and placed choice there instead. It wasn't merely lower payments— it was time reclaimed, fewer urgent conversations about bills, and the ability to redirect attention and capital toward growth, relationships, and meaning. That structural shift made later risks manageable and opportunities actionable; the payoff was both financial and profoundly personal.

My wish for you: My wish is that you treat this book as a toolkit and a companion: start small, learn fast, protect your downside, and celebrate the micro-wins that create momentum. Use the templates, adapt the governance to your life, and surround yourself with at least one accountability partner. Above all, may the discipline you build here buy you more than time and money—may it buy you the freedom to choose how you live, give, and lead.

APPENDIX A:

Glossary of Terms

HELOC: A Home Equity Line of Credit; a revolving credit facility secured by your home that lets you draw, repay, and redraw during the draw period. HELOCs typically carry variable rates and are used for short-term liquidity, strategic chunk payments, or contingency access.

Mortgage: A long-term loan secured by real property where scheduled amortizing payments cover interest and principal; mortgages typically have fixed or adjustable interest rates and a recorded lien until paid in full.

Principal: The outstanding balance of a loan on which interest is calculated; reducing principal is the core objective of acceleration strategies because it lowers future interest costs.

Interest: The cost of borrowing expressed as a rate applied to the principal; interest on HELOCs is commonly variable and often calculated on the average daily balance.

Amortization: The scheduled process by which loan principal is reduced over time through periodic payments; an amortization schedule shows how each payment divides between interest and principal.

Chunk payment: A deliberate, sizable principal payment applied to a mortgage to materially reduce balance and interest expense; in this book, chunks are financed temporarily with HELOC draws and repaid quickly.

Draw period: The portion of a HELOC term during which you may borrow funds; draws typically convert to a repayment period when borrowing ends and principal plus interest must be repaid.

Repayment period: The HELOC phase when no new draws are allowed and both principal and interest payments are required according to the lender's schedule.

Usable equity: The portion of your home equity available to borrow after accounting for lender LTV limits, liens, and required buffers; usable equity determines safe HELOC sizing for strategy execution.

Loan-to-value (LTV): A ratio that compares the loan balance(s) to the home's appraised value; lenders use LTV to set borrowing limits and underwriting risk.

Average daily balance: A method lenders use to calculate interest on revolving credit by averaging the outstanding balance each day over the billing cycle; minimizing days outstanding reduces cost.

Reserve (cash reserve): A liquid cash buffer held to cover payments and shocks; core reserves protect household solvency and are a non-negotiable guardrail in any HELOC plan.

Cooling-off period: A predeclared waiting time between contemplating a draw and executing it; this behavioral rule reduces impulse borrowing and improves governance.

Stop trigger: A predefined condition—such as reserve depletion, missed payments, or a rate threshold—that requires pausing new draws and initiating remediation steps.

Variable rate: An interest rate that moves with an underlying index plus a margin; HELOCs commonly have variable rates, exposing borrowers to rate volatility.

Index and margin: The index is a public benchmark (e.g., Prime) and the margin is the lender's spread; together they determine a variable rate on a HELOC.

Rate cap and floor Contractual limits on how high or low a variable rate can move during a period or over the life of the loan; caps limit upside rate risk, floors prevent rates below a set minimum.

Fixed-rate conversion: A HELOC feature or separate product that allows converting outstanding balances to a fixed rate for stability; useful when you want to lock repayment costs.

Refinance and cash-out refinance: Refinance means replacing an existing mortgage with a new loan (often to change rate or term); a cash-out refinance extracts equity as cash and increases mortgage principal.

Payoff statement: A lender document that states the exact amount required to satisfy and release a mortgage lien as of a specified date; necessary to confirm final payoff and record a lien release.

Lien release / satisfaction of mortgage: The recorded legal document showing the lender has relinquished its claim on the property after full repayment.

Average daily balance interest: Interest charged based on the average balance each day in the billing cycle; reducing days and balance lowers this interest.

Debt service coverage ratio (DSCR): A cash-flow metric used primarily for rental and business underwriting that compares net operating income to debt service; higher DSCR indicates greater ability to service debt.

Cap rate (for investors): A real-estate metric dividing net operating income by property value; it helps underwrite purchase yield and compare investment options.

Credit utilization: The percentage of available revolving credit in use; lower utilization often benefits credit scores, while sustained high utilization can harm them.

Credit mix and age of credit: Components of credit scoring that reflect the types and history length of accounts; keeping a long, well-managed HELOC can positively affect these factors.

Seasoning: The period a loan, property, or borrower must demonstrate performance before certain financing options become available; lenders may require seasoning before refinancing or new loans.

Bridge loan: Short-term financing used to bridge timing gaps between transactions; a HELOC can serve similar tactical bridge needs but uses residential collateral.

Opportunity fund: A purpose-driven pool of capital (cash plus contingency credit) maintained for time-sensitive investments or growth opportunities, governed by allocation and repayment rules.

Numbers Worksheet: A compact working document that centralizes key metrics—income, expenses, mortgage balance, usable equity, reserves, and repayment cadence—used for decisioning and stress testing.

Stress test / break-even analysis: Scenario modeling that evaluates outcomes under adverse rate or income shocks to determine whether a plan remains viable and to set conservative draw and reserve limits.

Escrow (taxes and insurance): A lender-held account for periodic payment of property taxes and insurance premiums; escrow shortages can create unplanned cash needs and should be monitored.

Automated repayment flow: An instruction that transfers funds automatically to repay HELOC draws; automation reduces behavioral leakages and enforces discipline.

Behavioral guardrails: Pre-committed rules—reserve minimums, draw caps, cooling periods, and accountability checks—that convert intent into reproducible, low-emotion execution.

Tax-deductible interest: Interest that may be deductible under tax law when used for qualifying purposes; consult a tax professional because deductibility depends on loan use, filing status, and current rules.

Documentation trail: A maintained record of draws, payments, lender statements, invoices, and decisions; a clear documentation trail supports reconciliation, taxes, and any future refinancing or sale.

Exit strategy: A planned sequence to eliminate or refinance HELOC exposure—sale, refinance, cash repayment, or converting to fixed rate—defined before large draws are made.

Governance cadence: The rhythm of reviews and checkpoints—weekly dashboards, quarterly stress tests, and annual plan updates—that keeps the strategy aligned, measured, and safe.

These terms form the operational language of the HELOC acceleration strategy. Keep this glossary accessible as you plan and execute so decisions remain precise, repeatable, and governed by the conservative rules that protect both your home and your future.

***

APPENDIX A: Glossary of Terms — Continued

Amortization schedule: A detailed table showing each payment over the life of a loan, how much goes to interest versus principal, and the remaining balance after each payment; useful for planning chunk payments and visualizing time-to-payoff.

Balloon payment: A large, lump-sum payment due at the end of a loan term when periodic payments did not fully amortize the balance; avoid unexpected balloons by confirming loan terms before using temporary credit.

Borrowing base: A lender's calculation of the amount available to borrow, often used for business credit but applicable when lenders set dynamic HELOC limits based on value and outstanding liens.

Cash-on-cash return: A simple yield metric for real estate investors that divides annual pre-tax cash flow by the cash invested; used to assess short-term returns on HELOC-funded deals.

Charge off: A creditor's declaration that a debt is unlikely to be collected, typically after prolonged delinquency; maintaining timely payments on HELOCs prevents severe credit and legal consequences.

Collateral: An asset pledged to secure a loan; with HELOCs the home is collateral, which increases lender priority and borrower responsibility.

Cross-collateralization: A lender practice where multiple loans or properties secure each other; it can complicate refinancing and title transfers, so disclose and understand any cross-collateral terms before drawing.

Debt consolidation: Combining multiple debts into a single payment or loan, often to reduce interest or simplify payments; using a HELOC for consolidation is effective only with disciplined repayment plans.

Default: Failure to meet loan obligations (missed payments, covenant breaches); defaults on secured credit can lead to foreclosure, underscoring the need for conservative exposure limits.

Due diligence: The research and verification process before making a financial move—inspections, market analysis, legal review, and financial modeling; mandatory for HELOC-funded investments.

Equity cash-out: Withdrawing home equity as cash via refinance or HELOC draws; treat cash-out as a resource that must be paired with a repayment and risk plan.

Fixed payment conversion: A lender option or product that converts a variable HELOC balance into a fixed monthly payment and amortization schedule to create certainty in repayment.

Good faith estimate (GFE) / Loan estimate: A lender disclosure that outlines estimated loan terms and closing costs; compare loan estimates across offers to understand true cost differences.

Hazard insurance: Property insurance covering physical damage; ensure premiums are current and escrowed appropriately to prevent unexpected shortfalls that strain reserves.

Imputed interest: A tax concept where below-market loans or certain transactions may carry taxable interest imputation; seek tax counsel when structuring intra-family loans or creative finance deals.

Indexation risk: The exposure that comes from the index component of a variable rate moving unpredictably; model indexation risk into worst-case scenarios for HELOC-driven plans.

Lien priority: The order in which creditors are paid from proceeds of a sale; first liens (primary mortgage) are paid before junior liens (HELOC subordinates), which affects refinancing and sale strategies.

Margin call (for leveraged investors): A demand for additional capital when leveraged positions fall below maintenance thresholds; while not typical for HELOCs, leveraged investment strategies should anticipate analogous liquidity calls.

Mortgage recycling: An advanced strategy where freed mortgage cash is redeployed into investments while maintaining some mortgage-like discipline; requires robust governance and risk controls.

Origination fee: A one-time charge by a lender to open a loan or HELOC; include origination fees in cost comparisons when deciding between debt options.

Payment holiday / forbearance: Temporary lender allowances to reduce or suspend payments; while helpful in emergencies, reliance on forbearance can erode credit and should be a last-resort contingency.

Prepayment penalty: A lender fee for paying off a loan early; verify whether your mortgage or HELOC carries prepayment penalties before planning aggressive principal reduction.

Recourse vs non-recourse: Recourse loans allow lenders to pursue borrower personal assets beyond collateral in default; non-recourse limits recovery to the collateral only—know which applies to any loan you consider.

Refinance seasoning: A lender requirement that a property or loan be held for a minimum period before qualifying for favorable refinance terms; account for seasoning timelines in exit strategies.

Retention reserve: A dedicated portion of proceeds or cash set aside for anticipated future costs (e.g., tenant turnover, capital projects); increases portfolio resilience when using HELOCs for investment.

Risk-adjusted return: A measure that evaluates potential return relative to the risk taken; use risk-adjusted metrics when comparing HELOC-funded opportunities to alternatives.

Servicing transfer: When the administrative servicing of a loan moves to a different company; transfers can cause temporary statement confusion—keep documentation current and verify balances after any transfer.

Sweep account: An account that automatically moves excess cash into interest-bearing instruments or to pay down debt nightly; sweeps can accelerate HELOC repayment when set up between checking and the HELOC.

Tax lot accounting: Methods for tracking individual investment lots for taxable accounts to optimize capital gains and tax loss harvesting; important when reallocating freed cash into taxable investments.

Title insurance: Insurance protection against defects in property title; necessary during purchases and when coordinating HELOC draws tied to property value.

Underwriting covenants: Conditions set by lenders for loan maintenance (e.g., minimum DSCR, maximum LTV); violating covenants can trigger repayment accelerations or penalties—monitor covenants when leveraging for investments.

Variable installment plan: A repayment structure where installment amounts change over time; some HELOC repayment plans are flexible but should be modeled conservatively for affordability.

Yield maintenance: A prepayment provision that compensates lenders for lost interest if loans are paid early; check for yield maintenance clauses in commercial mortgage contexts and understand implications for payoff strategies.

Zero-balance buffer: A deliberate small cushion kept between available credit and maximum limit to prevent inadvertent over-advances and fees; a practical habit for preventing technical breaches of HELOC terms.

These additional terms expand the operational vocabulary you'll use when planning, executing, and scaling HELOC-based strategies. Keep definitions close at hand as your decisions grow in complexity so language remains precise and governance effective.

APPENDIX B:

Resource Directory — Quick Guide

Recommended HELOC reading on clauses and lender risks Start by understanding HELOC acceleration clauses, triggers, and borrower protections so you know what can force repayment and how to avoid surprise risk; practical explainers and industry posts walk through common triggers, remediation steps, and borrower rights to preserve optionality and avoid foreclosure.

Online places to compare lenders and current market context Use major editorial aggregator reviews to narrow candidates quickly — they compare rates, fees, closing speed, and borrower suitability across national and regional banks and credit unions, and they update lists of top HELOC providers regularly so you can shortlist lenders to shop locally or online.

Community education and strategy guides Community-driven platforms and strategy guides offer structured playbooks, sample cashflow worksheets, and step-by-step pilots from people who have implemented HELOC acceleration; these resources help translate theory into practical next steps and checklist items before you speak with lenders or advisors.

Peer support and real-world discussions Forums and subreddits focused on homeowners and HELOC experience are invaluable for hearing real cases, lender quirks, and operational tips (what to ask, common gotchas, behavioral guardrails); treat anecdotal threads as idea prompts, then validate them with professional advice and your own stress tests.

Online calculators and scenario tools Before approaching lenders, model multiple scenarios with dedicated HELOC calculators that handle draw vs repayment periods, average-daily-balance interest, extra-principal effects, and amortization schedules; exportable amortization tables and rate-shock scenarios help set conservative draw caps and reserve requirements.

Practical how-to articles and credit comparisons Actionable articles and institutional explainers describe the mechanics, costs, and qualification rules for using a HELOC to pay down a mortgage, including stepwise examples and cost/benefit illustrations you can adapt to your Numbers Worksheet when sizing opportunities and worst-case scenarios.

Where to shop and how to evaluate lenders Once you've modeled your plan, shop multiple lenders and compare sample APRs, LTV limits, fixed-rate conversion options, fees, and customer service; trusted review sites publish regularly updated top-lender lists and market snapshots to help you identify national banks, regional banks, and credit unions that match your priorities.

APPENDIX C:

Forms and Templates

HELOC comparison worksheet A focused worksheet that helps you compare HELOC offers side-by-side so cost and flexibility drive your choice. Key fields include lender name; draw period length; index and margin; current APR range; initial and ongoing fees; LTV and usable equity limits; fixed-rate conversion options and costs; rate caps and floors; repayment period terms; escrow requirements; prepayment or yield-maintenance clauses; and customer service notes. Use the worksheet to score each lender across the attributes that matter most to your plan (stability, cost, flexibility, speed) and to record sample payoff scenarios using your Numbers Worksheet inputs. The goal is a single page that makes tradeoffs explicit and reduces selection by emotion.

Monthly tracking spreadsheet A reusable monthly tracker that captures cash flows, HELOC activity, and performance versus plan so you can see progress at a glance. Include dated rows for income, mandatory expenses, savings and investment flows, mortgage balance, HELOC beginning balance, draws, repayments, interest charged (by billing cycle), and ending HELOC balance. Add computed columns for usable equity, average daily balance, reserve level, and a running count of cooling-off periods used. Visualize key trends with simple sparklines or conditional formatting for when reserves drop below threshold or utilization exceeds target. Use this sheet weekly during active periods and monthly for reconciliation to statements.

Annual review template A structured one-page review to evaluate strategy health each year and to reset governance for the next 12 months. Sections include: current net worth snapshot; mortgage and HELOC summary (balances, rates, and LTV); performance versus targets (principal reduction, interest saved, reserve adequacy); stress-test results under a defined rate shock and income reduction; policy changes needed (draw caps, cooling rules, reserve targets); and goals for the year (acquisitions, repayment milestones, investment reallocations). Close with an action list that assigns owners and deadlines—this converts insight into accountable change and preserves institutional memory for the strategy.

Budget optimization worksheet A tactical worksheet for converting the former mortgage payment into prioritized funding buckets without undermining reserves or lifestyle needs. Begin by listing current net monthly cash flow and the mortgage payment now available. Provide configurable allocation rows for emergency reserve top-up, increased retirement contributions, opportunity fund, HELOC repayment acceleration, education savings, and discretionary margin. Include a "what if" slider to test different allocation mixes and an output that shows time-to-goal for each bucket (e.g., months to fund three months reserve, years to X additional retirement savings). The worksheet forces explicit tradeoffs and prevents the freed payment from diffusing into lifestyle creep.

Success metrics dashboard A compact dashboard that tracks the high-value KPIs that tell you whether the HELOC acceleration strategy is working and safe. Suggested KPIs: mortgage years shaved (compared to original amortization), cumulative interest saved, HELOC average utilization, reserve coverage (months of essential expenses), number of cooling-off periods invoked, and rate-shock solvency (months household can cover payments if rates rise by X%). Present these metrics as numeric tiles with a short trend line and a green/yellow/red status based on pre-set thresholds. Review the dashboard with your accountability partner each quarter to ensure the plan is both advancing goals and protecting downside.

Implementation and automation tips Use cloud spreadsheets with permission controls so you can access and update templates from any device; protect formula cells and keep a documented change log. Automate data imports where possible (statement CSVs, bank feeds) to reduce manual entry errors and to keep the monthly tracker current. Build simple alerts—email or in-sheet notifications—when reserve levels fall below threshold, when HELOC utilization exceeds target, or when a scheduled repayment fails. Finally, pair each form with a short procedural note (one paragraph) that explains how and when to use it so the templates function as operational tools, not aspirational documents.

About the Publisher

Janice Green is a legal educator and estate planning advocate dedicated to helping homeowners protect their property and secure their legacy. With years of experience guiding families through trust administration and title transfers, she specializes in making complex processes simple and practical. Her clear, step-by-step approach empowers readers to confidently use tools like living trusts and quitclaim deeds to safeguard their homes for future generations.

Read more at https://thebreakthroughcollective.online/.

www.ingramcontent.com/pod-product-compliance
Lightning Source LLC
LaVergne TN
LVHW052226200926
848481LV00001B/228
9798232956288